D0824521

POMONA

GODDESS OF FRUIT

Photo Research
by Betsy Brady

"Partners in Progress"
by W. Robert Finegan

Produced in cooperation with the
Pomona Chamber of Commerce

Windsor Publications, Inc.
Northridge, California

POMONA

GODDESS OF FRUIT

A CENTENNIAL HISTORY

Gloria Ricci Lothrop

Western
Amer.
Tall
F
869
.P7
L67
1988

Windsor Publications, Inc.—History Books
Division

Managing Editor: Karen Story
Design Director: Alexander D'Anca

Staff for *Pomona: A Centennial History*
Manuscript Editor: Nora Perren
Photo Editor: Larry Molmud
Production Editor: Kim Hogan
Editor, Corporate Biographies: Judith L.
Hunter
Production Editor, Corporate Biographies:
Phyllis Gray
Senior Proofreader: Susan J. Muhler
Editorial Assistants: Didier Beauvoir,
Thelma Fleischer, Kim Kievman,
Rebecca Kropp, Michael Nugwynne,
Kathy B. Peyser, Pat Pittman,
Theresa J. Solis
Sales Representative, Corporate Biographies:
Charlie Dresser and Will Lee
Layout Artist, Christina L. Rosepapa:

Designer: Tanya Maiboroda

Library of Congress Cataloguing-in-Publica-
tion Data

Lothrop, Gloria Ricci
    Pomona: a centennial history / Gloria
Ricci Lothrop. —1st ed. p. 192 cm. 22 × 28
    "Produced in cooperation with the Po-
mona Chamber of Commerce."
    "Partners in progress, by W. Robert
Finegan": p. 125
    Bibliography: p. 185
    Includes index.
    1. Pomona (Calif.)—History. 2. Pomona
(Calif.)—Description—Views. 3. Pomona
(Calif.)—Industries. I. Pomona Chamber of
Commerce (Pomona, Calif.) II. Title.
F869.P7L67   1988   88-17597
979.4'94—dc19   CIP
ISBN: 0-89781-263-8

©1988 Windsor Publications, Inc.
All rights reserved
Published 1988
Printed in the United States of America
First Edition

Windsor Publications, Inc.
Elliot Martin, Chairman of the Board
James L. Fish III, Chief Operating Officer

"To the City of Pomona on its Hundredth
Birthday"
by Richard Armour printed with permission
of the author.

C O N T E N T S

TO THE CITY OF POMONA ON ITS HUNDREDTH BIRTHDAY

By Richard Armour

As one whose people, seeking Heaven,
Arrived in 1887,
I feel myself an old Pomonan
And older daily, I keep moanin'.
I triked and biked and skipped my feet
On Garey and on Second Street,
On Main and Holt and Alvarado -
There tasted first an avocado.
I knew the smudge before the smog,
I knew the egg before the nog.
Such movies as I then did see
If rated would be rated G.
The orange groves on every hand
With fruit-filled branches greened the
        land,
For shopping centers, supermarts
Had not yet reached these tranquil
        parts.
I went to Central School, then Garey,
Pomona High, the cemetery.
This last, where friends I often met,
I've only visited as yet.
So now Pomona, my home town,
Has reached a hundred, quite a crown,
And I, if you would care to know,
Have still a little while to go.

The Pomona High School
football team posed for this
picture in 1905. Courtesy,
Pomona Public Library

ACKNOWLEDGMENTS

Every book is a joint enterprise. This volume, like others, has resulted from the research, generous cooperation, and assistance of many colleagues. I am particularly grateful to Professor Donald Pflueger who proposed that I undertake this interesting project. I am most appreciative of his careful review of the text. I also wish to acknowledge the constructive suggestions of Professor Doyce B. Nunis, Jr., who was generous enough to read the manuscript and share his insights.

This book would not have been possible without the support of California State Polytechnic University, Pomona, which provided release time to complete the text. I am also grateful for the Henry E. Huntington Library/Haynes Foundation Fellowship which provided an opportunity to study land promotion, town development, and agriculture in the Pomona area.

I also wish to thank Beth Page, president of the Historical Society of the Pomona Valley, for the invaluable resources she provided, and the Pomona Sesquicentennial Committee which encouraged my original study of Rancho San Jose.

I appreciate the knowledgeable assistance of David Streeter and the staff of the Pomona Public Library Special Collection, Walter Roeder of the Cal Poly University Library, and Melissa Paul of the University Archives staff. Their efforts considerably facilitated my research tasks.

I wish to take this opportunity to acknowledge the gracious assistance of the Pomona Unified School District, the Pomona Chamber of Commerce, and the Pomona Community Coordinating Council, whose history project provided much useful information. My thanks also to Mt. San Antonio College, Fairplex, and the Los Angeles County Department of Regional Planning, for analysis as well as data.

I am especially grateful for the expert support provided by Nora Perren and Kim Hogan, who made it a pleasure to work with Windsor Publications. Finally, my sincere personal thanks to Sandy Sharp and Gayle Savarese for their patient assistance in the final preparation of this study.

The Pomona Police Department Pistol Team #1 posed for this "shot" in 1936. From left to right are Ben Hite, Fred Shinogle, Rollie Caffey, J.B. Ashurst, and E.S. Hillier. Courtesy, Pomona Public Library

INTRODUCTION

Pomona, "The Town with the Right Mix," is made up of descendants of early settlers, post-World War II suburban residents, and recent exurbanite arrivals who represent the leading edge of expansion eastward from a coastal megalopolis which extends from Ventura to San Diego. In 1988 these diverse constituencies join together to celebrate Pomona's century of progress, transformation, and reinterpretation of the city's image and its citizens' expectations.

A review of the city's past 100 years reveals that Pomona is far more than a suburban haven accommodating an ever-increasing urban spillover. In 1887, when the Pomona Land and Water Company sold lots to the first 5,000 residents of this town dedicated to the Roman goddess of fruit, it was with the promise that the new residents would live in an urban garden lined with citrus groves and fruit orchards. Along with proven agricultural production from these lands formerly known as Rancho San Jose, the developers promised the amenities of a developing community and the aesthetics of the natural environment.

Today residents are still attracted by the mountain views and the residential space, but they are also lured by the growing number of employment opportunities in the various valley communities as well as by the array of educational offerings available in the proximate vicinity. Pomona's promise has been enhanced as a result of its key location between the expanding conurbation of Riverside and San Bernardino and the explosive edge of the 60-mile economic circle centered in Los Angeles County. This sphere of influence represents 28 percent of the spendable income of the 13 western states. If it were an independent sovereignty, its aeronautics, entertainment,

and clothing and furniture manufacturing, among others, would make it the 12th most prosperous nation in the world.

To further enhance this strategic location astride a historically important traffic artery, Pomona lies at the threshold of a weekend recreational hinterland interspersed with retirement communities and military bases that sustain an active commerce with the metropolitan center. As a result Pomona has become important in the development of the region's economic and civic life. It is a community that contributes human resources, research, and production to the centrifugal metropolitan center. In addition to its urban appeal, its open space has attracted light industry, and its centrality and accessibility to both air and maritime commerce have attracted international trade interests that augur continued growth into the twenty-first century. The region, a key banking center with port facilities unparalleled on the Pacific Coast and a foreign influx making it the nation's major point of entry, has become a major anchor of the Pacific Rim. This dynamic growth affects Pomona as well as her neighbors.

The centenary year marks more than a celebration of a city that has evolved from an early Indian settlement of Toybipet to the prosperous Rancho San Jose and later, to the boomtown of the 1880s. It heralds another phase of growth as the region assumes its position as a key Pacific Rim marketplace. But present and promised growth present challenges. Development must be consonant with transportation capabilities. In-migration must be complemented by adequate support services. Diminished low density must be offset by thoughtful planning. The rich ethnic diversity represented by the population that has funneled into this inland valley must be, on the one hand, welcomed into the mainstream, and, on the other, allowed the opportunity to sustain its uniqueness. In addition Pomona must implement a policy of regulated growth that both protects the fragile environment and nurtures a quality of life befitting a city dedicated to a goddess of abundant harvest.

Although Pomona's prosperous agrarian tradition, which helped make the region the nation's leading agricultural county until 1950, is no longer consistent with its contemporary development, the city's centennial can serve as a reminder of the dream of the urban garden that inspired its early promoters. In 1909 the verdant valley community, with its neatly plotted farms, rows of fruit trees, and bustling commercial center, inspired turn-of-the-century traveler George W. Burton to extol that not in the entire world was there "a spot to be compared with the valley around Pomona as viewed from the top of the city's new park." That same vista held the attention of early rancheros as well as real estate speculators, and catches the eyes of today's suburban commuters, who look down on a smooth, alluvial plain somewhat resembling an expansive fruit basket set amid the curving oak-dotted hills edged with brush and chaparral. To the north the inviting valley is framed by the San Gabriel Mountains' broadly contoured transverse branch of the coastal range, its mile-high summits dominated by Mount San Antonio. The San Bernardino range and to the east the San Jacinto range complete the protective perimeter. To the southwest and west the La Puente and San Jose hills yield entry to the largest coastal plain in California.

Before European settlement the inland valley floor was accented by olive-colored bunchgrasses and clusters of wild buckwheat, sage, and pigeon berry, indigenous oaks and walnuts, and stands of willows and sycamores growing along the banks of mountain washes. Clusters of green bracken, miner's lettuce, and wild onion marked the half-dozen springs that bubbled to the surface. They supplemented the water provided by San Jose Creek, which flowed near the western edge of the valley, and the larger Arroyo de San Antonio, which carried mountain waters southward within the network of the south Pacific drainage basin.

Located on an inland portion of the basin, Pomona shares an intermediate valley climate which is equable but distinctive in its combination of warm summers with comparatively mild winters, providing the image of Southern California most frequently held by visitors. Although the valley is part of the only region with a Mediterranean climate in the continental United States, it is sunnier and warmer than the region's maritime fringe because of the heat conduction characteristic of a valley. The desert border makes the region drier, averaging only 15 inches of rain per year, than Mediterranean regions on other continents. In winter when the effects of inversion are at a minimum, Pomona still offers the views of snow-capped mountains rising above green foothills and framed by high blue skies that formed the background of many California orange crate labels. In its unique isolation the region became known as "the island on the land," as described by Western America novelist Mary Austin.

BEFORE SPANISH SETTLEMENT

During the period preceding European contact, the portion of land later to be called Pomona was occupied by Indians of Shoshonean linguistic stock, who were part of a larger Uto-Aztecan family extending from Panama to Idaho and Montana. Although Indians first appeared in California about 30,000 years ago, they are presumed to have arrived in this valley at the end of a prolonged drought 3,000 or 4,000 years ago. Stone mortars and pestles found in Ganesha Park in this century suggest that these early inhabitants gathered seeds and other natural food products. Excavated stone points made for their light spears and darts suggest their hunting practices.

After the establishment of the Mission San Gabriel in 1771, the Indians of the area were called Gabrielenos. But their identity was well-established before the arrival of the missionaries. They were considered the most advanced of the southern Indian groups with the exception of the Chumash, whose culture, but not language, paralleled that of the tribes to the south.

The Gabrieleno Indians of Southern California traditionally performed a ceremonial Eagle Dance, dressing in eagle feathers. Courtesy, Corona Public Library

Above: Orange crate labels reflect the history of the valley's once flourishing citrus industry. Labels included the area, the packing association, and other information. The domestic market stopped using wooden crates in 1950 due to the high cost of material and their weight. Courtesy, Pomona Public Library

Right: This postcard by Edward H. Mitchell was printed in 1909. A blank line allowed the sender to fill in the name of the community. The larger-than-life fruit gave the impression that California was the land of plenty. Courtesy, Pomona Public Library

Left and below: In the early decades of the twentieth century, before the advent of television, color-tinted penny postcards showing magnificent scenes lured people to Southern California. Pomona, one of the most thriving and cultural communities at the time, was the subject of many of these postcards. Courtesy, Pomona Public Library

Street Scene, POMONA, Cal.

Above: Plank canoes were used extensively by the Gabrieleno Indians for transportation. Courtesy, Corona Public Library

Below: These Gabrieleno Indians are building a "jakal," or thatched dwelling. Courtesy, Corona Public Library

LIFE IN THE VALLEY

Recent anthropological research has refuted the earlier portrayals of Gabrielenos as primitive Stone Age digger Indians. They instead displayed keen sensitivity to the environmental capacity of their lands. Consequently they lived in tribelets with closely regulated populations in order to best utilize riparian resources, small game and wildlife, berries, nuts, and, above all, the acorn which was their dietary staple. Under the leadership of a hereditary chief, craftsmen plied their inherited crafts, and widows and orphans were cared for by means of tribute mandated by the chief. The local Indians were governed by laws that carefully regulated intermarriage and provided a graduated system of adjudication in which intertribal disputes were submitted to the binding arbitration of a representative from a neutral tribe.

The community consisted of circular brush huts, known as *wikiups*, which were clustered in three lodges or rancherias located at Indian Hill, the springs near present-day San Dimas, and along the banks of San Jose Creek in what is today Ganesha Park. From these settlements the inhabitants ranged across the valley gathering the favored locusts and grasshoppers, and hunting coyotes, raccoons, squirrels, and snakes. They rarely hunted bears, which were surrounded with superstition, or owls and eagles, which were held in great reverence.

The Gabrielenos also ventured into the foothills for the seasonal gathering of red manzanita berries, mountain cherries, and energy-giving chia seeds. In addition they engaged in a brisk trade, sometimes exchanging thick, rounded shells for the pinon nuts gathered by the Serrano Indians who lived in the surrounding ranges. Recent research has revealed the widespread practice of barter among California Indians, which included the exchange by northern Indians of obsidian blades for the salt, smoked fish, and dentalia of the coastal Chumash Indians. The commerce, which ranged from Pomo baskets to the red, brown, and black pottery of the Gabrielenos, reveals the vitality and variety that characterized the life of the California Indian.

Within their village of Toybipet, the Gabrielenos observed an elaborate protocol surrounding birth, marriage, and death. Contrary to earlier misconceptions, their labor extended beyond simple hunting and gathering. The upper rank of the social structure was occupied by artisans skilled in making ceremonial objects and musical instruments as well as jewelry, clothing, utensils such as coiled baskets and twined food-gathering equipment, and infant baskets.

The dark-skinned and long-haired Gabrielenos used both tattoos and body paint for cosmetic purposes. The women wore bark back-skirts and string aprons, while the men wore breechclouts. As needed, both sexes donned rabbit skin blankets and foot coverings made of woven mescal or yucca fiber.

In a series of letters published in the *Los Angeles Star* in 1852, Hugo Reid, a Scots settler whose wife Victoria was a Gabrieleno, provided insight into the lore and language of these Indians. Their rich language, he observed, containing nuances having no parallel in English, was replete with legends and fables that reflected the tribe's oral history and belief system. Theirs was a monotheistic cosmology that recognized a "giver of life" who, after having given order to the earth, placed it on the shoulders of seven giants whose periodic movements caused the earth to quake. The worship central to the culture was conducted in a consecrated dwelling or *yobagnar* where par-

ticipants, wearing feathered kilts and carrying feathered sticks, joined in ceremonial dances.

Given this religious tradition it is not surprising that upon meeting the first European expedition in 1769, the Gabrielenos welcomed as deities these visitors so unlike themselves in appearance. "They remained still more impressed with this idea," Reid adds, "when they saw one of their guests take a flint, strike a fire and commence smoking, having never seen it produced in this simple manner before."

Subsequent events convinced the Indians that these were not "givers of life" but potential harbingers of change and even death. The world would unalterably change for the inhabitants of the village of Toybipet as rivalries among the sovereign powers of Europe and imperial Spain's efforts to secure her colonial perimeter led a handful of soldiers and faithful Franciscans to this outermost edge of the Spanish empire.

This depiction of Gabrielenos in a ceremonial dance is visualized by Donna Preble, in her book *Yamino-Kwiti.* Courtesy, Corona Public Library

RANCHEROS RULE THE LAND

There had been reports about this land by various travelers, including a party marching west from Primeria Alta (Arizona) in 1774 under the leadership of Juan Bautista de Anza. The group had camped by the creek at the mouth of San Antonio Canyon which the Indians called Chuckawalla. Impressed by the number of bears in the vicinity, the pioneers named the stream Arroyo de los Osos, a name changed to Arroyo de los Alisos by Father Pedro Font, a member of the second Anza expedition, which camped at the site in 1776.

During the next 57 years, between 1776 and 1833, the land was administered by the Franciscans. Representing a transitional phase of colonial settlement, they were charged by the Spanish crown with converting and acculturating the native population to patterns of industry and socialization. In 1771 they established Mission San Gabriel, the fourth California church outpost to be organized as part of Spain's protective perimeter of presidios, pueblos, and missions. With the aid of neophyte labor San Gabriel soon became a major food source. In 1834 when the mission lands were secularized and redistributed, more than 16,500 cattle ranged across the mission lands, which were 21 miles wide and extended 42 miles southward to San Pedro and 84 miles inland toward the Muscupaibe range. These vast range lands were ad-

From 1774 to 1776, Don Juan Bautista de Anza and his followers traveled twice from Mexico to California, crossing the Pomona Valley. De Anza later founded San Francisco. Courtesy, Pomona Public Library

This San Jose Ranch house
was built by Francisco
Vejar and later became the
home of Louis Phillips.
Courtesy, Pomona Public
Library

Facing page: The Mission
San Gabriel was founded
September 8, 1771, and the
famous bell wall at the
mission still stands today.
Courtesy, Corona Public Library

ministered by mission outposts called
asistencias.

ESTABLISHMENT OF RANCH LANDS

Despite the hostility of Indians in the inland region, the Franciscans from Mission
San Gabriel established an outpost in San
Bernardino as well as two other ranches
located midway between the mission and
San Bernardino. Ranchos San Antonio
and San Jose, about six leagues (16 miles)
from the mission, were considered the
first stop on the dangerous seven-day
journey between Mission San Gabriel
and the Colorado River, following a road
running northeast toward Cucamonga.

Rancho San Jose was also on the route
from the Cajon Pass to Mission San Gabriel traversed in 1826 by Jedediah Smith
and his band of fur trappers.

The administration of San Gabriel by
the Franciscan priests came to an end
with the Secularization Act of 1834. This
act declared that mission lands had come
under the jurisdiction of the king of Spain
by virtue of the Laws of the Indies when
the Spanish occupied California in 1769.
Ownership had then passed to the new
nation of Mexico on April 9, 1822, when
Mexico became independent of Spain.
Thus empowered, the governor of California, Jose Figueroa, and his successors
began generously apportioning the lands
which for more than six decades had been
administered by the mission fathers.

By 1841 nearly 100 ranchos had been
apportioned from mission lands in California. In the next five years the number
would increase to 800. Among the successful petitioners were two young Californios who in March 1837 determined
to explore the grazing lands lying to the
east of Mission San Gabriel which the
two had first visited in 1833. During that
historic survey the party camped along
the banks of a creek which meandered
near the base of the gently rising San Jose
hills, swathed in the fresh green of early
spring. Among the travelers were six to
eight soldiers and several Indian retainers
who had joined the young men. Their
survey began that morning on the ridge
of the sheltering hills. From that airy vantage point the pair, Ignacio Palomares
and Ricardo Vejar, beheld a vision filled
with favorable portents for their future.

On this spring morning in 1837, the
two eager young supplicants determined
to appeal to the governor for a grant of
these lands which had once been a part
of the eastern outpost of Mission San
Gabriel. The area suited their plans for a

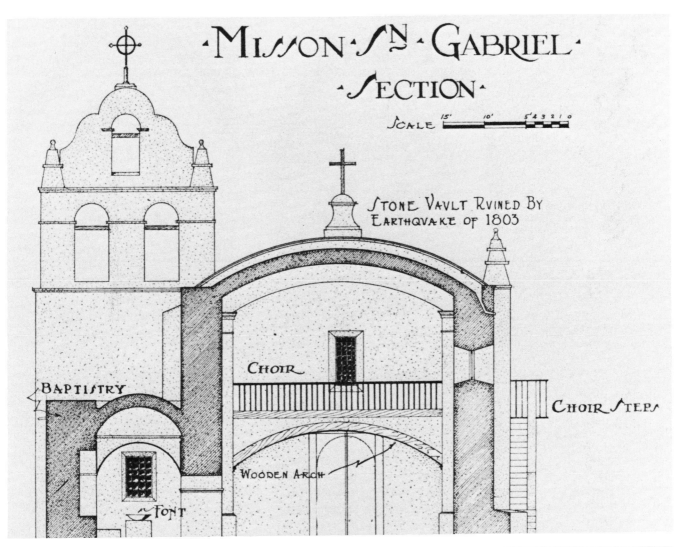

joint ranching enterprise.

Both men were residents of the small, dusty Pueblo de La Reina de Los Angeles some 12 leagues to the west. Both were active in the public affairs of the town. Vejar served as *juez de campo* (judge of the plain) in 1833. Palomares assumed the same responsibilities the following year and in 1835 became *regidor* (councilman). For some years they had worked as partners, running their cattle on the 4,000-acre Rancho Rodeo de Las Aguas held in co-ownership with Maria Rita Valdez de Villa. The young men aspired, however, to larger herds grazing on more expansive

Right: Don Ricardo Vejar was one of two men who are considered to be founders of Pomona. Vejar was given a grant in 1837 by the Mexican government to settle on land now known as Pomona. Courtesy, Pomona Public Library

Far right: Don Ignacio Palomares and Don Ricardo Vejar appealed to the governor in 1837 for a grant of land in the Eastern outpost of the Mission San Gabriel. Courtesy, Pomona Public Library

pastures.

As they sat astride their impatient mounts, the two presented a handsome image. Vejar, the shorter of the two, rode with a particularly easy assurance. Like most Californios he had acquired the skill of riding during his childhood, while living in San Diego. He was the proud son of Salvador Vejar, an expert wood-carver who had come from Spain via Mexico to artfully embellish the great mission altars at San Gabriel and San Juan Capistrano.

Young Palomares had been born in Los Angeles on February 2, 1811. Four days later he had been baptized at Mission San Fernando. His father, Cristobal Palomares, a native of Durango, had come to California in 1790 as a soldier assigned to the Santa Barbara presidio. At the conclusion of his service in 1810, he settled in Los Angeles. There he reared a family that was ever mindful of its notable Spanish ancestry, linked to Don Francisco de Palomares, once governor of the Spanish castle of Saint Gregory at Oran.

NEW RANCH OWNERS

On March 27, 1837, a petition was sent to the Governor of California declaring:

We have a considerable number of cattle and Horses being our only means for the support of our families ... which are now upon a place very small and inconvenient, where they do not thrive ... and the place being vacant which is known by the name of San Jose, distant some six leagues, more or less, from the Ex-Mission of San Gabriel, a map of which place we will lay before your Excellency as soon as possible—we respectfully ask you to grant us the said place, considering the smallness of the place in which we now are, for which cause it is that we appeal to your Excellency's goodness ... praying that you will receive this on common paper there being none of the proper seal.

The plea was turned over to the *ayuntamiento* (city council) in Los Angeles for investigation. The Council's Committee on Vacant Lands reported after a review:

The parties interested ... are Mexican citizens by birth, have rendered repeated services to this jurisdiction and have a considerable stock of cattle and horses ... which stock is at present on a piece of land given to them temporarily, in common with the residents of this city, which is small and on which there is a scarcity of water and pasture. The place San Jose ... is now vacant ... Although it has belonged to the Ex-Mission of San Gabriel ... there is not upon it a single head of cattle belonging to this Community. Wherefore the Committee thinks that it is in a condition to be granted in conformity to the laws of colonization.

On April 15, 1837, writing from Santa Barbara, the governor declared the two young men owners of the place called San Jose, an action approved by the provincial council four days later. It was now time for the alcalde of Los Angeles to take the last formal step in the declaration of title.

On August 3, 1837, Jose Sepulveda, the alcalde, accompanied by two chain bearers and a surveyor, proceeded on horseback to the southeasterly corner of the rancho of San Jose, among the hills called the "lomas de Santa Ana." The party had a cord 100 varas or 333 feet long, and to each end was attached a wooden stake. The traditional surveying ceremony is captured by Will W. Robinson in *Pomona, A Calendar of Events in the Making of a City:*

Commencing at the foot of a black willow tree which was taken for a corner and between the limbs of which a dry stick was placed in the form of a cross, thence from the east towards the west nine thousand seven hundred (9700) varas to the foot of the hills called "Las Lomas de la Puente" taking for a land mark a large Walnut tree on the slope of a small hill on the side of the road

which passes from the said San Jose to La Puente, making a cut (caladura) on one of its limbs with a hatchet: thence in a direction about from south to north Ten Thousand four hundred (10400) varas to the Arroyo (creek) of San Jose opposite a high hill where a large oak was taken as a boundary in which was fixed the head of a beef, and some of its limbs chopped: thence in a direction about from west to east Ten Thousand six hundred (10600) varas to the Arroyo (creek) of San Antonio taking for a corner some young cotton wood trees which are near each other marking crosses in the bark. Thence from north to south Nine Thousand seven hundred (9700) varas to the foot of the black willow the place of beginning.

Legend has it that the occasion was also marked by a Mass of Thanksgiving celebrated under a sheltering oak by Father Jose Zalvidea of the San Gabriel Mission. Vejar chose as his homesite on the newly acquired ranch the southern hills near the Arroyo Pedregoso, while Palomares chose a site near or at the present-day 1569 North Park Avenue according to the 1936 statement of his grandson, Francisco J. Palomares. The latter site was not far from the *cienega* at the eastern slope of the San Jose hills where the men had first camped in the spring of 1837. Locally this northern part of the ranch was called San Jose de Arriba and the southern part, where Vejar had located, San Jose de Abajo.

Three years later, in 1840, the partnership was expanded to include Palomares' brother-in-law, Luis Arenas, who had served as the first alcalde of Los Angeles. To accommodate him, an additional league was granted. It was subsequently known as the Addition to Rancho San Jose. This arrangement lasted until 1844 when Arenas sold or "lost" his land as well as the adjoining Rancho Azusa to Henry Dalton, a Los Angeles merchant, who thus became part owner of Rancho San Jose.

On February 12, 1846, a petition was filed to divide the ranch, giving the southern part to Vejar, the northern section to Palomares, and the area in the west to Dalton. The division, surveyed by Jaspar O'Farrell, was upheld during subsequent investigations by the United States Lands Commission. It first met in Los Angeles in 1854, and finally in 1875 a land patent was issued by President Ulysses S. Grant, which was based upon the official survey of boundaries conducted by the staff of the United States Surveyor General.

RANCHERS PROSPER

California's growing prosperity, stimulated by the thousands of gold-seeking forty-niners who flocked to the northern part of the state, benefited Vejar and Palomares, who provided cattle to the growing population. Both constructed fine family homes from which they dispensed their widely admired hospitality. Judge Benjamin Hayes, while campaign-

ing in the region, noted in his diary that the valley was "full of agreeable people fond of festivities, industrious withal." With evident pleasure he described feasting among nearly 100 guests at Vejar's one-story home, which with its blacksmith's and silversmith's shops and stable encompassed a central courtyard large enough to accommodate 100 horses.

In 1852 Vejar constructed next to his home a beautifully appointed chapel to which neighbors were summoned by the tolling of a large bell hung in a nearby pepper tree. As a result it was no longer necessary to travel to Mission San Gabriel or the church at the Los Angeles plaza for christenings or to participate in the colorful Corpus Christi processions. On one occasion even the sacrament of Confirmation was conferred when Bishop Francisco Garcia Diego visited the chapel.

The welcome was equally warm at the Palomares' 13-room home, Casa Madera, which had been first planned in 1854 as a wedding gift for Ignacio Palomares' daughter, Teressa, and Ramon Vejar. When the young couple chose instead to live in a two-story dwelling built for them

Ramon and Teressa Vejar's two-story home was built by Don Ricardo. This picture was taken in 1946, six years before the house was considered unsafe for occupancy and torn down. Courtesy, Pomona Public Library

by Ricardo Vejar on a site now occupied by Lanterman Hospital, Palomares and his wife, Concepcion, considerably expanded the dwelling to accommodate themselves and the five children who still lived at home. The house, with its vine-covered corridors, large *sala* (drawing room), dining room, five bedrooms, kitchen, storage areas, and *tienda* (shop), which together comprised an area of 3,500 square feet, was by far the largest home in the region. Its distinctive roof was made of hand-hewn shakes, the interior plastered with a mixture of lime and ground cactus pulp, and it featured walled gardens beneath shady pepper trees.

The spacious home was filled with the bustling sounds of family life, for though Teressa had married, Ignacio and Concepcion were surrounded by Luis, Tomas, Francisco, Manuel, and little Josefa. Palomares' guests also gathered at the home to witness cockfights or fast-paced rounds of *sacando el gallo* (pulling the rooster). With pleasure they accepted invitations to dance *La Zorrita,* or with their partners circle the gaily decorated *sala.* On occasions like San Juan Day, the guests gathered for horse racing, trick riding, and a barbecue under the willows in what is now Ganesha Park.

But Rancho San Jose was a working ranch devoted to raising sturdy Mexican cattle valued for market. One single northward drive of 4,000 cattle headed by Ricardo's son Chico netted a return of $14,000. In addition to tending the stock, there was the regular routine of branding during the semiannual rodeos at which Ignacio Palomares and Santiago Martinez, each serving as *juez de campo,* adjudicated disputes. Other tasks included processing the dressed beef into *carne seca* (dried beef), and rendering the tallow, which was poured while still

Francisco "Poncho" Palomares was one of six children of Ignacio Palomares. Courtesy, Pomona Public Library

melted into bags made of skins. Ranch retainers farmed, milked the cows, made cheese, and herded the sheep, which were sheared by a group of Indians from the former *asistencia* at Pala, who twice a year traveled northward to Rancho San Jose. Workers, drawn from the local community of approximately 200 former mission Indians, were paid 50 cents a day to repair the seven-mile aqueduct which brought water to the Palomares property. The disciplined harmony of these various operations was maintained by the grandees themselves, Palomares sometimes resorting to placing a lump of rock salt in the mouth of a hired hand who dared utter a vulgarity.

Despite the demands of ranch administration, Palomares remained active in public affairs. In 1838 he again served as *regidor.* In 1840 he was made *juez de campo,* and he was named *juez de paz* (justice of the peace) the subsequent year. He also served as an elector representing Los Angeles in 1843 and as one of six *suplente* (alternates) representing the south in the Assembly of 1845. He was elected alcalde during the American occupation but refused to accept the position.

VISITORS' OUTPOST

Among his responsibilities Palomares operated a *tienda* in the front wing of his house where he provided flour, needles, and spirits to the thousands who over the years stopped to refresh themselves at the ranch. Some were headed for Santa Fe by way of the Old Spanish Trail. Some were headed for the wagon road to Salt Lake and even beyond to Colorado. Others were headed for Los Angeles, having taken the Southern Route past Fort Yuma and Warner's Ranch.

The cavalcade of travelers was colorful and distinctive. Californios passed by in creaking wooden-wheeled *carretas* (carts). Their cargo was strapped in chests beneath canopies keeping the sun from occupants who rested on mattresses, which somewhat softened the jostling ride. They were followed by lumber wagons from the Mormon mill at San Bernardino. Somewhat later there appeared the lightly sprung, green Concord stages whose passengers gladly paid $200 to ride in leather upholstered splendor from St. Louis all the way to California. There was occasional excitement, as in 1851 when two members of the U.S. Army's ill-fated Camel Corps arrived. The imported camels were supposed to police the newly acquired Mexican Cession territory, but according to Bess Adams Garner in *Windows in an Old Adobe,* their appearance in the company of Hi Jolly,

an exotically costumed cameleer, "created great curiosity, and scared all the horses, mules, and children." Even a tired and tattered circus troupe paused for rest and water at Rancho San Jose in 1863.

Attracted by the promise of water, a number of stages also stopped at the home of Ricardo Vejar. By 1847, as a result of his purchase of Rancho Los Nogales, he had become one of the wealthiest men in the county, and his lands had an assessed value of $48,000. The number of stages arriving at the Vejar homestead increased after 1858 when the well-known Butterfield Stage started making regularly scheduled stops. There were visits as well by various stages operated by its Los Angeles competitors, Phineas Banning and Remi Nadeau.

AMERICAN OCCUPATION

The road across the valley was also traveled by United States troops in one of the few exchanges fought between the Americans and the Californios in the Mexican War. Shortly before that confrontation between the two factions at Isaac Williams' Rancho Santa Ana del Chino, the Palomares family slightly tasted the fruits of war when an American soldier unceremoniously appropriated a horse belonging to Ignacio Palomares' son. Palomares himself was to play a key negotiating role in the aftermath of the larger exchange. With William Workman he successfully interceded with Captain Jose Maria Flores to prevent the captives, including Benjamin D. Wilson, from being sent to Mexico.

The encounter at Chino was among the few hostile exchanges which marked the transition from Mexican to American rule in 1848. Of greater significance to the landowners was the resurveying of ranch boundaries and the review of owners' patents, as well as the establishment of American governmental institutions that declared the area an official township of the county in 1851. According to Roy M. Fryer in *Pomona Valley before the Americans Came:*

By a decree of the Court of Sessions on August 7, 1851, the County of Los Angeles was divided into six Townships or Towns as they were also called. These were Los Angeles, San Gabriel, San Jose, San Bernardino, Santa Ana and San Juan Capistrano. The Township of San Jose was created at this time partly from the former townships of San Bernardino and San Gabriel. According to the records it included Cucamonga, San Antonio, San Jose, El Pedregoso, San Jose en Medio, Los Nogales and Rancho de los Ybarras.

The new American regime also altered the system of taxation. Very quickly the lightly populated, pastoral region of Southern California experienced the imposition of unparalleled land taxes, approved by a legislature dominated by Northern Californians representing an exploding population of gold-seeking forty-niners.

The burden of increased taxes did not diminish the halcyon spirit of Southern California's rancheros, however. The onrush of settlers had fanned prosperity, and the promise of rail connections bespoke added opportunity. Amid this seeming affluence debts were incurred at high rates of interest and exchanges based upon honorable promises were accepted as sound business practice. Harsh economic consequences struck, however, as the population of gold-seeking miners diminished in the 1850s, and in the next two decades the railroad only slowly made its way southward.

DARK DAYS FOR RANCHO SAN JOSE

To the economic problems of increased taxes and diminished markets were added several other catastrophes which were of almost biblical proportions in terms of their scope as well as their wrath. At the outset in 1861 a series of unprecedented floods continued almost without cessation for a month. James M. Guinn in *Noachin Deluge of California* observed that the central basin of the state "became an inland sea," and on Rancho San Jose sodden adobes that could no longer absorb the rainfall simply collapsed. Roads were impassable, mail could not be delivered, the Los Angeles River overflowed its banks and permanently changed its course, and almost all the properties in the San Bernardino Valley were destroyed. Judge Benjamin Hayes, witnessing the scene, observed: "Here only a chimney, there a mere doorpost or a few scattered stakes of fence." The devastation was repeated in the winters of 1867 and 1868 when, noted Robert Glass Cleland in *The Cattle on a Thousand Hills*, "it looked as if the sea had moved inland."

The great flood of 1861 was followed by two years of uninterrupted drought. Almost no rain fell, and absolutely no grass was available for forage for the multitudes of starving, bellowing animals. Julia Slaughter Fuqua, born in 1866 near the south end of the present Garey Avenue, described the failed efforts of the wandering cattle to forage the few irrigated enclosures, when the animals, in trying "to reach the green leaves through the fence, died with their horns caught in the woven fence rails, too weak from starvation to free themselves." Those remaining were largely slaughtered for the trifling amounts their hides and horns would bring on the depressed market.

Their whitening bones strewn across the red and arid hillsides were soon made even drier by scorching desert winds bringing millions of grasshoppers sweeping across the country like a devastating fire. The earth was as hard as iron, and the sky was the color of brass. As John Forster wrote: "There was a perfect devastation—such a thing was never before known in California."

To these calamities was added the fearsome scourge of smallpox which claimed the Palomares' daughter, Maria de Jesus, as well as a grandson, Tomas. No general roundups were conducted at Rancho San Jose in 1863. In Los Angeles the church bell ceased to toll as the number of dead began to mount alarmingly.

The plague which broke out wildly in scattered localities could not be contained by the few physicians in the area using unfamiliar methods of inoculation. As a precaution against the loathsome terror, sentinels stationed at the entrances of the great ranchos checked the arrival of any stranger. At Rancho San Jose a tub, which contained some disinfectant in water to cleanse articles to be exchanged, was placed upon a post at the gate. Supplies for Indian workers were located at some distance from the ranch houses because the native population was particularly beset by the disease. In fact a large number of Indians encamped by the *cienega* east of the San Jose hills succumbed and were buried at the site where Ganesha Park is now located.

LOSS OF THE VEJAR HOLDINGS

"Everyone is down to his last dollar," wrote one settler, who added, "Everybody in town is broke . . . and the grasshoppers have taken possession." Southern California's economy was paralyzed, bedeviled by catastrophe. In the decade of the 1860s the number of cattle in Los Angeles County fell by 71 percent. The decline even affected the prosperous Vejars. To cover a seemingly temporary shortfall, Vejar mortgaged his Rancho San Jose de Abajo as well as all his stock property throughout the state for a loan of $19,763.62, payable in 90 days at 2 percent interest per month.

Los Angeles County records include a deed for Rancho San Jose made on April 30, 1864, by Vejar in favor of Isaac Schlesinger and Hyman Tischler for a consideration of $28,000.

The dispersal of the Vejar holdings by means of this "deed in lieu of foreclosure" aroused a bitterness that swept the entire Pomona Valley. As a result

William W. Rubottom built a house and a tavern on the land he purchased from Louis Phillips. A post office was later established there in January 1868. Courtesy, Pomona Public Library

Far left: Esther Blake Phillips was the wife of Louis Phillips. Courtesy, Pomona Public Library

Left: Louis Phillips was a founding father of the Pomona Valley. Courtesy, Pomona Public Library

Schlesinger and Tischler did not live at the ranch. Instead they employed young Louis Phillips, who was living in Paredon Blanco, now the community of Boyle Heights in Los Angeles, but like Schlesinger had been born in the Polish town of Kempen. In early 1863, for a consideration of $100 a month plus half of all the colts, calves, and lambs born each year, Phillips agreed to operate Rancho San Jose de Abajo.

Phillips administered the ranch with care, making improvements, avoiding debt, and maintaining a careful inventory of the herds and supplies, all the while cultivating the goodwill of his neighbors. By the spring of 1866 Phillips had signed a mortgage for $30,000 in exchange for the 12,000-acre San Jose Ranch. The following year he drove a band of horses raised on the ranch to Salt Lake City where they fetched more than enough to retire the mortgage.

Soon after Phillips obtained title to the land, he sold William W. Rubottom 100 acres of it for $1,000. Uncle Willie, as he was called, named the site Spadra in honor of the Spadra Bluffs in his native

state of Arkansas. He established a hostelry where stages changed horses and passengers refreshed themselves in the restaurant or the tavern, where a usually genial Rubottom maintained discipline, using a gun or knife if necessary.

The traffic increased at Spadra as rail lines were laid and freight cars exchanged cargoes with wagon trains from San Bernardino, Salt Lake City, and even Colorado. In 1876 more than 12 million pounds of building materials and livestock arrived at Spadra. Shipments consisted of wool, wine, hides, honey, and fruit. All was bustle as trains of 5 or 6 wagons drawn by 16 horses milled about the station platform, driven by weary teamsters impatiently anticipating a welcome respite at Rubottom's.

All was silenced, however, when in 1875 rail connections were made through Colton. Though settlers continued to pick up their mail and to vote in Spadra, it lost its status as the western terminus of the valley, and the surge of events to come would transform a large portion of the Rancho San Jose into the town of Pomona.

CHAPTER THREE

THE CITY
TAKES SHAPE

Change was rapid by the 1870s when the United States entered a phase of industrial development nourished by newfound resources, a growing work force, a widening array of inventions, broadening international markets, and a railroad network which connected Southern California with markets that had been previously inaccessible due to natural barriers of sea, desert, and mountains.

The lands of Rancho San Jose, which straddled the routes through the El Cajon and San Gorgonio passes long used by travelers journeying the southern trails, would be directly affected by America's railroad expansion. Although the golden spike connecting the Central Pacific and the Union Pacific had been driven at Promontory, Utah, in 1869, the Southern Pacific did not reach Southern California until some time later. In 1871 federal legislation was passed that allowed the Southern Pacific Railroad to join the Texas Pacific Railroad at Fort Yuma.

RAIL ACCESS

Fearing that the Southern Pacific might bypass Los Angeles in favor of the port city of San Diego, county voters approved an agreement, drawn up by Francisco Palomares and the railroad, which acceded to the railroad's demand for a subsidy of $600,000 and a new depot pre-

These cars were parked in front of the Palomares Hotel at the halfway point of the annual run of the Automobile Club of Southern California on April 27, 1904. The trip was made from downtown Los Angeles to Pomona and back. Courtesy, Pomona Public Library

31

liminary to its completing 25 miles of track north to San Fernando and laying tracks an equal distance to the east. As a result in 1873 track was laid through the Rancho San Jose lands into San Bernardino County. On April 21, 1874, the line between Spadra and Los Angeles was completed. In October 1875 a Southern Pacific station opened east of Spadra in the vicinity where Pomona would shortly be founded.

The line reached Colton, bypassing San Bernardino which had been unwilling to meet the Southern Pacific's requested subsidy, and it snaked through the San Gorgonio Pass. By 1877 the line had reached the west bank of the Colorado River opposite Yuma. By 1881 the

Above: Some of the workers who built the Southern Pacific Railroad from Los Angeles to Pomona posed for this turn-of-the-century photo. Timothy Bresnahan, right, was the foreman. Courtesy, Pomona Public Library

Right: These men are paving the Southern Pacific Railroad depot in Pomona. Courtesy, Pomona Public Library

Construction was under
way on the Southern Pacific
Railroad in the early 1880s.
Courtesy, Pomona Public
Library

further development of this route gave Southern California a direct connection with the eastern part of the nation. It complemented the existing cross-country connections via the San Joaquin Valley to the Pacific Coast rail terminus of San Francisco, which had been established in 1876.

Rail access quickly prompted the development of town sites in key locations including land adjacent to what would become the Pomona rail depot. The Spadra post office was soon moved to Pomona, and real estate sales gradually increased. Some of the sales were to disenchanted gold seekers attracted by the inexpensive acreage. A number of the buyers were agriculturalists attracted by the location and the good weather that caused the valley to have few winter frosts or desiccating desert winds.

Many of the newly arrived landowners became members of the Los Angeles Chapter of the National Grange of the Patrons of Husbandry, an agricultural cooperative founded in 1867. The master of chapter number 36, Thomas Andrew

Garey, was to affect the fortune and the future of the town that was beginning to take shape. Garey, proprietor of the Cooperative Nursery and an expert on citriculture, also served as the Grange organizing deputy for the Los Angeles-San Bernardino District. The energetic Garey, born in Cincinnati in 1830, had started for California in 1850 as part of a pioneer company journeying from Independence, Missouri. After a brief sojourn in Albuquerque, where he married Louise Smith, Garey proceeded west with his new wife to San Diego. He ultimately settled in El Monte in 1852.

Pomona's old Post Office
on Second Street between
Garey Avenue and Thomas
Street was quite the model
of efficiency at the turn of
the century. Courtesy, Pomona Public Library

Right: Cyrus Burdick, along
with Patrick Tonner and
Francisco Palomares, developed the first cooperative
citrus grove in Pomona.
Courtesy, Pomona Public
Library

Far right: Thomas Andrew
Garey was the proprietor of
the Cooperative Nursery
and became a respected authority on citrus cultivation.
Courtesy, Pomona Public
Library

PLANS FOR A TOWN

Garey, who also farmed land in La
Puente, Rialto, and later Los Angeles,
conducted a nursery with a stock of
1.25 million trees, raised silkworms, and
became a respected authority on citrus
culture. He wrote regularly for the Los
Angeles Chamber of Commerce and published a pioneer study, *Orange Culture in
California.* In 1870 he developed the
Mediterranean sweet orange and, from
cuttings provided by C.R. Workman, the
popular Eureka lemon.

It was to Thomas Garey that early Pomona residents turned when organizing
a local Grange, which was appropriately
named the Eureka Chapter. The ensuing
success of the organization led several
members, including Cyrus Burdick and
Patrick C. Tonner, who together with
Francisco Palomares held 3,000 acres
with water rights on Rancho San Jose de
Arriba, to propose a cooperative organization of landowners to develop citrus

groves along San Jose Creek. They pointed
out that harvests could be conveniently
shipped along the new rail lines which
spanned California and reached mining
districts in southern Nevada, Arizona,
and beyond. The proposal was made
doubly persuasive by the recent demise
of the cattle industry and the increasing
competition from Australia that threatened the local sheep industry.

At a general Grange meeting held in
El Monte in the summer of 1874, a committee on immigration was formed to
propose ways of attracting a more stable
agricultural population which might support the potential market expansion the
railroad promised. After some delibera-
tion the committee proposed the creation
of an association to buy and sell land-
holdings. With the support of several
businessmen, the group organized the
Los Angeles Immigration and Land Cooperative Association (LAILCA) with
Garey as president. Its first project was
Artesia, a land subdivision in southeast-

ern Los Angeles County.

The success of the venture led Tonner, Burdick, and Palomares to offer their obviously underfinanced project to the LAILCA. The principals, including several members of the Eureka Chapter familiar with the land and aware of its potential, purchased 2,750 acres for $10,000. Patterning their plans after the successful Artesia model, the group first surveyed the land, which was soon increased to 5,000 acres. They then divided it into 10- and 40-acre sections which were on a mesa relatively free of frost and therefore suitable for citrus. In the area adjacent to the railroad, a town site was plotted that measured one square mile, and streets were graded. Two-mile-long Garey Avenue, named for the respected president of the association, was bordered by Monterey cypress trees which were, according to an early account, "planted at such a distance apart as will allow the planting of Australian blue gums." Nurseryman Solomon Gates won the prize of a town lot for proposing that the community be named Pomona in honor of the Roman goddess of fruit. Po-

tential buyers from far and near were deluged with copies of *The New Italy,* later absorbed by *Halls Land Journal,* which promised readers unexcelled fruit country within 32 miles of Los Angeles. On November 11, 1875, a preliminary excursion, no doubt organized by publicist Luther M. Holt, brought the first newsmen to town. Initial impressions evoked a positive report from the *Los Angeles Star,* which announced: "The tract is a rich, friable loam of exhaustless fertility, and adapted to the growth of all fruits and cereals indigenous to this section." The reporter from the *Los Angeles Evening Express* included in his glowing description news that deductions in lot prices "will be made to those who actually plan to settle on the land."

The first people to respond to the energetic promotion arrived by excursion train on George Washington's birthday in 1876, welcomed by a brass band and the promise of a free meal at the newly built, two-story Pomona Hotel. The potential investors were not easily persuaded, however, despite the fact that the town's apparent water supply had been consid-

Far left: L.M. Holt was one of the early American settlers who designed the city of Pomona. Much of his vision still exists today. Courtesy, Pomona Public Library

Left: When Pomona was founded in 1874, Solomon Gates suggested its name. He is also noted for bringing the first eucalyptus trees to the area. Courtesy, Pomona Public Library

erably enhanced by the diversion of San Jose Creek to the open ditches lining each street, a brazen promotional scheme not unusual for the period. The middling land sales led Holt to the doleful assessment that "the excursion was a success, but the auction was a failure." Opening day sales amounted to $18,000; the price of the lots averaged $64. Among the buyers there had been little evidence of the speculation that characterized the promotion and would have promised significant profits for the organizers. The greatest profits may have been garnered by the enterprising Garey, who furnished the plantings for the new community.

Although the settlement did not immediately burgeon, it soon had 8 or 10 houses, a blacksmith shop, a livery stable, a drug and provisions store, a saloon, and a branch of George Egan's Spadra butcher shop, all clustered near Second and Main. Most importantly the town claimed a fine new railroad warehouse and a depot from which residents could venture to Los Angeles for $3. The pioneer settlers included several rail conductors, Luther Holt's brother, who purchased substantial acreage and lived for some years on the avenue that bears his name, and nurseryman Caleb E. White, a Massachusetts-born forty-niner who had sailed around Cape Horn. White also settled on Holt Avenue, where he planted an orchard considered to be a model by many throughout the valley.

Despite the best efforts of White and others, agricultural fortunes soon faltered. Following the abundant rain of the first two or three seasons, a series of dry years beset the valley. Artesian wells dried up, and landowners turned to the cooperative for assistance. With loans from the Temple and Workman Bank, the Pomona Water Company was organized to meet the most critical need confronting any Southern California agricultural venture. On July 23, 1875, the organization was incorporated with a capitalization of $25,000. With the promise of an assured water supply, Luther Holt supervised the planting of oranges and budded lemons on 40 acres north of the railroad and 120 acres to the south. But hope turned to despair when on the evening of July 30, 1877, the town was engulfed in flames, destroying much of the property owned by the approximately 300 residents of what cynics had come to call "Monkeytown."

Although the economic depression following the Civil War and the subsequent Panic of 1873 caused little economic disruption in the region, the area was deeply affected by rampant speculation on the fabled Comstock mining shares in Nevada that ultimately brought about the downfall of the Bank of California in San Francisco and, with it, the Temple and Workman Bank. The bank closed its doors in 1876, bringing an abrupt end to Pomona's development. In 1881 the land was returned to Louis Phillips.

SECOND CHANCE

Pomona's prospects were somewhat revived when the Reverend Cyrus Mills and his wife, Susan, the administrators of Mills College of Oakland, California, visited the area early in 1882. Impressed with the potential for a flourishing inland city, Mills, in association with M.L. Wicks of Los Angeles and several Northern California financial interests, secured land and water rights in order to incorporate the Pomona Land and Water Company in October 1882.

In December additional land acquisitions to the north and east increased the site to 12,000 acres. That same year the

THE CITY TAKES SHAPE

first flow from a newly drilled artesian well ignited a new spirit of expansion that was further spurred by the completion in 1883 of a cement pipeline costing $63,000, which carried water from San Antonio Canyon. Encouraged by the renewed growth, the editor of the *Pomona Weekly Times* observed: "By 1886 the hamlet had crossed the urban threshold: it was a city."

Pomona soon joined the rest of the region in a real estate boom that caused the number of Los Angeles County resi-

dents to rise dramatically and Pomona's population to increase from 300 to over 3,000 by 1889. The influx of prospective land buyers in the mid-1880s was occasioned by a substantial rate war between the Southern Pacific and the Santa Fe railroads, launched by the Santa Fe in an effort to weaken the Big Four's control over California rail traffic (Charles Crocker, Colis P. Huntington, Mark Hopkins, and Leland Stanford). On March 4, 1886, the fares from New York fell from $45 to $40. On that same day Chicago fares were cut

The first Pomona Water Company was organized in 1875 to meet the needs of the agricultural community. In 1882 the Pomona Land and Water Company was incorporated when the Reverend Cyrus Mills secured the city's land and water rights. Courtesy, Pomona Public Library

MAP OF
THE TOWN OF
POMONA
Los Angeles County, Cal.
SCALE, 5 CHAINS 330 FEET TO 1 INCH.
1885.

"By 1886 the hamlet had crossed the urban threshold: it was a city," observed the *Pomona Weekly Times.* Courtesy, Pomona Public Library

Crank's Los Angeles and San Gabriel Valley Railroad in February 1887, caused a continental shift in population that was to transform Southern California into what some have called "the seacoast of Iowa."

Farmers fleeing Midwestern winters, coughing pilgrims hoping to regain their health, and hopeful speculators captivated by the zealous real estate campaigns all made their way to Southern California. By 1887 boomtowns such as Long Beach, Alhambra, and Palms (near present-day Culver City) had assumed some of the reality described in their promotional literature. Along the foothills north of Pomona, instant towns such as San Dimas, Lordsburg, the short-lived Palomares, and Claremont sprang to life along the Santa Fe corridor, the new residents attracted by promises as generous as those listed on a real estate poster promoting the proposed town of Palomares:

Grand Railroad Excursion and Genuine Auction Sale!
No Chenanekin!!
Beautiful Palomares, Pomona Valley!
Lunch, Coffee, Lemonade, and Ice Water Free!
Full Band Music!

Lordsburg, now the city of La Verne, was typical of boomtown developments. The 600-acre tract was platted in the spring of 1887 by Isaac Wilson Lord. Dumke's chronicle indicates that more than $200,000 worth of lots were sold at its initial auction to the 2,500 visitors, who, arriving on a Santa Fe excursion train, were welcomed by three brass bands, a mammoth lunch, three auctioneers, and promoters who distributed literature urging:

to $32. The climax came two days later when, according to Glenn S. Dumke in *The Boom of the Eighties*, the competitors "settled down to a finish fight over the fares between Kansas City and Los Angeles. In the morning the Southern Pacific met the Santa Fe at twelve dollars. The latter then dropped to ten dollars and the Southern Pacific followed suit. Shortly after noon the Southern Pacific announced a rate of one dollar." Although this fare was short-lived, for the next year fares from points on the Missouri River to California did not rise above $25. This, along with the construction of James F.

These young men are enjoying watermelon near the YMCA in 1925. Courtesy, Pomona Public Library

Don't pass it by
At least to try
To go and buy
In Lordsburg

The town soon claimed a hotel, a business block, and several homes. But hopes for a promising future were quickly dashed when lenders foreclosed on Lord's mortgage and threatened to appropriate the buildings as well. As a result, explains J.M. Guinn in *The Great Real Estate Boom of 1887*, "the citizens of Pomona were aroused one Sabbath morning by the harsh grating of many heavy wheels; peeping through their shutters they beheld the city of La Verne moving down upon them—fleeing before the wrath of an outwitted creditor."

Ontario, located east of Pomona and developed by the Chaffey brothers on the land of Rancho Cucamonga, used similar promotional techniques but enjoyed greater success as a result of the Chaffeys' thoughtful planning. Along the wide streets of the "Model Colony," one could find a gravity railway and a mutual water system. Although saloons were prohibited, the construction of an agricultural college moved apace. From 1882 until 1886 the Canadian brothers witnessed a sixfold increase on their $60,000 investment.

To the southeast of Pomona, land developer Richard Gird, who had used profits from the sale of the Tombstone Mine in Arizona to purchase the vast Rancho Santa Ana del Chino in 1881, platted 23,000 acres into 10-acre lots and designed a town site one mile square. Gird's development of Chino, regularly reported in the weekly *Chino Valley Champion*, included a four-mile water conduit and reservoir system, a rail line between Chino and Ontario, schools, and an opera house. Despite such efforts a century would pass before the town fulfilled the

Students at Central School—first and second graders—learn first hand the art of gardening. Courtesy, Pomona Public Library

developer's expectations.

The uneven fortunes of these visionary villages of the 1880s underscored the singular vigor of Pomona's development. Hotels were filled, and visitors from Los Angeles, Pasadena, and Monrovia sallied forth to what promotional literature described as "a land redolent of orange blossoms and rich in every variety of fruit." As one brochure promised: "To visit Pomona is to create invariably a desire to remain in so lovely a spot." The developers promised that this community held something for everyone:

No one need go away dissatisfied. To the artist, her grand mountains and breadth of valley afford ever-varying studies in light and shade; to the worn out dyspeptic business man she offers rest and recreation; to the consumptive, a climate that in its equableness and freedom from malaria, will restore him to health, if not beyond redemption; to the mechanic and artisan, abundant opportunities to work at remunerative wages; and last and most important of all, to the tiller of the soil she offers inducements to stay as are not excelled and scarcely equalled in any portion of the state.

Above all, it was promised, "Pomona is the place for a home! And what a home can be created in this land of sunshine."

During the apex of the boom, 45 real estate agents initiated an intensive publicity campaign directed to the East and Midwest that resulted in substantial profits. In one six-week period the House and Dreher Company sold real estate amounting to a half-million dollars. In their enthusiasm journalists and realtors mailed newspapers and promotional broadsides everywhere. One group of zealous townsfolk carried their message to the St. Louis encampment of the Grand Army of the Republic, while the Pomona Board of Trade hosted a delegation of New England grocers. The boosterism was further reinforced by the fulsome praise for Pomona to be found in the increasing number of Southern California guidebooks.

As a result in 1887 alone $300,000 worth of new construction was initiated, including 50 houses per month. The value of the lots on which the structures were built rose even more rapidly. A town lot that sold for $200 in 1885 fetched $3,250 three years later. Another town lot which had been offered for $65 in 1876 was sold for $10,000 in 1877.

By the end of the decade, the boom had declined, but Pomona was left with a stable business climate and such up-to-date amenities as gaslights and cement sidewalks. In August 1885 the Sunset Telephone and Telegraph Company had installed a toll station at Hamner's Drug Store. Within the next two years the Taylor Opera House was built, a railroad powered by oil (unique at the time) was constructed connecting Pomona with North Pomona, and three mule-drawn streetcar lines bisected the town. When

The city's Pomona Valley Telephone and Telegraph Union had a working switchboard and operators hard at work receiving telephone calls in the early 1900s. Courtesy, Pomona Public Library

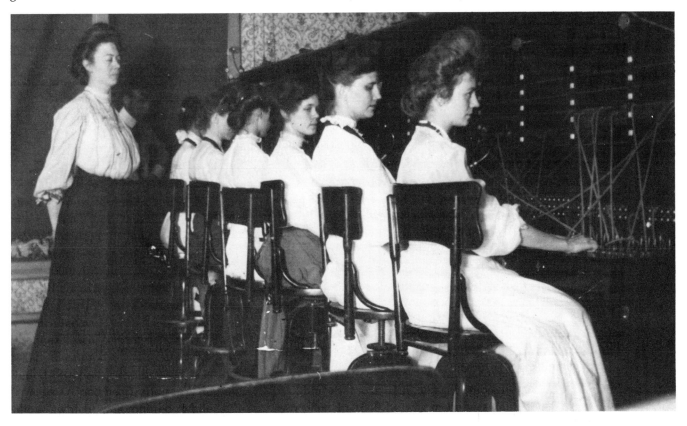

Delivering groceries to a
Pomona neighborhood was
common in 1923. Courtesy,
Pomona Public Library

in January 1888 Pomona was incorporated, it was the fifth largest city in the
county.

CIVIC DEVELOPMENT

The new municipality had a skating rink
and 23 saloons, which were bereft of customers by the end of the year when the
majority of the residents voted to make
the city "dry." Although only one under-
taker and embalmer served the town, demand was sufficiently light for him to
also trade in wood and coal. The town's
213 businesses included a flour mill, a
gun and lock shop, several dressmakers,
tailors and milliners, 3 drugstores, and 4
dry goods stores. There were 5 black-
smiths, a feed store, and 2 harness shops,
as well as 4 confectionary and book
shops. Among the several hotels, Mother
King's Pomona Hotel was favored by

those who visited the town for their
health. Boots and shoes were sold by Mr.
and Mrs. P.J. Tarr, who covered the coun-
tryside with signs urging "Try Tarr on
Shoes."

The growing population was supplied by 10 grocery stores, 2 bakeries, 2
meat markets, and a score of vegetable
markets belonging to the town's Chinese
population, which numbered about 200
and operated many of the town laun-
dries as well. The several restaurants included the Maison Francaise. It catered
to, among others, a significant population
of French settlers. By 1888 the newly incorporated city of 4,000 had dedicated a
city hall with a jail conveniently located
in the basement. Upon incorporation
the town replaced county constables
and justices of the peace with a locally
elected constable. From December 1886
until his death in 1922, former blacksmith
Frank O. Slanker served in that capacity.

He was repeatedly returned to office by admiring townsfolk who respected his sometimes unconventional but effective methods for assuring Pomona's peace and harmony, which included patrolling the town on bicycle and innovative methods for crime prevention. On one occasion, his coal miner's disguise and clever ruse captured a group who had been preying on visiting miners and sheepherders.

During the eventful year of incorporation, a semi-private town library was organized, and newly founded Pomona College began offering classes in facilities located at Fifth and White. Construction was under way on 125 buildings, a number of which were being financed by the Pomona Valley Bank (known after 1886 as the First National Bank of Pomona), H.A. Palmer's Pomona Bank, and the American National Bank, which from its offices in the Caleb E. White block conveyed an air of prosperous stability.

With the close of the decade, the community claimed 10 churches, half of them (including the Episcopal and Methodist churches as well as St. Joseph's Roman Catholic Church) located in permanent houses of worship. Others, including the Congregational and Unitarian churches, which were organized in Taylor's Opera House, were energetically raising funds for construction.

The community also fostered a varied social life, which was centered in the three-story Palomares Hotel erected in 1885 by the Pomona Land and Water Company. The grandly designed build-

Below: The three-story Palomares Hotel at the intersection of Garey Avenue and Holt Boulevard was built in 1885 by the Pomona Land and Water Company. The hotel did much to foster the area's social life, and was built at a time when land sales surged with the coming of the Southern Pacific through Pomona in 1875. Courtesy, Pomona Public Library

Left: The Palomares Hotel was expanded in 1887, and an addition providing 100 more rooms was built. Courtesy, Pomona Public Library

On June 14, 1911, fire broke out in the Palomares Hotel, completely destroying the 132-room Pomona Tavern and Hotel. The hotel had been an area landmark for 25 years and a social hub of the entire Pomona Valley. The hotel was located on the corner of Garey Avenue and Holt Boulevard, the current location of the city's YMCA building. Courtesy, Pomona Public Library

ing had interior woodwork and furniture of oak and ash. Appointments included brick and marble fireplaces and plate glass. Gaslight accented the ample public rooms and the graciously furnished guest rooms, which were expanded in number by a 100-room addition in 1887 and were equipped with electrically powered bell service. At that time the new owners, made up of a syndicate including Richard Gird of Chino, moved the original structure and attached it to the new construction. In addition to the $46,000 invested in construction, the new proprietors invested $15,000 in rich Brussels carpets, quality silver, elaborate wallpapers, and potted palms.

Despite these efforts and the services of a nationally acclaimed hotel staff, the passing of the boom augured ill for the enterprise. In 1891 a local newspaper ad

appealed: "Try our Christmas dinner, it will be a hummer." Not until a decade later, when E.H. Pierce purchased the hostelry for the sum originally spent on the furnishings alone, did the development of the automobile and better roads usher in a more profitable era. In 1904 the hotel was the official destination of a cross-country tour sponsored by the Automobile Club of Southern California. Only one of the 42 cars failed to complete the round-trip rally back to Los Angeles. In the course of that year, the hotel passed through the hands of several more owners, and the prominent landmark, with its central observation tower flanked by two end towers, was renamed the Pomona Tavern.

It was during this era that the hotel was designated as the site of Greater Pomona Day, which was celebrated on

January 7, 1911, to mark the completion of the Pacific Electric Railway to Pomona. The festivities included a baby show, a balloon ascension, and a biplane flight which overshot the festivities and landed in the town. These winter revels were to usher in the final phase of the hotel's history. Six months later the building, recently refurbished with electric lights, steam heat, and private baths, was engulfed in flames. After two and one-half hours, as one observer remarked, all that remained was charred brick and "a vast heap of smoking ashes."

The hotel's complete destruction was hardly a reflection on the city's inattention to fire fighting. As early as 1883

Pomona Hose Company #1 had been organized. By the end of the year, volunteers had used funds raised in large part at a Firemen's Ball staged in November to purchase uniforms, equipment, a 300-foot hose, and a cart. By December they had purchased six fire hydrants, and plans had been drawn up for a wooden reel and hose house. Within six months the town had a well-equipped volunteer fire department that was to serve until incorporation in 1888 led to the establishment of a city fire department. Beginning with the city's first volunteer fire chief, C.C. Zilles, the number of volunteer companies expanded, and equipment and technology were developed to meet the

The volunteers of Pomona's First Hose Company Number 1 posed for this group portrait in 1903. Courtesy, Pomona Public Library

needs of the growing mercantile sector and the specialized needs of the expanding citrus economy.

The skill of the three volunteer companies was particularly tested on November 9, 1895, when the opera house and the nearby Gosline Stables went up in flames. Although volunteers were not paid for their services, the prestige associated with occupying one of the 30 volunteer fireman positions was such that applicants far exceeded the openings.

As Pomona grew so did the fire hazards. In 1908 the city approved the purchase of a Rambler. It was converted into an "automobile hose wagon," which was used to fight the increasing number of fires. In 1911 the fires numbered 32, including the conflagration at the famous Palomares Hotel.

Though Pomona was bereft of its fashionable gathering place, its social life continued. Over the decades the towns-

folk frequently convened at McComas Hall on Second Street. There were card parties, concerts, and the presentation of an occasional play at the opera house by troupes coming out from Los Angeles. A favorite fair-weather pastime for Pomona residents was boarding the old pleasure wagons called tallyhos, which carried 20 or 30 passengers all about Southern California. They rode from the seashore to the nearby Chino Ranch, joining in picnics and socials or as rapt audiences watching the latest stereopticon presentation.

Pomona social life was reported in the town's three weekly papers, one of which was the *Pomona Times*, first published in October 1882 on a small press formerly located in Santa Ana. Within two years the paper combined with the *Courier*, established in December 1883, and it reappeared on April 26, 1887, as the *Times-Courier*. It was published daily until its demise in May 1891. The third

Pomona townspeople flocked to the Jackson Opera House at Third and Thomas streets to watch live entertainers perform. This picture was taken before the performance of Donald Bowles and Arthur Dole in 1892. The opera house was destroyed by fire in 1895. Courtesy, Pomona Public Library

paper was the four-page *Pomona Progress*, first published in January 1885, which was described as "a readable, live, wide-awake newspaper" and published by young Edward Stowell with the financial assistance of local bank officer Charles Lorbeer. It was produced in a board shack measuring 10 by 12 feet, using a hand press operated by the 21-year-old Stowell, who had recently emigrated from Illinois as part of the ever-increasing army of health seekers. With "keen, dusty dry humor," according to historian John Baur, Stowell reported on the real estate promotions of the day and campaigned to make Pomona the capital of the future state of Southern California.

The *Progress* disappeared with Stowell's death in 1888. That same year the ownership of the *Times-Courier* changed hands and in 1891 part-ownership was assumed by General John Wasson, editor of the neighboring *Chino Champion.* "Courier" was dropped from the newspaper's name, and the *Times* plunged into the national temperance controversy as editor Wasson championed Pomona's anti-saloon faction. The result was a readers' boycott and a marked decline in advertising. Before Wasson's death around 1910, the partnerships changed several times, and the paper appeared in 1915 as a semiweekly publication, *The Bulletin.*

POLITICAL INFLUENCE

The Pomona press provides ample evidence that this agricultural community was not isolated from the political issues of the day. Not only was the town considered a likely capital for the proposed state of Southern California, but it also was envisioned as an ideal county seat for a new governmental unit proposed by Pomo-

General John Wasson, editor of the *Chino Champion,* shunned advertisers and provoked a reader boycott when his newspaper supported Pomona's anti-saloon proponents. Courtesy, Pomona Public Library

na's state senator, Joseph E. McComas. He drafted legislation in 1889 and 1891 which would have created a county encompassing the area extending from the San Gabriel River to an undesignated spot beyond Cucamonga and from Whittier to "the summit of Old Baldy."

Supporters like Chino neighbor Richard Gird argued that the economic

Judge J.H. Gallup is shown in his Pomona office, left, when he was justice of the peace. Also shown is A.B. Caldwell, Pomona's Marshal, second from left. Courtesy, Pomona Public Library

homogeneity of the region not only provided a singular cohesiveness among the region's 10,000 residents but it also required informed representation sensitive to the region's unique concerns. Furthermore proponents observed that the creation of an additional county would be a step toward correcting the imbalance which allotted the "Southland" only 5 counties out of California's 53. Ultimately the victorious opponents in the north made light of the proposal and attempted to mollify the defeated crusaders by noting that the creation of Orange County out of part of Los Angeles was an adequate adjustment of the regional balance.

Pomona and its elected officials were also stirred by other political issues of the day. Echoing the vituperative anti-Chinese attacks uttered on the sand lots of San Francisco by Denis Kearney and the supporters of his Workingmen's party, some Pomona citizens in 1886 organized the Nonpartisan Anti-Chinese League. Their platform, in addition to such hotly argued issues as temperance and suffrage, both championed by State Senator McComas, was freely debated in the local press.

Pomona Senator J.E. McComas envisioned the city as an ideal seat for a new county. McComas served as state senator for four years. Courtesy, Pomona Public Library

Of particular interest to the residents of this orange-producing community in 1888 was the prospect of a free trade policy allowing unlimited imports if Democratic President Grover Cleveland were to be reelected to a second term. Prodded by Colonel Harrison Gray Otis, the Republican publisher of the *Los Angeles Times*, Pomona resident George Osgoodby, using the pseudonym of Murchison, pretended to be a former British subject assessing candidate Cleveland's position on free trade and directed an inquiry to British Ambassador Lord Lionel Sackville-West. That official's unguardedly candid reply to the "Murchison letter" conveyed his strong conviction that once reelected Cleveland would abandon his support of protective tariffs in favor

President William McKinley visited Pomona while campaigning for reelection in 1900, but stayed for less than a minute. As throngs of supporters surrounded the railroad tracks, McKinley's train only stopped long enough for the president to utter a few words. Courtesy, Pomona Public Library

of free trade. The Pomona Republicans had their answer, and the gleeful Colonel Otis waited until October to release the full text of the response to the Eastern press. The ensuing public debate grew heated, resulting in a demand that the British ambassador be recalled. Despite efforts to minimize the fracas, doggerel set to a popular tune captured the public's fancy:

I've a letter from Pomona
Baby mine, baby mine;
And to us it is a stunner
Baby mine, baby mine;
Mr. Murchison had the zeal
To trap the English Veal
Which has made the Demi's squeal
Baby mine, baby mine.

By election day 1888 the issue had not faded, and an informed consensus held that as a direct result of the "Murchison letter" drafted in Debrunner's grocery store in Pomona, Republican Benjamin Harrison was elected president.

Three years later Harrison visited Pomona, greeted by a throng of 4,000 people. It is not recorded whether Osgoodby, a pivotal figure in Harrison's political career, was present.

Another president passed briefly through the town in 1900. William McKinley, a Midwesterner as were many Pomonans, was campaigning for his reelection in nearby Redlands when, through the intercession of Otis, the president agreed to visit Pomona. His acceptance of the town's invitation was received a mere two-and-a-half hours before McKinley's arrival at 1:12 p.m. on Wednesday, May 8. Despite the haste Pomona was bedecked in flags and bunting, and 4,000 citizens gathered at the Southern Pacific depot, momentarily unmindful of a growing feud between the railroad and the local growers. It was a startling surprise to them and to the president, therefore, when in the midst of his

At the local level candidates and party organizations maintained a close kinship with the town's legal community. In 1875 there were only two lawyers between Los Angeles and Riverside, Patrick C. Tonner and John J. Mills, both of whom resided in Pomona. By the end of the decade, Tonner had acquired two partners, several other offices had opened, and the court dockets were filled.

No case generated more community

Judge J.H. Gallup was a well-known attorney and public official in Pomona. He would regularly bicycle past Pomona's once famous Hotel Palomares, which was destroyed by fire in 1911. The YMCA now occupies the land where the hotel once stood. Courtesy, Pomona Public Library

first sentence, there was, according to local press reports, a "scream of the whistle, a burst of steam, the clank of couplers and the train rolled forward." McKinley's visit lasted less than a minute. The residents had to satisfy themselves instead four years later with a speech that William Jennings Bryan, the Boy Orator of the Platte, addressed to them in July 1896.

concern than the battle over Lugarda Palomares' quitclaims to Pomona's water-bearing land, which she had conveyed to Tonner. The discovery that Tonner had transferred title to an out-of-state relative of a Pomona Land and Water Company official aroused both suspicion and ire, exacerbated by the fact that Richard Gird of Chino had been allowed by Tonner to

bore and tunnel for water north of San Bernardino Avenue and had laid a large pipe to carry Pomona water to the Chino community. Citizens vehemently expressed their wrath at mass meetings held at the opera house in early November 1891. At the fourth meeting on Monday, November 9, a series of questions was put to Palomares, and her answers made manifestly clear that she had not intended to defraud the townsfolk. Not until January 1892, however, was the Los Angeles Grand Jury able to announce that "the cloud on the title of the land in question had been removed."

INSTITUTIONAL LIFE

Although the uproar was slow to subside, life in Pomona reflected a reassuring continuity. Dr. Von Bonhurst and Dr. J.H. Dunn were well-established as the town dentists while Dr. Kirkpatrick, who had arrived in the early 1880s, indefatigably

made housecalls on horseback. The same was true of Dr. Homer Fairchild, who had spent time in the valley in the 1860s before driving cattle from Texas to California. In his later years he was described in the *Pomona Valley Times* as "a pioneer spirit . . . full of enterprise." Fairchild's colleagues included former Confederate officer Dr. Rolling Burr, whose saddlebags, filled with over 100 medicines, served as a kind of traveling drugstore. After 1888 he served as the town's health officer, vaccinating 2,000 Pomonans during a smallpox outbreak. In 1898 he served as surgeon first to the United States Volunteers in Cuba and then in the Canal Zone before returning to Pomona.

The medical ranks also included Dr. Frank Garcelon of Maine, who was respected for his diagnostic ability and admired for the fact that, believing people would pay what they could, he never sent a bill. A similar unconcern for pecuniary matters was displayed by homeopathic physician F. Dewitt Crank. Carrying his

A snowman was built complete with a pipe and derby hat during unusually cold weather in April of 1896 in front of the Palomares Hotel. Courtesy, Pomona Public Library

umbrella and usually in the company of his faithful dog or one of his cats, he would venture to Armour's drugstore and fill his prescriptions, for which he left a dime. Even when the prescription pharmacy section was terminated and he carried away the remaining supplies, he left one slim dime as recompense. He then freely distributed the medicine to those who needed it.

The several medical families included Drs. H.A. and Addie Whitefield, a husband-and-wife team who arrived in 1894. There were several other female doctors, including Dr. Hannah Scott Turner and long-time practitioner Dr. Hazel Forester. Her father, Dr. George Forester, was typical of a number of medical professionals who had been attracted by Pomona's citrus economy as well as by the restorative qualities of the climate. In the words of Dr. Edward J. Hadfield, who came to Pomona from Philadelphia in 1896, the town had the "best climate, altitude, water, soil, and surrounding country" for the cure of pulmonary troubles.

Pomonans understood that the continued vigor of their community rested largely on the education of their youth. On May 2, 1870, the County Board of Su-

pervisors approved a petition, organized by Cyrus Burdick on behalf of the citizens of Pomona, to establish the San Jose School District in order to locate a school closer to Pomonans' places of residence. The first classes in the newly formed district were conducted in the Thomas Palomares home at Orange Grove Avenue and Kenoak Drive by Anna Cuzad, a 19-year-old Anaheim girl who soon despaired of instilling "school ways" in her pupils. She was followed by a more formidable Mr. Eskridge, who did not speak Spanish and so was soon followed by Irishman Patrick Tonner who despite his brogue could speak Spanish as well as Latin and Greek.

Tonner was the first teacher to occupy the newly constructed schoolhouse near the northeast corner of Park and Orange Grove avenues. As the town grew, that site was traded for a lot on Holt where the Central School was built in 1876, its second story financed by the Odd Fellows, who used it as a meeting hall for a short time. It was surrounded by three acres of acacias, peppers, cypress, and shrubs. As the real estate boom of the mid-1880s began, the district constructed three more schools for the nearly 500 students and created the separate

Pomona College, now located in Claremont, first began offering classes in buildings located at Fifth and White streets. The original building, known as Ayer College, was dedicated on Founder's Day, October 14, 1937. Courtesy, Pomona Public Library

school districts of La Verne and San Dimas.

After the city's incorporation in 1888, the district became the Pomona School District with a board of education composed of the most respected civic leaders. On June 11 of that year, the community gathered at the opera house for a commencement ceremony honoring the 11 graduates who had completed the ninth grade. The three years of high school were added between 1890 and 1892, and accreditation was conferred on Pomona High School by the University of California in 1894. After the kindergarten was added in 1893, reported the press, Pomona citizens could boast of "13 grades from top to bottom."

The social institutions of the new community also included a Freemason organization and a thriving WCTU (Women's Christian Temperance Union) chapter organized in 1883. In the first bustling years of growth, the Knights of Pythias, the City Guards, Company D, the Pomona Women's Club, and the Ebell Club were each chartered. By mid-decade the YMCA had opened and furnished reading rooms in the Palmer Block, helped the sick and dying, and found employment for several members.

In a brief decade the community had blossomed. During the course of its rapid growth, it had developed an articulated infrastructure of institutions and services, all of which had only the faintest connections with the culture, language, and people who had been the sole residents of the area two decades earlier. It was a dramatic reorientation that was somewhat portentous of the adjustments the community would make as a result of Southern California's post-World War II growth.

On July 4, 1889, many of the community's 3,634 residents gathered to hear

General John C. Fremont speak at the dedication of the statue of the goddess Pomona, which had been given to the city by the Reverend Charles F. Loop. The minister had been so moved upon seeing the original in the Uffizi Gallery in Florence that he chose to endow its Southern California namesake with the symbol of agricultural abundance. The ensuing decades, when Pomona played an essential part in the nation's citrus production, were to underscore the appropriateness of that symbol.

The Reverend C.F. Loop arrived in Pomona in 1874, and the first Episcopal church services were held in his home. However, he is better known for giving the city the *Goddess Pomona* in 1889. The marble statue now makes its home in the Pomona Library. Courtesy, Pomona Public Library

One of the earliest Pomona Day Parades caused this street scene in the early 1900s. Courtesy, Pomona Public Library

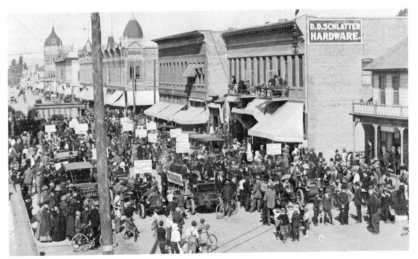

CHAPTER FOUR

POMONA PROSPERS WITH AGRICULTURE

Pomona was about to become unexpectedly prosperous from the cultivation of the orange, the mythical golden apple of the Garden of Hesperides, which some have described not as a fruit but as a romantic symbol of abundance and wealth. Indeed, "the fruited orb of the Hesperides" first described in classic literature soon transformed the foothills stretching from Pasadena to San Bernardino into the gold coast of California agriculture, where latter-day argonauts joined in a second great gold rush made considerably more lucrative by the fact that the golden citrus was a renewable source of wealth.

The orange empire—which extended from the relatively frost-free upland regions where the Washington navel orange flourished to Orange County, where the summer-ripening Valencia orange thrived—formed a "Citrus Triangle" anchored by Santa Ana, Redlands, and San Fernando. Within this area 95 percent of Southern California's oranges were harvested. Pomona was at the center of this region, which between 1890 and 1940 produced more than $2 billion in income from citrus, making Los Angeles and Orange counties the two richest agricultural counties in the nation.

These employees of the Claremont Fruit Growers Association posed for this photo in the late 1890s. Courtesy, Pomona Public Library

BOUNTIFUL HARVESTS

A significant portion of this citrus economy flourished in Pomona, which, located at an elevation of 900 feet, was generally above the frost line. Situated 60 miles from the ocean, at the heart of the region's intermediate valley, and protected by the transverse coastal range to the north and the San Jose hills to the west, Pomona literally became the city of bountiful harvests, with its soil, rich in decomposed granite, providing ideal drainage for citriculture.

Between 1890 and 1900 the number of orange trees in Southern California increased fivefold as retired businessmen and professionals from New England and the Midwest ventured westward to settle a new El Dorado. They coaxed unparalleled profits from small agricultural parcels costing a seemingly exorbitant $1,000 an acre at a time when farmland across the nation was being offered at an average price of $72 an acre. As a result the neatly planted citrus groves were designed to make the most of the land while at the same time providing lustrously green and fragrant settings for the newcomers' retirement homes and the sojourners' winter retreats.

The influx of these new settlers was to markedly affect the development of Southern California communities, particularly Pomona. The recent arrivals brought with them much-needed investment capital along with a willingness to experiment and learn. Many were novices, while the rest had had no experience in coaxing harvests from an arid land. As a result they improvised cultivation, pruning, and irrigation techniques and heeded the sage injunctions of Professor Eugene Hilgard, who headed the University of California Agricultural Experiment Station located adjacent to Pomona on

land donated by Gird. They presented the results of their own research at the Pomological Institute and heralded the glories of the Washington navel orange in journals around the world. The arrival of these well-heeled and well-educated experimenters, a pilgrimage, according to respected author Carey McWilliams, "of the rich and well-born," created a unique type of rural-urban aristocracy at the apex of a carefully stratified society consisting of the managerial elite, local entrepreneurs, and resident immigrants, both Asian and Latin, who soon became expert at picking, packing, and pruning. Consequently a uniquely stratified society developed that had no parallel in the other farm towns and cities of America.

In most orange-growing communities the typical pattern of growth was reversed. Small communities, often stimulated by a successful real estate promotion, preceded the planting of solid compact groves which soon flanked the two-lane roads that led to the town. Many of these towns, like early Pomona, were sedate suburban communities composed of a small commercial section, anchored by a fine hotel, several churches, and perhaps a small private college, exuding withal a quiet and complacent charm. It was a scene reproduced on orange crate labels and countless postcards, dispatched by thousands of California visitors who were treated to the panoramic mile-a-minute tour past acres of the flawlessly arrayed fragrant green trees which produced the golden glory of the citrus triangle.

EARLY AGRICULTURE

Pomona's successful citrus economy had been preceded by a number of other agricultural experiments. The lands on which

This was Olivia Ranch during the olive picking season sometime between December and January 1897-1898. Courtesy, Pomona Public Library

cattle and sheep had pastured—where Ignacio Palomares' fine horses had grazed—were rich and productive. As a result residents began growing everything available north of the tropics. Successful harvests of peaches, pears, and berries were soon surpassed by bumper crops of apricots and prunes. Although some grains cultivated near the present Los Angeles County Fairgrounds were beset by an invasive cereal rust stimulated by the occasional marine fogs, olive production was successful from its start in the 1870s. Under the leadership of the Reverend Charles F. Loop and nurseryman Caleb E. White, who jointly experimented with dozens of native and European varieties, Pomona soon became one of the nation's major centers of olive production as well as of plant stock. Pomona, where more olives were propagated than anywhere else in the world, was, as reported in the *Pomona Centennial History* published by the Pomona Centennial-Bicentennial Committee, soon acclaimed "the home of the American olive." At the Howland Brothers Olive Mill, the nation's largest, townsfolk produced olive oil that was distributed throughout the United States. By the turn of the century, however, markets diminished as Italian imports drastically undercut domestic production.

During the eventful decade of the 1880s, as the small settlement developed into an established town and Pomona's economy shifted from livestock grazing to agriculture, early resident Grat Mirande disposed of his flock of 9,500 sheep and turned to growing Mission grapes. He was followed by others until, by the mid-1880s, the valley was lined with vineyards and Mirande's winery on South Garey Avenue was producing 6,000 gallons of wine annually. In 1886 the establishment of the competing Pomona Wine Company led to the planting of an additional half-million vines, which represented a smaller capital outlay and came into production much sooner than deciduous trees. During harvest season as many as 50 wagons waited to unload their grapes into its elevators.

By the end of the decade, winemaking was the largest industry in the town, although a significant portion of the grape harvest was processed and shipped as raisins. These soon became the valley's second most important product and a major California export

Women inside the Waters Company prepared fresh fruit for shipping. The name of the plant was eventually changed to Sunset Canning Company and was located on Towne and Commercial streets. Sunset packed and shipped peaches, apricots, prunes, apples, and pears. Courtesy, Pomona Public Library

amounting to a total 250,000 boxes shipped by 1892. By the next year, however, valley growers were receiving only $8 a ton, half of what they had received for their wine grapes a decade earlier. Not only had the grapes lost out to drier varietals harvested in several Northern California valleys, but the industry had also been beset by the dreaded Anaheim's disease, which had vanquished the German winemaking community to the south. Of the 166 acres of vineyards still under cultivation in 1893, 25 percent were infected by the disease or affected by mildew. Pomona's winemaking efforts had also been foiled by temperance advocates and Italian imports, which proved superior to local wines produced from the sweet Mission grape.

Pomona's Mediterranean climate, which was so conducive to growing grapes and olives, was equally favorable

for growing deciduous fruits. Apricots, peaches, and prunes, and even pears and apples, grew in hundreds of acres of orchards. Some of the crops were processed at a vast 10-acre drying yard on South Grand Avenue, which in 1892 prepared 532 acres of fruit, including figs, which at harvest sold for $50 a ton with an acre yielding up to 6 tons. A clearer measure of profitability was the market price of 25 cents a pound for fancy packed dry fruit, 3 or 4 cents of which covered the actual costs of production.

To preserve the perishable harvests the town opened its first cannery in 1889. The next year the Loud and Gerling Packing House, conveniently located near the Southern Pacific Railway station, opened just in time to accommodate Pomona's bumper crop of 460 tons of apricots. Between 1894 and 1895 nearly 3,000 tons or 328 carloads were transported along a railroad network to which Pomona had ready access. Utilizing the latest technology the Sunset Canning Company (formerly Water's) and the Golden State Canning Company annually shipped canned and dried fruit, processed between July and October by local women, children, and men recruited from the resident farm labor population.

Growers were soon concerned about overexpansion of production, particularly of plums which sold for $1,000 an acre in 1888. This, coupled with brisk competition from several varieties of plums produced in the San Joaquin Valley and the increasing cost of acreage, led to an abrupt decline of the deciduous fruit industry and the financial ruin of many local growers. Subsequent efforts to cultivate the native black walnuts and the English walnuts introduced by the Franciscan missionaries resulted in more sustained success. By the 1920s the annual crop harvested from 6,000 acres which extended from near Garey Avenue southeastward to Chino amounted to more than a half-million dollars.

Equal success was claimed by barley and alfalfa farmers. The latter annually shipped 6 or 7 crops of up to 10 tons a year until the early 1900s when the land was converted to the more profitable citrus and, for a time, sugar beets. In 1917 the American Beet Sugar Company in neighboring Chino produced 326,535 bags of sugar from beets harvested locally and in adjacent communities. Despite the increasing cost and scarcity of land, citrus growers continued to appropriate valley acreage. Chinese truck farms along Arrow Highway and dairies throughout the valley were sufficiently productive to meet community needs. Beekeepers tended hives set amid sagebrush in the foothills to the north, and all along south White Avenue poultry ranchers, with flocks averaging about 1,000 of the favored white Leghorns, supplied eggs and poultry for county residents. Since each laying hen produced a revenue of one dollar per year, even into this century, the poultry business remained viable despite increasing land costs.

CITRUS PRODUCTION

The efficient land utilization characteristic of citriculture made it particularly attractive to Southern California agriculturists concerned about profit margins as acreage costs continued to increase. They were further encouraged by the fact that oranges and lemons consistently sold for higher prices than deciduous fruits. Inflated prices resulting from increased demand following the Civil War had attracted Italian producers, who by the end of the 1880s had engaged a fleet of more

Workers at the Loud and Gerling Packing House stand outside the business which was located near the Southern Pacific railroad station. Courtesy, Pomona Public Library

Colonel Frank P. Firey planted the first navel oranges in Pomona. Courtesy, Pomona Public Library

than 100 steamers, each carrying a cargo of 20,000 crates, to export fruit from southern Italy and Sicily. Southern California, with its similar climate, winter and summer crops, and recently completed rail connections with eastern markets, potentially appeared to have the competitive advantage.

The example had been provided by Cyrus Burdick, who as early as 1872 planted five acres of seedling oranges along Old Country Road (now Orange Grove Avenue). Believing that the young trees, purchased from a French nurseryman in Los Angeles, would fare better if planted at night, Burdick and his workers laid out the valley's first orange grove by the light of Mrs. Cyrus Burdick's lantern. A decade later Solomon Gates reported a nursery stock of 100,000 sweet oranges. By 1890 the Loop-Meserve citrus nursery had 200,000 orange trees, half of which had been raised to order. The anticipated orchard development was devastated, however, by a Christmas Eve freeze that killed stock throughout the valley and dramatized one of the limiting conditions

which would periodically overwhelm the local citrus industry.

During times of optimistic expansion growers debated the relative advantages of various types of fruit. Banker and agriculturist Charles Lorbeer was convinced that the greatest profits lay in planting 16,000 acres of midsummer ripening valencias, while citrus specialist Thomas Andrew Garey favored a mix of Mediterranean Sweets, Malta Bloods, and Paper-Rind St. Michaels, with the preponderance of the acreage given over to the Washington navel, a Brazilian mutant grown on trees of the Selecta variety. A dozen young Washington navels had been budded in Bahia and dispatched to appropriate regions of the United States by the U.S. Department of Agriculture in 1873. The fruit from a pair of these trees consigned to Riverside alfalfa farmers Luther and Eliza Tibbets soon garnered blue ribbons at fairs across the nation, causing growers to clamor for budded stock from this sweet, seedless orange, with its considerable rag as well as fine, firm texture. Its ripening cycle from November to April and its excellent shipping qualities made it an ideal product for eastern markets.

Within the decade Colonel Frank P. Firey planted the first navels in Pomona. In 1883 Seth Richards, a new arrival from Oakland, planted 250 acres of navels on his 306-acre orchard, described as the largest orange grove in the world. It stretched along Garey Avenue from the Santa Fe Railroad tracks to Foothill Boulevard.

The valley soon displayed a dense patchwork of dark green trees demanding attentive care as the expanding ranks of orchardists engaged in intensive farming on an increasingly extensive scale. Their lands stretched from the foothills, where lemons thrived in the well-drained soil, to the orange groves in the warmer lowland areas. Orchardists were assured that, with proper attention, the initial capital outlay of $3,500 associated with the purchase and cultivation of a typical 10-acre parcel during the five years preceding the first full harvest would be offset by annual revenues of $400 per acre after the eighth year.

Growers with average size orchards did much of the work independently, occasionally employing expert Italian pruners and seasonal workers for harvesting and packing; thus, the labor costs on a crate of citrus ranged between six and eight cents. To reduce loss, crews of 15 to 30 pickers directed by a field boss carefully worked a section, using gloves so as not to injure the fruit and special clippers to cut as close as possible without injury to the skin. As a further precaution the fruit was placed in sacks which opened at the bottom to let oranges, for example,

roll gently into field boxes that held approximately 200 of them.

Successive waves of Mexican, Chinese, and Japanese farm workers assisted in transplanting trees, furrowing and irrigating, and spraying such destructive blights as winter tip and black scale. Many were local residents. Their wives and children worked in the packinghouses and canneries, and their livelihoods rested upon the vagaries of production and distribution, although after a work stoppage during World War I when the labor supply was particularly scarce, Pomona growers did negotiate a wage of 25 cents per hour with the laborers.

MARKETING DIFFICULTIES

The distribution to distant markets of a perishable commodity relied upon an

These orange pickers posing with their mule-drawn wagon would pack the oranges right in the field, as the first packing house was not built until 1890. The man in the foreground is holding a pair of clippers used to cut the fruit from the vine. Courtesy, Pomona Public Library

the transcontinental railroads and highways, which roughly paralleled routes followed by pioneer fur traders and teamsters traveling to Los Angeles, local growers did not enjoy unlimited access to the rails. Transportation was sometimes withheld, or shipments were shunted to a siding and allowed to rot. At the height of an easement dispute between Pomona residents and the Southern Pacific, local railroads provided the growers with only half the boxcars needed. As a result the unshipped fruit rotted, and recently solicited eastern distributors became disaffected. As orange production began to exceed demand, these jobbers offered minimum prices to the hapless growers and sometimes refused to purchase fruit FOB (free on board), accepting it only on consignment at the growers' expense.

Above: Women commonly worked inside the packing-houses. These workers are cutting peaches at the Evergreen Ranch in Lordsburg for twenty-five cents an hour. Courtesy, Pomona Public Library

Top: Minority workers performed a variety of tasks for citrus growers in early Pomona. Courtesy, Pomona Public Library

effective transportation system. The fortunes of the expanding industry were closely linked to the Southern Pacific and the Sante Fe, which established connections in 1886, the same year a special train loaded exclusively with oranges left Los Angeles. Soon cooling and refrigeration techniques were improved, but fees—in the estimation of growers—were arbitrary and excessive. Costs rose to $600 for a carload shipped to the area of the Missouri River.

Although Pomona lay at the nexus of

Of equal concern to the citrus growers was the fact that their product was harvested simultaneously and in a counterproductive marketing effort sold simultaneously in eastern markets where demand had not been stimulated to meet supply. Finally valley agriculturists, keenly aware of the effect of foreign competition on their earlier efforts to raise

grapes and olives, recognized the importance of legislative lobbying on their behalf.

From the late 1880s when the great real estate boom faded through the hard times of 1893, many an orange grove was abandoned, marking the low point of the Southern California citrus industry. Orange prices had fallen from 25 cents to 15 cents a crate when, according to Peter J. Dreher, on April 4, 1893, he and other growers met at the offices of the Los Angeles Chamber of Commerce "to provide for the marketing of all citrus fruit at the lowest possible cost under uniform methods, and in a manner to secure to each grower a certain marketing for his fruit and the full average price to be obtained in the market for the entire season."

GROWERS ORGANIZE

The organization developed to meet the growers' needs was to be modeled on several local citrus cooperatives, particularly the Claremont Fruit Growers Association formed in 1892 by 11 growers in the upper Pomona Valley to handle the

packing and marketing of members' crops either by auction, direct contracts with jobbers, or through export. To strengthen their marketing negotiations the members agreed to ship only high quality fruit which would bear the "Indian Hill" trademark along with the individual grower's name. The remaining oranges were classified as seconds or culls, which were processed as pectin, orange oil, or a variety of other by-products.

On April 14, 1893, the group launched an innovative direct marketing and advertising campaign by shipping a carload of Washington navels to England with one box directed to Queen Victoria. Within each container was a letter introducing the product and the association. It concluded with the assertion: "Believing they will meet with . . . appreciation as to merit our further shipments, we most respectfully commend them to lovers of choice fruits."

Dehrer, president of the Claremont organization which would provide a helpful model to the concerned growers attending the Los Angeles meeting in 1894, was appointed secretary to a committee convened to draft a proposal for a Southern California growers association. Later, when the county growers met in Pomona at Dehrer's invitation, they enthusiastically endorsed the committee's proposal that the Southern California growers organize a cooperative similar to the Claremont association. Southern California was divided into eight districts in which a number of local associations were organized with the Southern California Fruit Exchange serving as a clearinghouse of sales information.

After a number of reorganizations, the California Fruit Growers Exchange emerged with expanded responsibilities in all phases of production from quality control to advertising. With the appoint-

Left: Floods were common in Pomona throughout the turn of the century. This picture was taken in 1916 on East Holt Avenue just east of the reservoir. Courtesy, Pomona Public Library

Workers pose inside the Pomona Fruit Growers Exchange Packing House at East Second Street in 1908. Courtesy, Pomona Public Library

ment of its first publicity committee in 1895, it launched a promotional program ranging from premiums to poetry contests, from the distribution of carloads of free oranges to joint promotion with the railroads of fruit trains bearing such familiar slogans as "Oranges for Health—California for Wealth."

In the Pomona Valley, or District 3, several growers organizations were represented by the San Antonio Fruit Exchange. Dreher served as its secretary and general manager. He also was a director of the California Fruit Growers Exchange, and he became its president in 1920.

CHALLENGES FACING GROWERS

After three decades of cultivation more than 5,000 acres in the immediate vicinity of Pomona were devoted to citrus production. By 1916 the San Antonio Fruit Exchange shipped from its two packinghouses fully 20 percent of the worldwide production of Washington navel oranges. This was part of a total local output of 426,351 crates of citrus fruit, which represented 36 percent of the entire shipment of the California Fruit Growers Exchange.

This accomplishment is more impressive when measured against the difficulties that confronted the growers. For each challenge, however, remedies were soon developed. To reduce spoilage, growers developed techniques for careful harvesting, selective washing, and painstaking wrapping. The Australian "ladybird" beetle was introduced to successfully bring to an abrupt end the devastation wrought by the cottony, cushiony scale *(Icerya purchasi)*.

A reappearance of black scale, which had devastated Pomona orchards in 1862, defied scientists from around the world until Sheridan A. Stowell of San Dimas devised a successful system of fumigation in 1895. It also proved successful against the scale bug, marking Stowell as a leading exterminating specialist in the state. As nocturnal application of cyanide under "government twill" tents gave way to spraying, Pomona became a center from which crews and lumbering spraying rigs were regularly dispatched.

Local orchardists were equally resourceful when the annual Santa Ana winds uprooted countless trees in 1887 and again in 1891. The growers planted windbreaks of cedar, cypress, and eucalyptus, many of which still stand, marking the forgotten perimeters of yesterday's orange empire.

To offset the effects of sudden frosts, the most devastating of the climatic hazards, orange grove owners attempted to raise orchard temperatures by placing slow burning buckets of coal, paper sacks filled with apricot pits, or mill shavings mixed with crude oil beneath the trees. In 1910 frost fighting efforts were aided by the introduction of the smudge pot, a five-gallon container to which a smoke stack was attached. In extreme cases a few growers resorted to burning abandoned tire casings, which significantly

phone lines were first used to summon the owners' smudging crews. Within a few years subscribers were able to obtain the minimum temperature predicted by the Pomona facility from local telephone operators, although only limited information was provided.

In the fall of 1930 the late Floyd D. Young began his nightly reports, broadcast by remote control from the weather station at Pomona, on radio station KNX. The frost warnings, delivered at eight each night between November 15 and February 15, provided growers with critical information regarding the rate of temperature decline as well as the number

Pomona Produce Growers organized a Pomona Fruit Growers Exchange Packing House, located on the northeast corner of Park Avenue and the Southern Pacific Railway. These employees posed outside the packinghouse in 1906. Courtesy, Pomona Public Library

added to the pall of smoke that often clouded the morning sun in the citrus belt region. The unpleasant side effect was somewhat overcome by the introduction of wind machines, which substantially raised orchard temperatures.

Strategies for combating the deadly frost were considerably enhanced with the establishment in Pomona of the United States Weather Bureau frost warning service. On dangerously cold nights the agency would telephone forecasts to key growers who were in turn responsible for calling others. Often, however, the

of nights the "freeze" would continue. Through various configurations and with successive announcers, the service to growers continued until citrus culture had been largely displaced from the region. During the critical years when production was at its height, however, technology helped growers to surmount critical challenges.

WATER SHORTAGE

The citrus growers were equally beset by

Fumigation crews were dispatched into the Pomona orchards as early as 1895 to save the produce from the devastating Australian Beetle. Courtesy, Pomona Public Library

deluges and droughts. The rainfall for the first half of the 1880s consisted of four years of drought and one year of flood when Los Angeles County reported a record rain of 40.29 inches. In the latter half of December 1889, a tremendous downpour that destroyed many highway and railroad bridges was followed by 20 days of uninterrupted rain and another storm in early January. Together they brought the greatest rainfall in county history. In November 1900 heavy rains caused flooding throughout the area, rendering impassable every avenue of transportation except sections of the Southern Pacific Railroad.

Pomonans, however, experienced a significant decrease in rainfall from 1895 to 1904. At the same time water usage increased considerably. As a result in 1894 residents began employing pumps on the town's artesian wells. To meet the new demand the Pomona Manufacturing Company was organized in 1902 to build Pomona Duplex Reciprocating Water Lubricated Deep-Well Pumps. The pumps, powered by large internal combustion engines, were soon used nationwide by water companies. In the foothill orchards the double-action pumps were supplemented by triplex or duplex plunger pumps designed for high lift as well as the

deep-well turbine pump applicable to various pumping problems throughout Southern California. To compensate for the outflow through pumping, some residents concerned with conservation made an effort to raise the water table by diverting surface water into spreading areas where it was quickly soaked up by the highly absorbent beds of gravel and boulders which make up much of the alluvial land lying south of the San Antonio Canyon region.

The innovative effort helped restore the level of the local water table. But with the drought of 1907, neighboring communities began to tap Pomona water, resulting in the formation of the Pomona Valley Protective Association. It intensified spreading operations south of San Antonio Canyon and, under the management of former Chicago water engineer Willis Jones, successfully defended its water claims against outside users, particularly the San Antonio Water Company to the east. In a well-supported brief the association not only proved continued local usage of the area's water but also illustrated the southwesterly flow of the canyon waters toward the San Jose hills of Pomona. In 1912 significant limits were placed upon the exportation of water by the San Antonio Company. The association also repurchased a number of wells, further limiting outside use. Within five years, however, more than 4,500 additional acres were ready for citrus production. This increased future water requirements to 43,309 acre feet, 33 percent more than the region's capacity.

TURNING POINT

The center of the golden triangle had blossomed and produced. It had surmounted infestation, aridity, wind, and frost to become a world leader in citrus production. But its rise was doomed by the scarcity of water and land costs.

Russell K. Pitzer, a Pomona philanthropist, was at one time the largest individual citrus grove owner in California with holdings of more than 1,000 acres in Pomona and Riverside. He was quick to realize the mushrooming real estate value of orange grove property. After the major setback caused by the Big Freeze of 1913, which killed entire orchards, Pitzer, a former president of the San Antonio Fruit Exchange and a member of the board of the California Fruit Growers Exchange, began purchasing citrus acreage. With the appearance of real estate subdivisions in the 1920s, and more significantly after World War II, Pitzer's holdings accommodated housing developments as well as the needs of expanding cities. In a newspaper interview he conceded: "I'm sorry to see the orange groves go but they had to make way for an increasing population."

The era of oranges was fast approaching an end as bedroom communities appeared amid the groves. The destructive quick decline, a suspected virus that attacked sour stock trees, claimed many more. Nevertheless the ethos of the era had left an impression.

In the view of one citrus belt resident, historian Robert Glass Cleland, the mutual interests of citrus growers had drawn them together. In *California in Our Time* he ventured the observation that the citrus growers of California are:

typically conservative, prosperous, self-satisfied, cultured, clannish, intensely loyal West-of-the-Hudson-River Americans. As a group they vote the Republican ticket with unquestioning fidelity—at least since the demise of the Progressive Party. Those in

Southern California . . . regard a high protective tariff as the Keystone of American prosperity; send their children to college; give liberally to churches, charities and every other good cause; support women's clubs, lectures and concerts; build and maintain the best schools; look with suspicion on Wall Street and even upon their Republican brethren among Eastern manufacturers and bankers; show genuine and intelligent concern for the welfare of their employees, but decry labor unions and all forms of farm labor organization; regard socialism, communism and the New Deal as synonymous; and condemn all forms of federal aid to the individual—except when such aid is needed by the citrus industry itself.

This forceful but insightful assessment rendered by a native son not only captured the spirit of California's "second gold rush" communities but also suggested that in the process of cultivating the citrus, a remarkably productive and renewable source of wealth, orange-growing communities like Pomona had developed a unique spirit with both strengths and weaknesses that would affect the town's responses to the challenges presented by the ensuing decades.

Floyd D. Young prepares to make his regular frost warning broadcast to the agricultural industry. Courtesy, *Progress-Bulletin Newspaper*

CITY OF CHURCHES AND SCHOOLS

Progress and prosperity were reflected in Pomona at the dawn of the new century. The town, with 5,526 residents, was served by four banks and two building and loan associations. A sanitation system had been established, and by 1902 the first train on the Salt Lake Railroad (now the Union Pacific) had reached town, and a new station had been built. That same year townsfolk approved bonds for the construction of a high school and development of Central and Ganesha parks. A $15,000 Carnegie grant was obtained for the proposed library, and the Home Telephone Company was organized.

The first decade of the century was marked by expansion. In 1906 alone the city committed $218,000 to street grading and the construction of cement sidewalks and curbs. An armory was built for Company D, the local National Guard unit. In 1909 the fire department obtained its first motorized equipment, and the city acquired an electrified streetcar system.

By the end of that eventful decade, Pomonans had organized an Elks Club and three PTA chapters. A Masonic Temple had been erected, and Company D had been dispatched to San Francisco to assist in fighting the devastating fire that followed the 1906 earthquake.

The Pomona High School girls' basketball team stopped shooting hoops long enough to pose with their 1907 championship trophy. Courtesy, Pomona Public Library

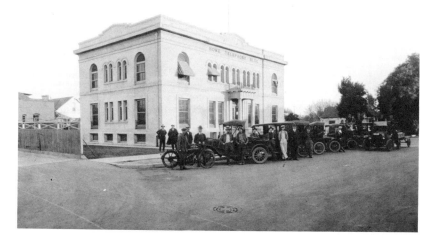

Above: Employees of the Home Telephone Company pose outside of the Pomona Valley Telephone and Telegraph Union building in 1917. Courtesy, Pomona Public Library

Above right: This was the view of the intersection of West Second Street and Main Street—the business district—in the 1920s. Courtesy, Pomona Public Library

TRANSPORTATION PROMOTES GROWTH

In 1911 the electric interurbans, crucial to the diffusion of Southern California's population into widely dispersed streetcar suburbs, were consolidated under the Pacific Electric Company, owned by Henry E. Huntington. As early as August 31, 1912, the Pacific Electric's Covina-Pomona Line made 12 round trips daily from Pomona to downtown Los Angeles, each trip taking 83 minutes, according to transportation historian Spencer Crump. The Pomona-Upland Line, which was originally owned by the Ontario and San Antonio Heights Railway Company in 1910, became part of the Pacific Electric Line in 1912. Thirty-three times each day between 1911 and 1933, rail cars made the round trip to North Pomona or followed longer routes to Claremont, Upland, and Ontario. At each of these stops, connections could be made with the Pacific Electric's Eastern District trolley which by 1937 was transporting passengers to Los Angeles in 105 minutes, nine times per day. Henry E. Huntington's big red cars whisked passengers at a brisk 40 m.p.h. past pepper-trees and ostrich farms to bungalow-filled

garden towns like Pomona, reminiscent of the Midwestern villages where many of the newly arrived riders had spent their childhoods.

Heeding the PE's imperative to "Live in the Country and Work in the City," children of citrus growers as well as newcomers commuted from low-density suburbs to jobs in the urban core. As a result Huntington's network not only encouraged the region's horizontal growth but also helped Los Angeles to become a forerunner of the post-industrial city in which production and consumption are widely dispersed. The power of the transportation network and its owner was keenly felt by Pomona residents when, after a controversy with townsfolk, Huntington delayed completion of a streetcar line to the town for nine years. Although he extolled Pomona as the richest town of its size in the world, Huntington took his revenge for the town's earlier recalcitrance by finally providing it in 1912 with a sec-

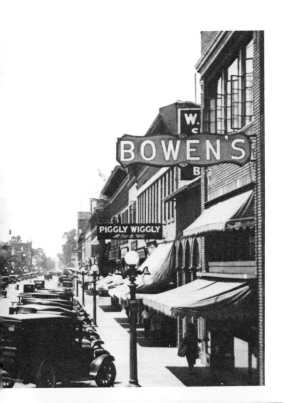

ondary line connecting Pomona to the Pacific Electric's interurban station in Claremont.

The energetic development evident in Pomona was reflected throughout the region. By the end of the decade, engineers had accepted nature's challenge and created Los Angeles Harbor. Its opening coincided with the opening in 1914 of the Panama Canal. Another avenue of growth was created by William Mulholland, who helped drill one of Pomona's earliest artesian wells. In 1913 he directed the channeling of water from the Owens Valley into the chronically thirsty Los Angeles basin. The region's bond to technology was further evidenced in 1915, when county residents' ownership of 55,000 cars led the nation and pointed to an emerging phenomenon which would impact upon Pomona, located on

A Company D ball was held at the Pomona Opera House near the turn of the century. The opera house building was used by the city's national guard unit until a new armory was built at West Second Street in 1904. Courtesy, Pomona Public Library

Above: This early street
scene shows the evolution
of downtown Pomona.
Courtesy, Pomona Public
Library

Right: The first traffic but-
ton in Pomona was installed
at the intersection of Second
Street and Garey Avenue.
This "silent policeman" was
actually just an 18-inch
painted white disc. In this
1913 photo, Otto Schwich-
teuberg points at the disc.
With him were Police Chief
H.P. Tracey, front seat,
Judge Gallup in the Panama
hat, and City Mayor Vaude-
greff. Courtesy, Pomona
Public Library

Southern California's historic avenues of travel.

BUSINESS ISSUES

Pomona was also affected by international political events ranging from the annexation of Hawaii, which growers hoped would provide export access to the Pacific Rim, to the Mexican Revolution of 1911, which stimulated immigration of the Mexican nationals who soon became the primary agricultural work force. At the national level residents mindful of the vagaries of the citrus economy favored protective tariffs and the construction of an Isthmian canal. Consistent with other regional voters, Pomonans favored bimetallism, a bias shared with such illustrious visitors as Theodore Roosevelt, a local favorite who visited Claremont in 1903, and William Howard Taft, who came to Pomona in 1911.

Local issues included division from Los Angeles County and designation of Pomona as the county seat, an issue resurrected by the local press in 1906 and intermittently championed for the next nine years by the Board of Trade, which advocated the economy of such a measure.

In 1911 the city not only organized a police department and dedicated a new city hall, but also adopted a new charter providing for administration by a mayor and city council. A charter provision prohibiting the sale of alcohol underscored the successful lobbying of the disfranchised members of the Women's Christian Temperance Union. As a result of strong Southern California support, equal suffrage for women was approved that same year on a ballot listing numerous Progressive reforms which Pomona voters endorsed, recognizing their practi-

President William Howard Taft visited Pomona via railway on October 17, 1911. Taft received a basket of fruit from Pomona residents who had come out to see the president. Courtesy, Pomona Public Library

cal advantages. The less laudatory aspect of the Progressive agenda—an intense anti-Asian sentiment—resulted in the statewide passage in 1913 of the Alien Land Act. To this, local residents added the Alien Poll Tax in 1920.

Continued growth, which caused Pomona's population to double between 1900 and 1913, tended to diffuse community leadership, though officials continued to be distinguished by their dedication, probity, and support of temperance. By 1913, however, a score of merchants and businessmen had petitioned the city council for protection from the effects of the widespread smudging necessitated by the Big Freeze of 1913. Recent arrivals who were less sympathetic to the growers than earlier Pomonans succeeded in electing a city administration committed to regulating orchard heating. The ensuing community dispute climaxed in April 1919 when voters approved a local initiative outlawing orchard heating altogether.

On June 17, 1913, in response to the disastrous freeze earlier that year, the local Board of Trade, the Pomona Businessmen's Association, and the Pomona Realty Board consolidated to form the Pomona Chamber of Commerce. To offset the effects of future freezes, the chamber undertook to assure better weather forecasts. Preliminary activities also included supporting the construction of a dam in the San Antonio wash and launching an ongoing advertising campaign designed to attract residents and businesses to the valley.

While orange groves still provided the economic base for Pomona and the region, the geography and climate were attracting imaginative entrepreneurs. Filmmakers established studios in Hollywood and Santa Monica, and pioneer aviators took to the Southern California skies.

BATTLE OF THE CLOUDS

Early experimenters recognized the importance of weather and climate in the flight of heavier-than-air machines. Among the earliest of these machines was a pusher-type biplane which Glenn L. Martin succeeded in keeping airborne for 12 seconds above the Irvine Ranch. By 1900 Martin had mastered the technology sufficiently to fly to Pomona from Santa Ana. In 1910 the city was again the intended destination of an adventurous flyer, this time a French aviator by the name of Dadier Masson. While he overshot Pomona and landed in Cucamonga, Masson held the record for Southern California's longest nonstop flight. That same year 20,000 spectators gathered at the Dominguez Ranch for the first international air meet, held for 10 days in January to highlight the mild winter climate.

An even more exciting aeronautical display occurred in 1914. To mark the ground-breaking ceremonies of a proposed automobile speedway, the Pomona Chamber of Commerce hosted the

"Battle of the Clouds." Aviation pioneer Glenn Martin was invited to demonstrate the practical use of the "aeroplane" as a military weapon. Despite contradictory claims it was during this demonstration that ground-to-air communication was successfully established for the first time. Only months before the outbreak of World War I, the 28-year-old Martin participated in a mock battle in which he synchronized the maneuvers of his army scout plane with the movements of land troops attempting to capture a mock fort.

The April air meet also marked the first time explosives were dropped from the air onto a ground target. The daring display involving Company D, Pomona's National Guard unit, was witnessed by officers from the United States Aviation School in San Diego as well as by nearly 12,000 spectators who arrived by train aboard Pacific Electric cars dispatched at five-minute intervals, or in autos which, according to the *Los Angeles Daily Times*, "lined every highway within miles of the park." Along Pomona's flag-lined thoroughfares, a carnival atmosphere gained momentum as schools and stores closed in observance of this event in which, it was promised in the *Pomona Progress*, "the world's greatest aviator" would present "one of the most elaborate productions of its kind ever held."

During the two-day show Martin also broke the United States altitude record by flying at 14,200 feet. Additional highlights included a demonstration of the Martin Life Vest by 18-year-old parachutist Tiny Broadwick. When the twisted cords of her chute caused her to veer some distance from the crowded grandstand, the doughty jumper ruefully observed that she had at least broken the long-distance record for walking back to her tent.

Another highlight was an aerial parade feature watched by Miss Pomona, Graciosa Vejar, the granddaughter of 84-year-old Ramon Vejar. She stood on a field where his sheep and cattle had once grazed, gazing at the sky where a miracle of technology was unfolding. Although the proposed speedway was never built, "the most perfect air meet ever staged in California," as the *Los Angeles Daily Times* pronounced it, presaged a future source of prosperity for Pomona.

WAR AND THE RETURN TO NORMALCY

Within a few months Europe was engulfed in war. Pomona residents supported the national policy of neutrality during the early years of the conflict, but as sentiments shifted citizens became concerned with preparedness and defense, planting vegetable gardens and surpassing local Red Cross quotas. The Home Defense League was organized and equipped with carbines provided by the city. Members of Company D were summoned to active duty. Nineteen of the 678 Pomonans who served did not return.

Members of the military who did return found that Pomona, as well as the nation, sought a return to "normalcy." For some whose nerves had been rubbed raw by war and whose idealism had been shattered by an imperfect peace, the antidote was political isolationism and the escapism of the jazz age. In its retreat from international responsibility, America celebrated the flapper and ignored the postwar plight of 4 million striking workers and the nation's farmers and growers, who had no share in the momentary prosperity.

Political leaders declared that "the business of America is promoters." The region's 43,000 real estate agents repre-

The "Battle of the Clouds," an aeronautical display staged to mark the ground breaking of a proposed automobile speedway, resulted in aviator Glenn Martin breaking the U.S. altitude record by flying at 14,200 feet in his "aeroplane." Courtesy, Pomona Public Library

Right: The Pomona High
School Class of 1896 made
this rather distinguished
portrait in 1896. Courtesy,
Pomona Public Library

Below: This was the Pomona
High School graduating
class of 1895. Courtesy, Pomona Public Library

sented the largest concentration in the
nation. As a result it has been observed
by one historian that "the lights went on
all at once in California and the blaze has
never dimmed." For Pomona it was a
time that saw the establishment of clubs
and schools, theaters and bus routes, and
above all, an unbroken trajectory of
growth and expansion.

THE LOCAL SCENE

Pomona in 1920 was a community largely
inhabited by prosperous, American-born,
middle-class people, who enjoyed lawn
tennis and polo as well as outings to Los
Angeles musical events. The hierarchy of
privilege included a number of Jewish
merchants and landowners, who were
appointed to civic offices and enjoyed
memberships in the community's organizations.

Pomona residents proudly celebrated
their achievements with a Pageant of
Progress staged in 1920. They also maintained well-established standards of

cleanliness, carefully enforcing health regulations curtailing both stray dogs and spittoons. In 1908 townspeople launched a "Clean Up Day," a tradition continued through the years by garden club members, who later burnished Pomona's public presence in preparation for the 1932 Olympics held in Los Angeles.

Pomona residents were equally attentive to the quality of their public education. The degree of civic pride was evident when 5,000 citizens gathered to see 82 high school graduates receive their diplomas from Pomona High School, which was ranked among the top four secondary schools in the state. Among the notable graduates during the transitional years were philanthropist Frank Seaver (1901), well-known author/humorist and professor Richard Armour (1923), and Cordelia Honaday (1909) who, with future husband Walter Knott (1909), would launch Knott's Berry Farm.

Curricular innovations included restructuring a postgraduate program in 1906. As a result Pomona became one of the first communities in the nation to

have a community college. The following year a junior high school component was introduced into the school program. Soon a night school was organized to serve a maximum-capacity student body, and the kindergartens, introduced in 1890 and later directed by the gifted Barbara Greenwood, achieved national acclaim.

By the turn of the century, Pomona had welcomed 15 major religious denominations, whose congregations constructed churches during the ensuing two decades. In 1905 the Christian Scientists completed an edifice, which was followed the next year by St. Joseph's Roman Catholic Church. They were joined by the Methodist Episcopal Church, the Free Methodist Church, and others, culminating before World War I with the construction at the intersection of Holt and Garey avenues of two imposing symbols of Pomona's religious life—the Greek Revival edifice occupied by the First Baptist Church and the Gothic-style structure occupied by the Pilgrim Congregational Church. By 1928 there were 28 church organizations in Pomona.

Pomona celebrated its prosperity with a Pageant of Progress in 1920. The town sponsored many parades downtown to display its civic pride. This aerial picture was taken at the intersection of Second Street and Garey Avenue. Courtesy, Pomona Public Library

Right: The Gothic-style Pilgrim Congregational Church still stands at the corner of Garey and Pasadena streets. This photo was taken in 1969. Courtesy, Pomona Public Library

Below: The First Baptist Church, on the corner of Holt and Garey avenues, was dedicated in June 1911. Courtesy, Pomona Public Library

Below right: This is the Seventh-Day Adventist Church in Pomona. Courtesy, Pomona Public Library

The Mount Zion Church at Eighth and Main joined the ranks of this city of churches in the early 1930s, when Pomona's small black community had grown large enough to sustain an independent congregation.

RACIAL DIVERSIFICATION

At the turn of the century, most of Pomona's 27 blacks lived in the 600 and 700 blocks of First and Second streets. They were employed throughout the community as laundresses and laborers. Some assumed managerial positions.

Local blacks did not experience the widespread antipathy directed toward Asian immigrants. Community concern about the arrival of enterprising Japanese workers and their families had surpassed the enmity expressed toward earlier Chinese male sojourners who hoped to return to China and their families after work in the orchards and fields of California.

Local Indians had all but disappeared from California by 1900, and the Latino culture had become alien in the lands once claimed by Palomares and Vejar. Descendants of the former landowners were designated as Spanish, but the families were described as being Mexican. Many of the latter lived in Pomona's original barrio along Second Street. Their children rarely graduated from high school. In the local theaters they were assigned restricted seating. After 1919 they were permitted to use jointly with "colored people" the newly constructed swimming pool in Ganesha Park on one day a week. Most worked in the community, and many served their country. Mexicans served in Company D, and several returned as veterans from World War I.

Pomona's Latino community was served by the short-lived newspaper *El Heraldo de Mexico*, which provided insights into the social and cultural life of the community. For two years beginning in 1927, the weekly *El Eco del Valle* carried local and international news as well as information about the remaining California pioneers and their descendants. A subsequent effort, *El Espectador*, was published for 28 years beginning in 1933 by valley resident Ignacio L. Lopez, who served on numerous governmental and civic committees promoting activities that drew together members of the local Latino community. Among the most successful was the four-day celebration in 1936 marking the centennial of Rancho San Jose. In September of that year more than 5,000 people gathered for Mexican Independence Day festivities, which were followed the same week by a 50-float pageant commemorating the early history of the valley that was presented in conjunction with the Los Angeles County Fair.

THE COUNTY FAIR

In 1922, 206 Pomona citizens organized a nonprofit stock corporation to support, with county assistance, an agricultural fair. The initial effort that same year was an unequivocal success. Forty thousand people visited the displays of citrus and livestock presented on 43 acres the city had purchased on the western edge of Pomona. As a result of a bond issued the following year, the city purchased an additional 62 acres.

Improvements included administration facilities and service sheds, a half-mile track, a grandstand that held 4,000, and horse and cattle barns. A decade later the site was deeded to Los Angeles Coun-

Above: This girl and her
sheep posed for this publicity
photo for the 1926 agricultural fair. Courtesy, Pomona
Public Library

Above center: This is an
aerial view of the first
County Fair, taken in October 1922. Courtesy, Pomona
Public Library

Right: These men are pre-
paring the ground for the
first agricultural fair in the
spring of 1922. Courtesy,
Pomona Public Library

Above: This picture of two boys and their roosters was used as a publicity photo for the 1926 county fair. Courtesy, Pomona Public Library

Left: Crowds of people were on hand to inaugurate the first Agricultural Fair held in Pomona in 1922. After 62 years, the Los Angeles County Fair is touted as the largest of its kind in the nation. Courtesy, Pomona Public Library

ty, which in turn leased the property to the Los Angeles County Fair. By the end of the decade, a half-dozen permanent exhibit buildings had been erected by the Works Progress Administration (WPA).

SPIRIT OF PROSPERITY

During what has been described as the golden age of capitalism, industrial giants like Ford and Goodyear established branch plants in Los Angeles County, a region hailed by promoters as a "center of destiny." Prosperity was also sustained by citrus-related enterprises such as pumping, spraying, and packing. In 1926

the California Fruit Wrapping Mill began operations in Pomona. Other enterprises included the Alpha Beta Food Markets, which were incorporated in 1928 by three Gerrard brothers—Albert C., Hugh A., and Alexander W.—who operated four stores in Pomona and Santa Ana dubbed the Alpha Beta Stores. The name was chosen to underscore the alphabetical arrangement of the stores' full lines of grocery items, which customers were invited to select directly from the shelves. The innovative arrangement had been first developed at Gerrard's Triangle Groceteria, an expansion of Albert C. Gerrard's meat market which had opened in Pomona in 1900.

The subsequent success of the supermarket chain resulted from both the efficiency of access and the development of suburban shopping malls. The neighborhood grocery was quickly rendered obsolete, its demise hastened by the increasing popularity of the automobile—despite warnings that the exertions of driving could contribute to misshapen legs for female motorists.

MERGERS AND EXPANSIONS

By the end of the 1920s, 200 companies controlled half the wealth of America. Reflecting the merger spirit of the era, in 1926 Pomona purchased the Consolidated Water Company and formed the Pomona Water Department. That same year Pomona, Claremont, and La Verne organized the Tri-City Sewage Treatment Plant. Through the plant's early recycling efforts, reclaimed water was sold to agricultural interests in Walnut and Diamond Bar.

The following year the Southern California Edison Company, which had obtained the Pomona franchise at the turn

The first graduating class of Pomona Valley Hospital's training school for nurses was photographed in June 1907. Seated is Clara Arbuthnot, superintendent of the hospital. The graduates are, from left to right, Addie Blewitt, Mauree DuBois Howard, and Opal Chaise Richardson. Courtesy, Pomona Public Library

of the century, purchased the Ontario Power Company and later the California Electric Company. These utility companies served a region which as early as 1892, it was later announced at the 1924 Pacific Coast Convention of Electrical Engineers, had used "the first high voltage long distance transmission in the world." It enabled 800 horsepower that had been generated from a powerhouse at Mount San Antonio Canyon to travel 28 miles to enthusiastic customers in Pomona.

News of this event was featured by the local papers which, through a series of purchases and reorganizations, emerged as *The Bulletin*, first published as a semiweekly in 1915 and later as a morning paper, and the evening *Progress*. In 1927 the two dailies merged to become the *Progress-Bulletin*.

A reorganization of services led to the establishment on April 1, 1927, of the Pomona Valley Community Hospital. Major donor Russell K. Pitzer served as president of a 15-member board and oversaw expansion plans which, by 1929, made the hospital the most modern facility in Southern California. The hospital, organized by local nurse Eliza B. Bradbury after witnessing the inadequacy of local services while caring for victims of a Southern Pacific Railroad accident in 1899, had developed considerably beyond the original 16-room facility. In 1905 the Nurse's Training School was established at the hospital under the direction of hospital superintendent Clara Arbuthnot. When that facility was destroyed by fire in December 1912, the Pomona Valley Hospital Board and the community, undeterred by the economic setbacks caused by the Big Freeze of 1913, succeeded in building a larger facility accommodating 30 to 40 patients.

Another health facility appeared in Pomona in 1927, when the Pacific

Pacific State Hospital was founded in 1927 by the Pacific Colony on a 300-acre site in West Pomona. Courtesy, Pomona Public Library

Colony moved from 1,800 acres in Walnut to a 300-acre site in west Pomona that provided better access to rail and highway transportation as well as a potable water supply. There it was subsequently renamed Pacific State Hospital and later Lanterman Developmental Center, becoming a facility for the developmentally disabled administered by the Health Department of the State of California.

DEPRESSION

The collapse of the illusion of prosperity that became evident on Black Thursday, October 24, 1929, had not been unheralded. The mergers and the margin buying on Wall Street were shadowed by the apocalyptic reality represented by rural America. The cosmopolitan areas of the 1920s ignored the plight of small town America and its farmers, who did not share in the prosperity of the era. Deprived of wartime markets and with no form of governmental support, agriculturalists represented the soft underside of the economy's inflated expansion. By the first week of December 1929, growers had begun to experience a market decline. By early 1920 citrus prices had slumped, and some local growers had at-

The Pomona Valley Community Hospital held the first of its annual baby shows on May 12, 1922. The winners were, from left, Kenneth Mautz, Janet Robbins, Margaret Adamson, and Ross Sanborn. Courtesy, Pomona Public Library

tempted to maintain prices by pouring kerosene on surplus crops. During the depths of the Depression agricultural prices nationwide declined by 65 percent. Bank failures caused capital assets to disappear, and increasing unemployment led to public antipathy toward the Mexican laborers employed in low-paying agricultural and construction jobs.

The decade of the 1930s, marred by the Long Beach Earthquake in 1933, a major freeze in 1937, and a fierce winter flood the following year, also witnessed the arrival of a new population. Vagrants, often victims of national unemployment (which reached 16 million by 1932), occupied "hobo jungles" adjacent to railroad tracks. They were joined after 1935 by the disinherited from the dust bowl, farmers fleeing the dust-filled winds which were choking the farms of the southern Midwest.

Penniless, disoriented, and with no prospect of state relief for at least the first year of settlement, the newcomers eagerly accepted the minimum wages paid the Mexican agricultural laborers,

150,000 of whom had been voluntarily repatriated between 1931 and 1937.

As the economic malaise moved west, merchants shared the growers' financial decline. Products disappeared from window displays, and prices for available items declined. In nearby Covina the price of a new 1935 Chevrolet fell to $465, down from $756 in 1929.

To reduce expenses the Pomona Valley Hospital discontinued its nursing school after the graduation of the final class of 10 students. Under Pitzer's judicious guidance the hospital's operation was uninterrupted, although in 1935 the entire staff was forced to take a 25 percent pay cut.

The downward financial spiral prompted a variety of solutions. In 1935 all of Southern California, captured by the latest pyramid scheme, began mailing chain letters containing a dime. The unemployed occupied themselves with jigsaw puzzles, the latest fad, and rolled their own cigarettes.

In 1934 the county began giving the needy cash doles in place of food baskets and housing guarantees. Two years later the state began distributing an old age pension of $35 a month.

In Pomona the chamber of commerce launched a program of prorating the work force to ease unemployment and redoubled its efforts to attract businesses and residents. An illustrated booklet publicizing "the fair city" was distributed internationally. By the end of the decade, enterprising chamber members had secured a full-page ad in the state's *Official Tourist and Guide* distributed at the California state border. While the city and the region were not as deeply affected as much of the nation, the decline brought changes. Even barnstormers, who had once thrilled weekend visitors at the air

as part of President Franklin Delano Roosevelt's New Deal program for economic recovery.

POMONA WOMEN ORGANIZE

A number of Pomona's 50 volunteer organizations, ranging from the PTA to the Southern California Council of Church Women, provided assistance to the needy. Women assumed leadership of many of these voluntary agencies. As had been true throughout the history of western settlement, Pomona women had long been involved as city builders and culture bearers.

In April 1887 Pomona women had

Below: The City Transit Taxi Company opened for business in Pomona next to the confectionery and barber shop. The gleaming taxis lined the streets while the drivers were visited by a city policeman on October 28, 1934. Courtesy, Pomona Public Library

races at Burnley Field, sought more profitable enterprises ranging from flying flowers to Chicago to hauling shrimp from Mexico.

As a community service the local YMCA continued its policy of providing free meals and lodging to men and boys unable to pay. Many of these young men joined the ranks of the Civilian Conservation Corps (CCC). The CCC was one of the many alphabet agencies that emerged

Left: These vats full of mash at a large illicit alcohol distillery were discovered by federal officials at Muroc Dry Lake. Courtesy, Pomona Public Library

The "Fruit and Flower Mission" was formed as a volunteer organization in the spring of 1889 by Clara Mueller. It later became known as the Pomona Welfare League. Early on, limited membership included 25 young women who were to cheer the hearts of the sick and lonely away from Eastern home and friends by offering them the choicest fruits and flowers. Later the service was enlarged to assist any family in distress. Courtesy, Pomona Public Library

raised $515 at a flower festival. The funds provided the basis for the Pomona Public Library and Floral Association, which was organized the following month.

Inspired by the women's club movement, local residents organized the Pomona Women's Club in 1892. Four years later it was joined by the Times Club of Current Events. Soon afterward Kate Bassett, supervisor of Pomona's kindergartens, convened the first meeting of the Saturday Afternoon Club. It soon became the Pomona Ebell Club and followed the guidelines of Dr. Adrian Ebell, a noted German scholar and founder of the International Academy for Women.

Caroline Severance, founder of the International Federation of Women's Clubs, asserted: "All things are possible to women if they organize." Pomona's club women campaigned for civic improvements and through their philanthropy responded to a wide range of social needs, including hospitals, youth camps, and children's services. In the depths of the Depression, five Pomona women organized the Junior Assistance League. Following its first spring garden party in 1934, a donation of $44 from the proceeds was given to Pomona Valley Hospital. By the end of the decade, the league's donations had increased to $5,000.

In 1915 Sarah M. Jacobus recommended to the Library Board of Trustees the organization of a historical society to preserve the history of the valley. She had begun preserving and cataloging records shortly after her appointment as city librarian in 1906. By the 1930s the Historical Society of the Pomona Valley had dedicated markers at several historic sites and successfully restored, with the assistance of the WPA, the Adobe de Palomares, reopened on April 6, 1940. In the early decades of the century, Pomona women had voluntarily assisted the needy through the Fruit and Flower Mission, using funds raised at their annual festival.

In nearby Chino the care of the disabled absorbed the attention of Frances Eleanor Smith, a nurse who suffered from the severe effects of infantile paralysis and who, with Dr. Lincoln L. Wirt, established Casa Colina Convalescent Home for Children in 1936. This rehabilitative center was relocated in Pomona in 1960. Headed by "Mother Smith," the facility was heralded by President Roosevelt at its dedication as "the future Warm Springs of the West."

The California Theatre opened in November of 1923 on the first floor of the investment building at Third and Main streets. The opening feature picture was *Hospitality* with Buster Keaton. Until the opening of the Fox in 1931, the California Theatre was the principal theater not only in Pomona but in the entire valley. These ushers are standing in front of the theater. Courtesy, Pomona Public Library

MOVIE TOWN

To escape the gray realities of the era, Pomonans joined the 90 million Americans who flocked to the movies each week. In 1931 the Sunkist and the Fox joined the other leading movie theaters, the California and the Belvedere. A decade later the State Theatre opened with a premiere of *Golden Hoofs*. It had been filmed largely at the county fairgrounds, where much of *State Fair*, starring Will Rogers, had been shot, and Bing Crosby and Fred MacMurray had enacted portions of *Sing You Sinners*.

The elegant art deco Fox Theatre, with its mighty Wurlitzer pipe organ, was often the site of movie previews which were announced on a banner hung from the theater's 81-foot tower. Hollywood had selected Pomona for trial showings of unedited films before final cutting and release to the general public. Using magnetic sound reproducers designed for projecting working prints, the Fox Theatre previewed films from all the major studios including *Vogues 1938*, one of the first produced in color. While producers, directors, and stars like Jeanette McDonald, Walter Pidgeon, and Merle Oberon studied audience reactions from the loge seats at the rear, theater personnel distributed postcards soliciting comments which not infrequently resulted in changes before commercial release.

KELLOGG RANCH

The community also claimed a film star. Jadaan, an Arabian horse from the W.K. Kellogg Ranch located in west Pomona, had been ridden by Rudolph Valentino. Soon film luminaries including Tom Mix, Rudy Vallee, and Loretta Young joined the crowds who flocked to the ranch each weekend to watch the Arabians perform in an area at the center of the 30-stall stable.

As the crowds reached the overflow point, Will Keith Kellogg erected a larger arena. In 1932 the general public was invited to free demonstrations in which both three- and five-gaited horses ran, jumped, and performed tricks Kellogg particularly favored. Tourist magazines featured the ranch in countless articles suggesting that the Kellogg Arabian Horse Ranch in Pomona was a major California tourist attraction. The publicity was welcomed by Kellogg, owner of the Kellogg Corn Flakes Company, who had envisioned his winter retreat in Pomona as a horse ranch devoted to promoting and improving the Arabian breed. Consequently Kellogg, although by nature a private person, utilized the publicity attendant upon Hollywood's fascination with his horses by featuring photographs with visiting stars in Kellogg advertisements. Arabian dignitaries were feted at special shows emceed by close friend Will Rogers, and Kellogg's Arabians marched in the Pasadena Rose Parade.

Life as a celebrated Southern California horse rancher and millionaire businessman was far removed from Kellogg's earliest days. The seventh child of a devout, hardworking couple, young Kellogg joined his father selling brooms. By the time he was 20, he had launched his own broom factory in Texas. For the next 25 years, however, he lived in the shadow of his well-known brother, Dr. John Harvey Kellogg of the respected and fashionable Battle Creek Sanitarium.

As his brother's assistant Will Kellogg experimented with digestible flaked cereals for the sanitarium patients. The corn flake, an outgrowth of these efforts, became increasingly popular, and in 1905 he established his own company. The product, popularized through innovative advertising and promotions, became a worldwide success by 1924,

making Kellogg a multimillionaire free to pursue his various interests and travel. On one such exodus from the winter cold of Michigan, Kellogg visited a niece, Josie. She had nursed and later married Louis R. Phillips, son of Louis Phillips, who had acquired Rancho San Jose de Abajo. Following Phillips' death Kellogg assisted his niece in securing her legal claim to Phillips' land, part of which he later purchased, acquiring additional land from other Phillips relatives.

The cereal magnate's visits to Southern California often included trips to Palm Springs and the Chauncey Clarke Arabian Ranch in nearby Indio. When he learned that all of Clarke's stable was being sold, Kellogg seized the opportunity to fulfill a childhood dream. Not only did he purchase all 11 Arabians, but he also contracted to hire Carl Schmidt, their trainer. Schmidt oversaw their transfer to Pomona, where they remained at the Pomona Fairgrounds for a time while Kellogg's 377-acre horse ranch was being completed. In 1926 the horses were transferred from temporary facilities on the ranch to permanent stables. Six more Arabians had been purchased from F.E. Lewis II of the Diamond Bar Ranch in Spadra, and in January 1926 Schmidt was dispatched to Europe where he purchased 14 Arabians from the Crabbet Stud in England. Subsequent additions were acquired from Polish, Spanish, and Egyptian breeders, increasing the stable to 55.

Animal lover Kellogg was also a precise taskmaster, who painstakingly oversaw the development of an ideal horse ranch. The renowned architect Myron Hunt, designer of both the Huntington Library and the Rose Bowl, was engaged to design the 19-room Mediterranean villa atop what later became known as Kellogg Hill. From that vantage point, using his binoculars, Kellogg could survey the carefully planned landscaping, the duplex occupied by the trainer and his chauffeur, and the Manor House, occupied at various times by several Kellogg children. With his second wife, Carrie Kellogg, for whom he installed a pipe organ in the living room of Kellogg Hall, he supervised the construction of curving roads and pathways, as well as several pools rising from natural springs. Sometimes riding his favorite horse, Antez, he would inspect the elaborate irrigation system with its pump house, wells, and double reservoirs, or simply behold the rose garden in full bloom, a fitting memorial to the Arabian steeds buried there.

On 100 acres Kellogg ordered the planting of olive, citrus, pomegranate, and avocado trees, the fruits of which were sold to local fruit companies. Much of the remaining acreage was devoted to horse pastures and the growing of feed. Fifty acres were set aside, however, for the nation's largest privately owned airport, rarely used for more than emergencies or Kellogg's personal mail deliveries. With the assistance of a staff of 14, America's king of corn flakes administered a modern-day barony, which in 1930 was expanded by the purchase of 325 acres that had been part of the former state hospital in Walnut.

In 1932, preoccupied with his imminent demise and deeply committed to public philanthropy, Kellogg turned over the facility to the University of California with the stipulation that the popular horse shows should continue at least until 1975. He retained 50 acres and the "Big House" where he lived until 1942, but at public ceremonies hosted by Will Rogers and attended by several thousand people, the facility became the Institute of Animal Husbandry.

By the end of the 1930s, it was evi-

dent that the university was not committed to the arrangement, and by mutual agreement the property was deeded to the federal government. The Pomona Quartermaster Remount Depot was established by the U.S. Army. During World War II the facility served as an internment center for Italian prisoners of war, who maintained the roads and built walls and trails.

Reality had altered Kellogg's dream, but new opportunities lay ahead for the Kellogg Ranch and the people of Pomona, who by 1940 numbered 23,539. Allen Nichols, a former law partner of Russell Pitzer, launched a residential development in the Ganesha Hills in 1937. The completion of Holt-Garvey Boulevard from Pomona to Los Angeles made driving to Los Angeles on the future route of the San Bernardino Freeway as fast sometimes as traveling on the Pacific Electric.

By the late 1930s, 50 acres of land adjacent to the county fairgrounds had been leased for an air strip. Pomona College students took flight training at what became known as Brackett Field, while students at Pomona Junior College, later Mt. San Antonio College, took their training at the Pomona (also known as Burnley) Airport. In September 1938 a branch of California State Polytechnic College, San Luis Obispo, was located at the Voorhis School for Boys in nearby Veus.

The elements contributing to renewed development were gradually appearing. The growth and challenge of the approaching years would be unprecedented as the entire region grew more prosperous and cosmopolitan, and technology and transportation integrated the suburbs ever more inextricably with the urban core. The ensuing decades would create a new world for the town of bountiful harvests.

POSTWAR CHALLENGE

United States involvement in World War II galvanized the nation and forced Americans to forget the woes of the Depression decade. The national commitment to the war effort resulted in the investment of more than $800 million for the development of industrial plants, 5,000 of which were established in California between 1940 and 1944. By June 1943 the state was receiving 9.54 percent of all United States military contracts. During these four years the production of aircraft in Southern California increased from 8,000 to 96,000 planes per year.

As the nation's industrial centers shifted westward, California's population leaped from fifth to third largest in the country. In addition industrial leadership brought an end to the state's seeming insularity. With the aid of air transport, its commercial hinterland had become international. Furthermore the island-hopping war against the Japanese had created a growing national awareness of the Pacific Rim. As a result of these myriad changes, a quarter of a century's development was telescoped within a few years, and postwar California was to develop new social and economic patterns as it responded to the challenges of the second half of the twentieth century.

The San Bernadino Freeway opened in 1954. Courtesy, Pomona Public Library

Above: During the war, the Pomona Quarter-master Motor Base was established on the Pomona Fairgrounds. This picture is of the transport school. Courtesy, L.A. County Fair/Official U.S. Signal Corps Photo

Right: An aerial photograph shows the rows of barracks, left, and trucks, foreground, which covered the Los Angeles County Fairgrounds during World War II. Courtesy, U.S. Army Signal Corps/L.A. County Fair

THE WAR YEARS

A number of the 7 or 8 million military personnel who trained, traveled through, or embarked from California had some contact with Pomona. As many as 6,000 troops were stationed at the fairgrounds, which in 1941 had been rented by the War Department at a monthly fee of

$1,700. In April 1942 the Pomona Quartermaster Motor Base was established on the grounds. By the end of the year, the shops, supply depot, transport school, and motor pool of 8,000 vehicles utilized the services of more than 1,300 military personnel and 800 civilians, one-fourth of whom were female assembly line workers and chauffeur mechanics. On February 15, 1943, the base became part of the famed desert training center.

Military personnel stationed at the fairgrounds and the Kellogg Ranch—including the 125th Infantry, which arrived on December 14, 1941—were welcomed by townsfolk, who gathered at the local railroad stations, and by volunteers at the local USO and the servicemen's center, established at the Pomona YMCA. During World War II more than 28,000 men used the Y's various recreational facilities. To advise civilians on how best to serve members of the armed forces stationed in the area, the chamber of commerce organized a Military Affairs Committee. Pomona's own fighting unit,

Company F, which had become part of the U.S. Army in 1941, fought its way across the South Pacific in a series of beachhead campaigns that claimed the lives of 40 Pomona residents.

From early May until August 1942, the county fairgrounds served as a temporary detention center for more than 5,400 of the 100,000 Japanese Americans on the mainland. Under the provisions of Executive Order 9066, issued by President Roosevelt on February 19, 1942, many evacuated residents were interned in a temporary detention camp located on approximately 80 acres in the west parking lot, which had been quickly transformed into a self-contained community. The tar-paper town had police and fire units, mess halls, churches, a post office, even a system of scrip used for transactions inside the internment camp. Most of the 425 prefabricated units were six-person residential units. The rest served as warehouses, offices, and a hospital staffed by 12 Japanese-American doctors and nurses, and a dentist. After the Japanese were assigned to more permanent quarters in August 1942, the facilities were used by military troops and later by German and Italian prisoners of war.

American military involvement also touched civilians in other ways. Pomona citizens prepared bandages and sewed more than 35,000 garments. Local Gray Ladies administered blood drives and worked in hospitals. Local schools were designated as sites of the National Defense Training Program, which prepared hundreds of men and women for war production. These programs became models for the increasing number of local adult education classes, in which enrollment increased by 75 percent between 1946 and 1950. Trainees were employed in local plants on facilities in adjacent communities. The plants included the

Kaiser Steel Plant in nearby Fontana where Henry J. Kaiser, aided by a Reconstruction Finance Corporation loan, transformed a vineyard into the largest steel mill in the West.

Along with the rest of the nation, Pomona residents recycled foil, rubber, grease, and empty toothpaste tubes. By early 1943, when they realized that the conflct could not be brief, citizens were adjusting to using ration coupons for coffee, meat, sugar, and shoes, and outings were curtailed by the limited allocations of gas and rubber as well as by the 35 m.p.h. speed limit.

As in other towns across America, members of the Civilian Defense Unit, authorized by the Pomona City Council in June 1941, conducted inventories of fuel and supplies. In addition they designated orchard spray rigs as emergency fire vehicles. As part of the war effort, the chamber of commerce organized the Pomona Valley War Housing Center in 1943 to assist the incoming thousands who vied for scarce apartments, houses, and rooms. From 1940 to 1946 Pomona's vacancy rate declined from 5.15 percent to 1.25 percent.

During World War II, the War Department rented the Pomona Fairgrounds for $1,700 a month to use as a military base and later as a detention camp for Japanese Americans. This picture was taken where the warehouse building stands today in the southwest corner of the fairplex. Courtesy, L.A. County Fair

Postwar Growth

After the conclusion of hostilities in 1945, the nation focused on its long-deferred civilian agenda. By September 1945, a scant two weeks after VJ Day, federal gas rationing had come to an end. Americans eagerly used wartime savings to purchase the cars, machines, and appliances that soon rolled off assembly lines hastily converted from the production of tanks and tools. Reunited and often relocated couples burgeoned into baby boom families inhabiting tracts of single-family dwellings which mushroomed from Levittown to Lakewood.

These dynamic postwar changes would profoundly affect Pomona. Contemporary California has been described by many as "America only more so." Similarly Pomona in the late 1940s epitomized the optimism and expansion that energized postwar America. More than 300,000 GIs and their families returned to California after the war to settle in communities where the quality of life matched their positive expectations for the future. Many used GI loans and savings to purchase homes in Pomona, a community of orchards and tree-lined streets that also served as a regional center at the nexus of a nationwide transportation system. As a result between 1946 and 1949 the town's population grew by 30.3 percent. Orchards and fruit stands along Foothill Boulevard, the famed Route 66, were soon replaced by trailer parks and motor courts filled with newcomers attracted by the area's low population density of 1.26 persons per acre, the appealing semirural environment, and the relatively low land values.

Unfortunately the declining price of land reflected the declining fortunes of the citrus growers. Their markets had been negatively affected by the end of government purchases in 1946. At the same time the export market diminished, protective tariffs were reduced, and Florida and Texas emerged as new competitors. Furthermore inflation had caused the costs of cultivating and harvesting to increase by 30 percent, and the burgeoning population resulted in sharp increases in property assessments and taxes. In addition the new subdivisions irreparably altered old irrigation systems, and air pollution drifted eastward from Los Angeles. It nearly choked the valley by 1948, affecting both the size and the quality of the citrus fruit. Consequently an increasing percentage of local fruit was rejected by packinghouses. Even more devastating to the orchards was the rapid advance of the quick decline disease.

The demise of the local citrus industry was further hastened during the winter of 1948 when the most severe frost in more than a decade destroyed 25 to 45 percent of the entire citrus crop. The yield of navel oranges declined from 341.5 to 289.1 field boxes per acre, while the harvest of valencias fell from 261.1 to 232 field boxes per acre.

Confronted with these realities growers converted submarginal land to avocados, persimmons, flowers, berries, and other valuable crops. Recognizing that commercial developments would utilize only the periphery of a grove while adversely affecting the productivity of the entire orchard, owners rejected strip sales or leases while also admitting it was impractical to plant field crops on increasingly valuable acreage. As a result, between one-third and one-half of the owners of 13,277 acres of orchard land, constituting 43 percent of Pomona's land, were favorably disposed to sell to large residential tract developers.

It was hoped that single-family dwellings on large lots in carefully planned tracts interspersed amid the remaining orange groves would not significantly alter the appearance of the community; rapid development soon shaped another reality. By the end of the 1940s, the number of acres devoted to agricultural production in Los Angeles County had declined from 311,000 to 293,000. Due to the inexorable postwar expansion, by 1950 industry had appropriated 50 percent of the pasture lands in the county.

Development throughout the region resulted in a suburban push to create new bedroom communities. Consequently, by 1950 Pomona had 17,146 residential units. Despite the call for greenbelts, parks, and golf courses, as well as planners' warnings against overdevelopment, housing developments mushroomed. The growth pattern was accelerated by the city's becoming a member of the Metropolitan Water District in 1950.

Dependence upon the limited local water supply had been made problematic when, after five successive seasons of subnormal rainfall between 1944 and 1949, the underground water tables had fallen. As a result voters approved the formation of the Pomona Valley Municipal Water District in 1949 as the initial step toward becoming part of the Los Angeles Metropolitan Water District with its enviable acess to the Colorado River. In 1950 residents overwhelmingly approved a bond issue to finance the affiliation, which was made possible by state legislation energetically supported by the local Citizens' Area Water Committee.

Pomona's resulting population growth rapidly surpassed local employment opportunities. One postwar survey determined that the 88 establishments in the immediate area could provide industrial jobs for no more than 2,762 workers. The shortage in employment was critical.

Unlike the earlier residents of Pomona, those living in the new subdivisions, particularly in the southern sections of the town, generally were below 40 years of age.

Despite the absence of rapid transit other than the Pacific Electric interurban line to the fairgrounds, which operated until 1950, more than 40 percent of the new arrivals commuted 15 to 45 miles to work. The largest number traveled to Alhambra and Pasadena. A 1948 survey of the residents in the recently completed subdivisions of Westmont, Town House, and Homes for Tomorrow revealed that 122 of the 440 employed residents commuted to Los Angeles or beyond.

In response to the residents' need for jobs, the chamber of commerce actively recruited industry. It emphasized the convenience of rail and other transportation facilities, the relatively low building costs, and the existence of a climate that permitted outdoor operations. Anticipating the postwar withdrawals of the Lockheed and Goodrich companies, the chamber launched a campaign which in 1948 alone attracted 41 new businesses to the area.

Among the new arrivals was the Wayne Manufacturing Company established in south Pomona by Charles Weinberg in 1947. Within a decade the popularity of the street sweepers, water trucks, and power vacuums manufactured by Weinberg and later his son, Gil Wayne, led to the employment of 500 workers at the 7.5-acre facility, as well as the establishment of 6 international subsidiaries.

In 1946 the United States Chamber of Commerce singled out Pomona as one of the two fastest growing communities in the United States. Its location near several major transcontinental trunk lines and within 45 trucking miles of a major

Pomona's electric streetcars, which operated until 1950, found a resting place at the car barn storage tracks in Claremont. Pomona's "Dummy" car is pictured on the right. Courtesy, Pomona Public Library

port facility, as well as the community's quality of life, made it attractive to American industry which was developing a pattern of plant decentralization. Pomona was to especially benefit from this dispersal pattern with the establishment of General Dynamics' Pomona plant, an industrial research ordnance plant owned by the navy but operated by General Dynamics. Admiral Charles F. Horne, longtime president of the plant, which employed 4,500, explained the reasons for locating in the community:

One of the key factors that helped determine Pomona as the site of our new 100,000 square foot engineering building was the area's ideal living and working conditions. We have found that people like to live here and to send their children to our excellent schools. I am certain this is one of the significant reasons why our personnel turnover rate is low.

The arrival of the General Dynamics plant and the American Brake Shoe Company brought 3,000 new jobs to Pomona and increased the local payroll from $12 million to $15 million.

Pomona's growth inevitably led to an increased demand for better transporta-

tion. As the community moved from agriculture to a balanced suburban economy, improving connections with the metropolitan center became a necessity. Garvey Boulevard, a major arterial highway, had become clogged with densely built business strips. In 1947 the approval by the state legislature of a 10-year highway construction program which called for state freeways connecting all communities of 5,000 or more with the federal highway system, assured the construction of an east-west freeway. A dispute quickly arose, however, regarding the route. The state highway engineer favored the "southern route" while a local citizens' committee campaigned for a route north of Ganesha Hills. After a bitter debate the route skirting the southern edge of the hills was approved by a four-to-one vote of the council. Construction of the Ramona Freeway (later known as the San Bernardino) was completed through Pomona in 1954.

By the end of the 1940s, the city's leadership was committed to expansion and progress. To facilitate the administration of the growing city, an administrative officer was added in 1949. This transformed the commission form of government stipulated in the 1911 charter into a council-manager form of municipal organization. Although a city charter incorporating this change was not approved in 1954, voters ultimately approved the council-manager concept in 1963.

During the decades of postwar expansion, the town acquired both the Garfield and the Park Avenue hospitals. Pomona also held 35 of the 42 churches in the valley. The city's library circulated 264,339 items in one year, and its wide-ranging services were considerably enhanced by the active support of the newly created Friends of the Library.

This is a view of downtown Pomona in 1944, looking north from Fourth Street up Garey Avenue. Courtesy, Pomona Public Library

By 1947 the Humane Society had been organized. Both a community band and a chorus began presenting public concerts. The Pomona Valley Symphony Orchestra was revived after a wartime interruption, and an opera support group was formed. By the summer of 1947 citizen efforts had resulted in the construction of a new campsite at Barton Flats in the San Bernardino Mountains, which was used by the growing ranks of Camp Fire Girls. The increasing organization of boy's and girl's clubs was reported by the Old Baldy Council of the Boy Scouts of America and by the Spanish Trails Council of the Girl Scouts of America.

By the early 1950s Pomona's population had regrouped into a solid pyramid. As a result of the large number of children, school enrollment increased to 7,900, served by an expanded staff of 316 full-time employees. Students included future television news commentator Robert Pierpoint and Olympic athletes Robert Seagren, 1968 and 1972 winner of

Olympic medals in the pole vault; and Mabel Ferguson, 1972 Olympic silver medal winner in the 1,600-meter relay competition.

Pomona's strides toward civic maturity also included providing for higher education. As early as 1945 local residents had agreed to terminate Pomona Junior College, which since 1937 had operated a 4-year, 11-14 program, in order to establish a junior college in cooperation with the neighboring Covina, Bonita, and La Puente school districts. That same year, on land which had once been the site of the state's Pacific Colony, Eastern Los Angeles County Junior College was established. It was renamed Mt. San Antonio College the following year when it officially opened for classes, attended by 600 students. A decade later in 1956 the Voorhis Unit, San Dimas, a branch of California State Polytechnic College, San Luis Obispo, expanded to the Kellogg Ranch, which it had acquired in 1949. The branch was known as Califor-

This aerial view of the San Bernardino Freeway route through Pomona was taken in 1953. Courtesy, Pomona Public Library

nia State Polytechnic College, Kellogg-Voorhis Campus, Pomona.

In 1948 the Los Angeles County Fair was held following a six-year interruption. It attracted a record-breaking 1,254,503 visitors. On September 25 alone, 28,300 jammed the race course, establishing a still unbroken attendance record.

CITIZENS TAKE PRIDE

As a new decade dawned California celebrated the centennial of its admission to statehood in 1850. While the cold war escalated into armed conflict in Korea, Southern California continued to be influenced by inflation, a population influx, and an unabated real estate boom. From new offices on East Third Street, the Pomona Chamber of Commerce joined the spirit of expansion, distributing promotional materials around the world. As a result of an advertising campaign on the radio and the newly available television, more than 20,000 inquiries were received in one year.

The chamber's slogan for the 1950s, "Clean up, Pick up, and Fix up," reinforced residents' pride in the community. It also inspired citizen support for the 13 separate community improvement bonds that provided funds for education, water supply, sewage disposal, and civic center development.

In 1953 a citizens' committee of 100 was created to propose the development of a 16-block center to house municipal and county services. By the end of the decade, Pomona, having invoked historic precedent, had fended off competition from neighboring Covina and been chosen as the site for a new superior court building.

To ease growing congestion on city streets aggravated by the city's 14 railroad crossings, Pomona led in the development of a statewide program to establish a formula for apportioning between railroads and public entities the financial responsibility for the creation of railroad grade separations. State legislation made matching funds available from the State Division of Highways. The following year, as a result of support spearheaded by the Pomona Chamber of Commerce, a bond providing the needed matching funds was approved, and railroad grade separations planned for Garey, Towne, and White avenues were undertaken. In 1959, on the hottest July 19 on record, the Towne underpass was the first to be dedicated.

Citizens were equally supportive of bonds for park improvements proposed in response to a state assessment noting the inadequacy of the facilities in relation to the community's growing population. Pomona, which had led the state in developing the concept of shared use of school grounds and parks through the 1943 Joint Use of Facilities Agreement, approved a major park improvement bond issue of $850,000 in 1956.

The area's recreational facilities were further enhanced by the state's purchase, using offshore oil funds, of 1,138 acres of the Puddingstone Dam and Reservoir originally developed in 1928. The park, later deeded to the county and subsequently renamed Bonelli Park in 1970, became a 1,975-acre facility with 98 species of plant life, camping and hiking areas, an equestrian center, and a 250-acre lake.

Puddingstone Dam had been created half a century before as a facility designed by the Los Angeles County Flood Control District to regulate runoff and restore the aquifer. Fifty years later Pomona took the lead among the League of California Cities in developing a storm drain program to further control runoff. It was approved by Pomona voters in 1952. The $4-million project was augmented with construction by the U.S. Corps of Army Engineers of a dam in San Antonio Canyon, which was completed in 1956.

During that eventful decade Pomona Valley Community Hospital expanded to include the short-lived Pitzer Home, a separate 31-bed facility for elderly patients, and a 4-story addition to house surgery, obstetrics, laboratories, and a nursery, which was completed in 1956.

Expansion also occurred at Pacific State Hospital in west Pomona. Severe overcrowding was relieved by an extensive building program which by 1954 had added a school and 12 new ward buildings for 2,800 patients. By 1957 the facility employed 1,355. Many of the workers were local residents.

Unfortunately the hospital's expansion during the 1950s resulted in the demolition of the historic Vejar adobe. In response to community concerns raised particularly by the Historical Society of the Pomona Valley, which had ascertained that one of the last remaining examples of typical Monterey architecture could have been restored for $110,000, a replica made of bronze and concrete, on a scale of eight to one, was constructed on the site.

Efforts to preserve evidence of Pomona's rapidly fading history also led the historical society to renegotiate the contract for the Casa Madera, the second Palomares home, with the city. According to the revised agreement the caretaking and maintenance duties were allocated to the City of Pomona and the historical society, which undertook the landscape renovation utilizing historic flora.

Volunteer efforts were marshaled to preserve Pomona's historic tradition, and with equal commitment local citizens worked through service clubs, the Assistance League, and the League of Women Voters to preserve the traditional quality of life for the burgeoning community.

By the close of the decade Pomona appeared poised at the threshold of promise. But challenges of unexpected complexity would delay this optimistic expectation.

REEMERGING PROMISE

W hen a huge population counter overhanging the Oakland-San Francisco Bay Bridge tallied 17,393,134 on November 24, 1962, California became the nation's most populous state. The growing number of residents settled in supercities stretching northward from San Diego created environmental challenges which were regional in scope. In the course of their expansion, these urban centers frequently challenged the autonomy of smaller municipalities. As Pomona businessmen soon discovered, they equally as often lured away clientele from established commercial districts.

As the region encompassing Pomona changed, Southern California was heralded as the bellwether in national trends. By the 1960s California cities were often described as being on the experimental edge of national change.

ECONOMIC EXPANSION

The region's growth resulted from advances in sportswear and furniture manufacture, food processing, tourism, and media entertainment. Most importantly California had assumed leadership in securing defense contracts that emphasized the development of complex weapons systems. By 1962, 40 percent of all military development contracts were being awarded to California companies, including the Pomona branch of General Dy-

These elephants are being readied for the town's circus in 1985. Courtesy, Pomona Public Library

namics, a participant in the development of the Atlas ICBM missile, and Aerojet General Corporation in nearby Azusa.

The transformation of the aircraft industry into a combination of aircraft, missiles, and electronics resulted in the commitment of more than one-third of the state's industrial production to defense and space exploration. It was a transition intensified by the Korean and Vietnam military conflicts, which made research and development of military equipment a permanent part of the economy. In the process, employment patterns in communities like Pomona came to directly reflect fluctuations in federal defense spending.

Predictably the economic expansion which stimulated population growth resulted in a residential building boom that consumed acres of semi-seasoned lumber, tons of cement, and vast numbers of bricks in the construction of housing

developments that soon covered the region's agricultural lands. Industry soon occupied 50 percent of the county's pastureland, and the acres devoted to crop production declined from 311,000 to 293,000.

Pomona was an inviting location for expansion. With moderate temperatures, little wind, and low humidity, it had a pleasant natural environment that permitted outdoor construction and assembling, and kept heating and lighting costs to a minimum. Pomona also had access to important markets via major transcontinental trunk lines and east-west highways. Furthermore, in the wake of the citrus producers' declining fortunes, property was comparatively inexpensive. Finally, the low density residential pattern which had distinguished Pomona as a "garden community" easily accommodated tract development. As a result developers and promoters replaced

Brackett Field was the location for an Abbott and Costello movie set on June 17, 1954. The crew of Universal-International filming the scene are gathered around a vintage biplane. Courtesy, Pomona Public Library

growers in shaping Pomona's future. Subsequent educational needs, sagging commercial profits, and such regional dilemmas as smog and traffic would command the attention of beleaguered civic leaders whose ranks were temporarily diminished as old-timers departed and newcomers slowly familiarized themselves with the issues.

MEETING NEW NEEDS

During the era of Southern California expansion, Pomona grew at an ever faster rate. In the 1940s and the 1950s, the population jumped by 51 percent. Between 1950 and 1960 the population increased by 90 percent. In order to plan for orderly expansion, the chamber of commerce appointed a 1981 committee in the early 1960s to estimate the future needs of the community that was celebrating its Dia-

The old Pomona Health Center, at the Main and Fifth streets intersection, was razed in 1966. Courtesy, Pomona Public Library

Opposite: Pomona residents
can find refreshing sum-
mertime fun at nearby Rag-
ing Waters, an aquatic
amusement park, in San
Dimas near Bonelli Regional
County Park, just 10 min-
utes northwest of the city.
Photo by Larry Molmud

mond Jubilee in 1963. After 75 years of progress Pomona claimed a population of 75,000. It had more than 60 churches and 25 public schools, including Ganesha and Garey high schools, which both opened in 1962 to help accommodate a growing enrollment of 19,000 students. The total number of students had increased by a thousand each year since 1954.

During the jubilee year a new public library housing 228,000 volumes and 700 periodical titles was dedicated. It represented one element in a planned civic center envisioned by the Pomona Citizens' Committee of One Hundred as a complex housing both municipal services and the services of a subregion of the metropolitan Los Angeles area. In keeping with the plan, in 1966 the Pomona Health Center was completed. The same year construction was begun on a new city hall and the East District Superior Court Building.

It was anticipated that the 12-block civic center, with its parklike setting, would complement the expected economic growth in a newly developed nine-block pedestrian mall. Inspired by Pomona's motto, "Beauty is Good Business," local citizens had successfully urged the passage of the Mall Law of 1960. This state legislation supported the development of the mall, the first one west of the Mississippi River. The landscaped pedestrian lanes, dedicated on October 15, 1962, were accented by fountains, murals, and sculptures. It was anticipated that the thoroughfare, anchored to the east by a Buffum's department store constructed at a cost of $4 million and to the west by the six-story Home Savings and Loan Building valued at $2.5 million, would relieve the traffic congestion in the town's established business district, thus stimulating trade as well as providing a graceful prototype for the nation's urban

planners.

The city's 75th birthday celebration was also marked by the dedication in October 1963 of a two-story Public Safety Building, which housed communications and civil defense units as well as the fire department. Through its ongoing fire fighting enhancement program, the department received a coveted First Class national ranking in 1975. The Pomona police, the fourth occupant of the complex, responded to increasing caseloads with the innovative use of helicopter surveillance (HALO) and the operation of an accredited police academy training center.

The cultural life of this growing community was enhanced by the activities of the Musicians Club of Pomona which, beginning in 1960, conducted auditions among local music students, awarding prizes and featuring finalists in concert performances. The arts were also supported by the Pomona Valley Art Association, founded in 1948. Its 300 members were responsible for a continuing program of classes, workshops, and open-juried shows, and a revolving art program that placed original art in public buildings. Residents also welcomed the opportunity to participate in a community chorus and the concert band, whose summer evening programs in Ganesha Park are today a continuing source of community enrichment.

The health needs of Pomona's increasing population continued to be met by local hospitals. In November 1963 a new East-West Wing costing $2,714,000 was added to Pomona Valley Community Hospital. Assisted by a federal grant the hospital opened a psychiatric division in 1967. Facilities were further augmented when an $8.5-million addition was completed in 1973, at which time the complex was served by 200 categories of

106

Above: These two youths take the opportunity to go one-on-one on an out-of-the-ordinary basketball court in Pomona. Photo by William A. Matthews

Right: Members of the Pomona Lawn Bowling Club compete with other clubs from surrounding communities. Photo by Mark E. Gibson

This four-level freeway interchange for the 10, 57, and 71 freeways provides access to Pomona from many surrounding areas. Photo by William A. Matthews

The sale of autos and auto parts continues to be first among Pomona's taxable transactions. This roadside mechanic finds it necessary to get a closer look at the problem along Garey Avenue. Photo by William A. Matthews

The setting sun marks the end of a long day for these two construction workers who are working on a development overlooking the Orange Freeway near Elephant Hill. Photo by William A. Matthews

110

A worker picks berries in one of Pomona's many strawberry fields that are scattered throughout the city. The boxes stacked at the end of the row are flats filled with berries picked during the morning, which are available to the public straight off the lot. Photo by William A. Matthews

Above: Located at the eastern end of the Pomona Mall, the College of Osteopathic Medicine greets students and visitors with this graceful entrance gate. Courtesy, Mark E. Gibson

Left: The distinctive design of Pomona's City Hall sets the building apart from other civic center structures. The hall is attractively illuminated at night. Photo by Mark E. Gibson

medical employees including 180 physicians and dentists.

Parallel growth occurred at Pacific State Hospital, later Lanterman Developmental Center, where the staff exceeded 1,500 by the end of the 1960s. The relocation to Pomona of Casa Colina, the expansion of other medical facilities, and the establishment of the Inland Medical Center and the Dialysis and Transplant Center, as well as the presence of numerous extended-care facilities, confirmed Pomona's leadership in health care.

Services continued to be provided by the Pomona Valley Red Cross, which had been organized in 1917 with the support of several hundred local citizens. These services included single-family and communitywide disaster assistance, expanded blood donor programs, and classes in first aid, earthquake preparedness, and CPR. The Pomona Visiting Nurse Association, was organized in 1952, and in 1965 it combined with the Ontario unit. It thus made available to more than 250,000 people assistance in physical therapy and nursing aid, as well as support to recently discharged medical patients and senior citizens.

CHALLENGES OF GROWTH

Amid evident expansion, complex themes began to emerge. As a result in 1966 a Redevelopment Commission was appointed to address such issues as the declining vitality of the central business district. Statistics indicated diminished pedestrian traffic and lagging sales. Pomona, once Hollywood's favorite sneak preview town, witnessed successive theater closings. By the early 1970s only the Fox Theatre continued to operate in the downtown area.

The seeming commercial inertia was inconsistent with various indicators of economic health. According to an analysis provided by Security First National Bank, the city's taxable sales between 1957 and 1963 had increased by 50 percent, a rate of growth sustained through 1967, when total sales led all San Gabriel Valley communities except Pasadena. A 113.5 percent increase in the sale of general merchandise between 1960 and 1966 was surpassed in the valley only by West Covina and Pasadena, while sales by Pomona's auto dealers and suppliers were exceeded only by Alhambra and, again, Pasadena.

Between 1958 and 1963 Pomona's service establishment grew from 422 to 505, and its 714 retail businesses employed 6,154 people. It led the East San Gabriel Valley in total sales, number of employees, and total payroll, surpassing the entire San Gabriel Valley except for Pasadena.

The vitality was not reflected by establishments along the Pomona Mall, however. Although in 1963, after one year of operation, foot traffic had increased by 75 percent, merchants soon moved elsewhere, citing the increased rents, inadequate parking, absence of government support and cooperation, and even the length of the mall itself. In addition buying behavior had changed when shoppers discovered the convenience of auto-oriented plazas with their concentrations of specialty stores. By 1972 the nearby Montclair Plaza was attracting 36.4 percent of the Pomona shoppers. Furthermore much-lauded alterations had removed many traditional meeting places. Without the lights and excitement of earlier days, there was little to attract pedestrians to the area.

By 1972, 42 of the 111 stores were vacant or being used for storage. The rest of Pomona's commercial areas also re-

Facing page: The spacious plaza of Pomona's Civic Center is bounded on the west by the Supreme Court Building. Photo by Mark E. Gibson

The construction of Montclair Plaza, the region's first enclosed shopping mall, hurt the business community in Pomona. Courtesy, Pomona Public Library

flected a decline. In 1963 Pomona had reported 13.5 percent of the pedestrian goods sales in the Pomona Valley. Two years later a more than 10 percent decline augured ill for the business sector, which was frequently bypassed by motorists traveling the surrounding freeway network. This network increasingly isolated the urban core and robbed the city's arterial streets of customers.

CHANGING RESIDENTIAL PATTERNS

Several other factors contributed to economic change in Pomona. Significant among these was a trend reflected in the doubling of the number of building permits issued by the city between 1959 and 1963. During this period Pomona led all San Gabriel Valley cities in the number of dwelling units authorized. Between 1960 and 1963, 74 tracts comprising 1,993 lots were developed. Between 1964

and 1967 another 25 subdivisions offered tract houses at prices ranging from $15,000 to $20,000 each.

The rapid construction of houses on former orange-producing land resulted in an unexpected glut, reflected in 1965 by the number of idle electric meters. They represented 18.6 percent of all the new single-family dwellings and 24.1 percent of all the multiple units recently constructed in the city. Significantly, three years later the figures dramatically declined to 2.8 and 6.6 percent respectively. The change reflected a major population influx that swept the city into the vortex of historically important population changes across the nation. It was to result in demographic adjustments that Pomona's civic services, employment sector, and transportation network had

not anticipated.

During the 1960s Pomona's population increased by 22,000 residents, 17,000 of whom were blacks responding to new economic opportunities and exploring new horizons implicit in the emerging civil rights movement. As a result Pomona's traditionally small black community, which had numbered about 900 for some years, grew from one percent to 12.2 percent of the population. It approximated the size of the well-established Latino community generally concentrated south of Holt Avenue, which represented 13.7 percent of Pomona's population in 1972.

As the nation endorsed the principles of the Great Society outlined by President Lyndon Johnson, increasing numbers of blacks followed other groups to middle

Pictured is a portion of the Civic Center in downtown Pomona. The large building is City Hall, while the City Council Chambers, the round structure, is located in front. Courtesy, Pomona Public Library

The Pomona-Lewis Business Center is an example of the graceful and modern developments cropping up in present-day Pomona. Photo by Mark E. Gibson

class-oriented suburbs. Los Angeles County, where the population had grown from 2 million in 1950 to 3.5 million in 1970, best exemplified this dispersal. During a decade of significant income advancement, blacks shifted to a patchwork of communities in the suburban ring, and in particular to Pomona, where low-cost housing was abundantly available.

Extensive promotion and special programs had at first lured white middle-class buyers from Los Angeles, 33 miles away. A year or more after purchase of the tract houses, however, the new residents recognized they were an inconvenient distance from places of employment and moved to newer tracts springing up on vacant lands closer to Los Angeles.

Most importantly the end of the Korean War and a consequent reduction in federal defense spending had caused a general economic decline in Southern California. By 1953 California had surpassed all other states in the net value of prime military contracts and awards for supplies, services, and construction. The cessation of hostilities, however, ushered in a period of major economic adjustment. Overtime declined, and layoffs followed. Soon the Veterans Administration (VA) and the Federal Housing Administration (FHA) began repossessing houses. It is estimated in a *Los Angeles Times* article that by 1960 between 50 and 75 percent of the houses in the tract later known as "The Island" sat "vacant, weed-grown and weeping glass slivers from broken windows."

The FHA and the VA, both eager to solve the vacancy problem, listed refurbished homes with local real estate agents rendered idle by the economic slump. In keeping with new government guidelines, many realtors reversed long-standing policies and signed nondiscrimination pledges. At the same time government agencies announced the availability of the repossessed homes to residents of the Los Angeles urban core. This coincided with the incendiary Watts riots, which resulted in 34 deaths and $46 million in damage, and impelled moderate blacks to flee urban violence and seek better schools. Pomona, where four-bedroom tract houses were being offered for $13,000, offered an affordable alternative. Additional urban out-migrants filled nearly 12,000 rentals, which constituted a significant portion of the available dwelling units.

As a result of the influx, the community known as "The Island" emerged in the northeast Pomona tracts adjacent to Pomona High School. A second concentration known as "Sin-Town" grew in northwest Pomona near recently opened Ganesha High School, while a third cluster settled in "The Flats" in southwest Pomona in an area served by newly built Garey High School. The pattern distributed the 100 recently enrolled black high school students among the district's three secondary schools.

The new residents were well-educated, the average years of schooling completed being 12.1. They were also better paid than the new black residents in northern and eastern cities. Their reported median income of $7,705, however, was not commensurate with the average of $10,253 reported by newly arrived white residents.

While voter registration records indicate that the majority of the new residents had moved from elsewhere in the state, a 1972 community survey indicated that 25.3 percent of all the respondents came from outside the state, and a special state census conducted in Pomona in 1977 revealed that 52 percent of all Pomona residents had lived in the city three years or

less. The complexity of the rapid population shifts was exacerbated because black residents had left behind their church congregations, fraternal organizations, and established leadership structures. Time was needed for new spokespersons to develop credibility and constituencies. On the other hand, local community leadership was diminished as a result of white flight.

Although by 1970 blacks had joined the police force and the school district's certified staff, a segment of the civic leadership was committed to the status quo. It tenaciously guarded the city charter provision calling for the election of council representatives for specific districts on an at-large basis. During this sometimes abrasive transition period, the city was reprimanded for discriminatory practices, and in 1973 it was sued for its police and fire fighter hiring practices.

The community was initially hostile. It accused government agencies of having generated Pomona's community problems and began to balk at paying higher taxes for civic improvements. Local merchants who objected to assessments five times higher, they claimed, than those for comparable sites, gradually relocated, and townsfolk who had voted in 13 successful bond elections were no longer supportive.

The debate was particularly sharp with reference to education. An Interracial Advisory Commission established in 1968 proposed a plan to pair elementary schools, one with a majority of black students and the other with a majority of white students, in adjacent areas. The plan was defeated by 13,000 white voters; a second plan met objections from black parents.

Student disturbances which had surfaced in April 1966 and February 1968 heightened in January 1971, causing the closing of the high schools for four days beginning on January 7. Despite the problems of internal adjustment, the school district continued to grow. In 1972, a total 22,143 students, 38.21 percent of whom were members of minorities, were enrolled in 21 elementary schools, 6 junior high schools, and 4 high schools. In combination with adult school and English as a Second Language programs, the schools were staffed by 1,021 certificated personnel.

The national unrest of the late 1960s and early 1970s, sometimes characterized as "the ungluing of America," also affected Pomona. In the summer of 1971 rock-throwing members of the long-established Latino community, which had grown to 16.3 percent of the town's population by 1970, laid siege to Pomona's new police headquarters, an increasingly visible community symbol. Reported crimes against property rose 59 percent and arrests nearly doubled from 2,007 to 3,841 between 1965 and 1970.

The public demonstration was an unprecedented activity for the highly stable Latino community, composed largely of descendants of residents of the states of Jalisco and Guanajuato in the central highlands of Mexico, who had migrated northward as railroad workers or fled the poverty and revolutionary conditions in Mexico between 1910 and 1930. By the 1960s the enclave had evolved into a tripartite community. The first two groups consisted of temporary residents and permanent immigrants. The descendants of the latter, in combination with descendants of long-term inhabitants, some from the days of Palomares and Vejar, formed the third group. All shared the national aspiration for education and economic opportunity. In the process they too heard the promises of the Great Society and turned to Pomona's civic leadership for their fulfillment.

Public protest was generated by economic as well as social needs. The 1970 census revealed significant increases in the youthful populations in census tracts 4021, 4030, and 4029. By 1972 one-half of the city's population was under the age of 30. It was a population group low in revenue production but in need of such public services as schools.

Many of the youthful residents claimed only entry-level job skills. Furthermore by the early 1970s opportunities within the city were fewer than 4,300 in nonmanufacturing areas. While manufacturing and aerospace positions had grown to 22,000 in 1971, the following year they were reduced by 25 percent as a result of federal cutbacks in aerospace spending. The resulting unemployment rate surpassed that of the Great Depression and also created demands for other public services which generated further demands upon a diminishing revenue base.

Limited local employment opportunities also forced residents to commute. By 1970, 12,000 residents commuted at least 25 miles to work, while the overwhelming majority commuted at least 12 miles. Many of the two-income families were employed in government offices in Los Angeles where affirmative action policies had recently opened job opportunities to blacks. Because of commuting time and employment demands, members of the newly established community were unable to assume positions of community leadership or participate in solving problems directly affecting them and their children.

The commuting challenge, which confronted 90.2 percent of the Pomona residents who drove to work, according to a 1977 Special State Census, was not lessened by Pomona's strategic location within the region's transportation network. In 1951 the Pacific Electric Railway had concluded its scheduled trips to the county fairgrounds. Charter air service from Brackett Field to LAX had proved to be a short-lived program, and Pomona's Greyhound Terminal had been relocated in Claremont. Although local transit systems provided transportation between nearby communities, freeway auto travel was essential despite the resulting low gray pall of smog which was relentlessly blown eastward by coastal breezes, forcing Pomonans to recognize that they were inextricably bound to both the opportunities and the problems of the regional community.

By the mid-1970s an expanded freeway network reaching the foothill communities as well as Orange County was conveying 129,000 cars through the vicinity of Pomona, resulting in renewed stimulation for residential construction. As improved highways conveniently linked the community to the Los Angeles urban metropolis, newcomers settled in the Phillips Ranch subdivision and the upper and lower Mountain Meadows residential developments.

A DUAL CELEBRATION

The national bicentennial in 1976, which was celebrated in conjunction with the centennial of the founding of Pomona, provided an appropriate opportunity for self-assessment with the publication of the *Comprehensive General Plan for the City of Pomona*. A major finding of the extensive analysis was that Pomona still was a "balanced community" offering a mix of residential and commercial opportunities to its citizens. Local manufacture, augmented by the development in 1968 of facilities in the Southern Pacific indus-

trial area south of the Pomona Freeway and east of the Corona Expressway, produced a variety of items ranging from hair spray to guided missiles. The commercial sector also reported continued steady growth. The public sector was another source of economic vitality, which employed 20,000 workers in regional and local government offices located in Pomona.

Festivities marking the national and local anniversaries ranged from the Pomona Centennial Horse Race run on September 13, 1975, to hosting the United States Freedom Train at the county fairgrounds. The historical thrust of the celebration was emphasized at the annual meeting of the California Conference of Historical Societies held at Cal Poly's Kellogg West Center and hosted by the Historical Society of the Pomona Valley. The society could point to an impressive list of preservation successes. They included the restoration and furnishing of the Phillips Mansion, the area's first brick structure which, with the active support of the society, was acquired by the city in 1966. Another important part of Pomona's centennial history, La Casa Primera, built by Ignacio Palomares in 1837, had been rescued from partial decline and public indifference in 1972 by the society, which later restored it through a state preservation grant.

Pomona's progress during its first 100 years was also reflected in the innovative Central Kindergarten, which had served the city from 1908 to 1974, when the historical society and other local preservationists succeeded in relocating it to an area adjacent to La Casa Primera. The refurbished kindergarten, renamed in honor of Barbara Greenwood, a local kindergarten pioneer, continues today to be used by community groups.

The 1976 celebration's theme, "Build-

Pomona City Hall was built after the Pomona Health Center building was completed in 1966. Courtesy, Pomona Public Library

ing on Pomona's Heritage," not only took into account the past and ongoing efforts to preserve it, but also underscored aspects of the city's continuing development, particularly in the area of education.

In 1978 the large number of institutions of higher education located in or near Pomona grew to include the College of Osteopathic Medicine of the Pacific, one of only 15 fully accredited osteopathic colleges to operate in the western United States. It opened in Pomona with an initial enrollment of 36, which soon grew to 440.

The region's continuing growth was also reflected in the enrollment at Mt. San Antonio College. By the mid-1980s it had 28,000 students representing all 16 communities within the community college district. Similar expansion was reported by California State Polytechnic University, Pomona, which in 1987 claimed a student body of 17,000 students enrolled in 47 bachelor of science programs, 10 bachelor of arts programs, 14 master's programs, and 6 credential programs. The university, established under the 1960 California State Master Plan for Higher Education, in 1966 became an independent unit of the 19-campus system

and in 1972 qualified as a university according to legislatively mandated criteria. The original campus, the 157-acre Voorhis School for Boys, was sold to the Pacific Coast Baptist Bible College for $2.3 million, and the university subsequently acquired a 100-acre addition northeast of the 813-acre Kellogg Campus. Cal Poly, famous for its annual Rose Parade float and monthly horse shows, has become a recognized center in international agriculture, small business administration, and hotel and restaurant management, among other fields.

ADJUSTMENT AND SUPPORT

Along with other public agencies educational institutions were forced to adjust to the revenue reductions resulting from the passage of Proposition 13 in 1978. The California property taxpayers' protest, which soon rumbled eastward across the continent, forced the fiscal reorganization of the school district as well as community colleges such as Mt. San Antonio Community College by centering authority with revenue sources in Sacramento. Cutbacks in revenues caused reductions in staffs and services throughout the public sector and increased the reliance on citizen groups such as Volunteers for Vital English, which was dedicated to teaching non-English-speaking adults to communicate effectively in English. The 100 volunteer teachers instructed more than 400 adult students in 18 local communities.

Numerous public agencies have also been served by the 1,500 volunteers placed each year by the Volunteer Center of Greater Pomona Valley, organized in 1978. Private citizens have completely staffed Pomona Meals on Wheels, as well as SCAMP (Senior Citizens' Activities and Meals Programs), the Organization for After-Stroke Resocialization, and Project SISTER Sexual Assault Crisis Services. Along with such well-established groups as the Pomona YMCA and the Spanish Trails Girl Scout Council, whose 336 local units in 34 communities have a total membership of more than 20,000, they are among the many community agencies that continue to serve because of the generous efforts of citizen volunteers.

In the wake of Propositions 13 and 4, the government spending limit initiatives, education allocations were reduced, causing California to fall from 17th to 35th among the states in per-pupil spending for public education. By 1986 it had the lowest teacher-pupil ratio among all the states. Volunteer support for underfunded school activities has included reading tutorial assistance, a variety of services provided by the PTA (which has served Pomona schools since 1907), and the Pomona Educational Partnership, organized in 1984 with the objective of inviting local businesses to provide various forms of assistance ranging from tutoring to career exploration experiences to students in an adopted school. The innovation offered citizens an opportunity to support the school district's commitment to:

provide each student in the multi-ethnic and diverse community of Pomona and North Diamond Bar an education which challenges that student to reach his or her highest potential in the areas of academics, critical thinking, occupational skills, and personal growth to prepare for individual education and career choices.

More than 24,000 students were enrolled in 1987 in Pomona's 34 schools, and the school district's commitment is designed to prepare them for the expanding challenges of a new century.

POSITIVELY POMONA

In the 1980s new prospects unfolded for Pomona, a community which had grown to 30,350 households and ranked 29th among all California cities. At the outset of the decade Pomona claimed a work force of 23,000 employed in the manufacture of durable goods and the provision of administrative support and personnel services. The median family income was $17,425.

To meet the needs of the growing community the city employed a staff to maintain its 21 park sites. Other essential services were provided by 218 fire fighters and a police staff of 130. To fund these growing programs a utility tax first authorized in 1969 was increased to 11 percent of residents' gas, electric, water, and telephone bills, yielding approximately $10 million annually.

Amid debate regarding utility taxes, other significant revenue sources emerged during the 1980s. Building permits rose 51.5 percent during the first three quarters of 1986 and 1987, contributing to a 10.4 percent increase in assessed valuation.

Increased construction is but one of several indications that in the 1980s Pomona was discovered as the gateway city to the burgeoning developments of the Inland Empire. Pomona, the third largest city in the inland region, strategically located 7 miles from the Orange County line and 30 miles from downtown Los Angeles, offers reasonable land prices when compared to much Southern California real estate. As a result building permits issued between January and September 1987 resulted in added residential development in Phillips Ranch, Cobblestone Creek, Grove Estates, and the 570-unit Pomona Town Center. The construction sustained a steady population growth of 21.9 percent and an increase from 112,775 residents in 1986 to 117,827 in 1987, making Pomona the 146th largest city in the nation.

In 1984 Pomona, the community "with the right mix" of residences and jobs, moved to provide increased employment for a population whose median age was 27.8. Inspired by the motto, "Pomona . . . Positively!" the Pomona Economic Development Corporation, a volunteer group dedicated to stimulating investment, employment, and tax revenues, attracted 1,600 new jobs to the area during its first year of operation. Today many in Pomona's labor force of 44,019 are locally employed in the 40,000 jobs available, particularly in nondurable manufacturing and retail sales. The largest employers are General Dynamics Corporation (8,821), the Pomona Unified School District (2,239), General Telephone (2,200), Pomona Valley Hospital (2,000), and California State Polytechnic University, Pomona (1,850).

In 1986 alone 551 new businesses obtained licenses and leased 2 million square feet of business space, a portent of the increased business activity throughout the region. An increase of 805,000 jobs has been forecast for Los Angeles County by the year 2000. The anticipated economic surge became evident in Pomona with the construction of University Corporate Center, Pioneer Electronics, Inland Envelope, and T.S. Park Plaza, as well as the development of industrial parks, including University Tech Center and the Bonita Business Center near Pomona's northern industrial border. There has also been a $4-million refurbishment of the Los Angeles County Fairgrounds including the construction of a recreational vehicle park. In order to better accommodate the 2.5 million visitors who annually attend events at the fairgrounds, plans have been developed for the construction of an equestrian sales and exhibition facility and the development of a hotel and exposition complex.

Other projects in the planning and development stages include the commercial center bounded by Mission, Temple, and the Orange Freeway; King's Plaza on Holt Avenue; the Phillips Ranch regional shopping center; and Foothill Square and the Auto Serve Mall, both located in the vicinity of Foothill Boulevard and Garey Avenue—an intersection traversed by 55,000 cars daily.

Characteristic of the economic expansion is the Pomona Auto Center in south Pomona. Its success has significantly contributed to the fact that the sale of autos and auto parts continues to be first among the city's taxable transactions. It was appropriate, therefore, that the River Ranch Road Interchange dedicated in February 1988 not only linked the commercial center of south Pomona with the residential areas of Phillips Ranch, but also, as a symbol of Pomona's renewed economic vigor, incorporates the very highway system which at one point was an agent in the decline of the central business district. The $5-million interchange, which Pomona's city officials have observed is the first in the California State Highway System "to be designed, constructed, administered and paid for by a municipality," has been called "the bridge to the second century." It could also be called "the bridge to a prosperous tomorrow."

Southern California's real estate industry, it has been observed, has attentively watched the dramatic growth and the impressive absorption rate in west

Pomona. In 1988, as Pomona celebrates its centennial, its past is closely linked to an optimistic future. The ranches granted 150 years ago to Ignacio Palomares and Ricardo Vejar have developed into a community lying at the threshold of a growing inland empire, participative in the economic activity of a 60-mile circle surrounding the Los Angeles urban core. It is a compact area which generates one-half of California's economy, employs 56 percent of all state residents engaged in manufacture, and is engaged in 67 percent of its international trade.

Pomona is a part of this complex region, which is simultaneously America's Ellis Island of the twentieth century, an economic center of the Pacific Rim, and the generator of a gross regional product that exceeds the GNP of all but 11 leading nations and states in the world. In addition to being an integral part of this dynamic area, the city of bountiful harvests offers a singular potential for progress composed of its available land, accessible transportation system, and resident labor force, easily augmented by the 10 colleges within or adjacent to the city.

Even more important is the fact that Pomona is a mature city that has adapted and accommodated to changing circumstances and expectations. Surveying the success of its first century, its citizens should confront the second century of progress with the enthusiasm, idealism, and hope exhibited by its founders, who at the dedication of the statue of the goddess Pomona were stirred by the words of southland leader J. DeBarth Shorb, who reminded them:

Agriculture and manufacturing, finance and commerce, science and mathematics, may make in able hands a nation great, strong and wealthy; but when this is accomplished at last, only the foundation stone is laid of true national greatness. Upon this foundation a higher civilization remains to be built; this must be the superstructure of which we are the architects and builders, and constitutes the debt we owe to the past men of our nation and the duty we owe to ourselves and future generations.

Though Shorb's observations were national in scope, the truth of his words has meaning for Pomona on the verge of its second century. While trends strongly predict the future economic prosperity of Pomona, its greatest wealth lies in the will and effort of citizens who have steadfastly recognized their duty to their city and its future generations.

Santa Claus greeted people at the Fox Theatre and was the master of ceremonies at the Christmas Eve party there. He presented to the audience a large assortment of Christmas gifts which had been donated by local merchants. Courtesy, Pomona Public Library

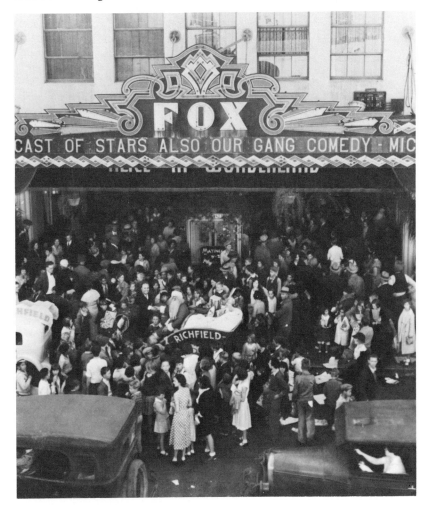

PARTNERS IN PROGRESS

··

In 1875, 13 years before Pomona was officially incorporated, a group of entrepreneurs formed the Los Angeles Immigration and Land Cooperative Association, and began to survey and subdivide the newly named settlement into lots and tracts on Rancho San Jose. The town already had a hotel, a drugstore and provision store, a saloon, and a butcher shop.

Blessed with fertile soil, abundant water, and an ideal climate, the area was soon filled with vineyards for wine and raisin production—the beginning of Pomona's economic leadership among the cities of the valley. Later, in the 1890s, these industries were largely replaced by citrus orchards and olive groves, which became the fledgling city's major source of income and employment.

While these agricultural activities were to be the backbone of Pomona's commerce for many years, the real future of the city had already started to take form as early as 1864, when thriving business and industrial enterprises began to locate in the community. Pomona led the way in the development of long-distance transmission of electricity, use of alternating current, the first semiautomatic switchboard west of the Mississippi, and direct-distance dialing. It had an unbeatable mix of agriculture, business, and innovative industry, all being shepherded toward the kind of wide-based economic stability envisioned for the city.

In time, this enlightened approach was to succeed beyond even the wildest dreams of those early planners. During World War II nearly 30 industries came to Pomona, with only 2 departing when the economy returned to peacetime. The construction of the Pomona and San Bernardino freeways became a reality, and the Los Angeles County Fair, today the largest county fair in the world, made its home in the city.

Currently, Pomona's large commercial, professional, and industrial base employs more than 35,000 people in the industrial sector alone. Products include high-quality optics, electronic software, beer, bakery goods, glass, paper, cosmetics, steel, and defense weapons systems.

Surrounded by colleges, Pomona has its own claim as an educational center with California State Polytechnic University, Pomona, and the College of Osteopathic Medicine of the Pacific located within its borders.

Major banks and other financial institutions, hospitals, health care services, churches, service organizations, parks and recreational areas, a broad range of housing choices, an excellent school system, retail stores, a new auto center, an antique center, restaurants, three main railroad lines, and easy access to nearby Ontario International Airport round out the attractions of this progressive and growing city of more than 110,000 people.

The stories of the organizations who have chosen to support this major literary and civic record of Pomona's first 100 years are detailed on the following pages. They represent the rich variety of enterprises that helped give the city the title of "The Gateway to the Inland Empire."

Facing page: This was the Pomona police force, as it appeared in 1924. Courtesy, Pomona Public Library

POMONA CHAMBER OF COMMERCE

The Pomona Board of Trade, later to become the Pomona Chamber of Commerce, was founded on November 15, 1888. Its task was to actively encourage the growth and development of what essentially was a rural community into a major metropolis.

There was no time to lose. That same year the first coast-to-coast paved U.S. highway was opened, and already there were two railroads serving the fledgling city. And the population was exploding: Within four years it would jump from 800 to 3,500.

Capitalizing on this sudden spurt of popularity, the board of trade began extensive promotion of Pomona and the valley. It produced a booklet describing the opportunities and attractiveness of The Land of Fruit and Flowers and circulated it nationally. In 1893 the board sponsored an exhibit at the Chicago Fair and began advertising in the *San Francisco Chronicle* to attract newcomers arriving in California by ship.

Looking west on Second Street between Garey Avenue and Thomas Street. The photo was taken around 1905 when the chamber was known as the Pomona Board of Trade. Courtesy, Pomona Library

The home of the Pomona Chamber of Commerce on Garey Avenue since 1977.

Eventually it became necessary to combine the efforts of the board of trade and two other organizations working toward the same goals: the Pomona Businessmen's Association and the Pomona Realty Board. This resulted in the formation of the Pomona Chamber of Commerce on June 17, 1913.

Today the goals and precepts of the chamber have remained unchanged in everything but scope since those early days. The organization's aggressive Program of Action has kept Pomona on the move. In cooperation with the City of Pomona, the Pomona Unified School District, the Los Angeles County Fair Association, and the Pomona Economic Development Corporation, plans and programs have been formulated and are being implemented to bring new industry, tourism, conventions, and entertainment to the community. Industrial and office buildings are being erected at a record rate; hotels, motels, restaurants, and shopping facilities are being built; and established business facilities are being upgraded and modernized in an un-

precedented display of confidence in the future of the area.

The Pomona Chamber of Commerce continues to bring job opportunities to Pomona, but it also has become increasingly concerned with the social and cultural climate of the city. The organization's sensitivity to the city's economic and ethnic diversity has prompted a broader look at the needs of the people and the design of programs to meet those needs.

A number of informational services are provided by the Pomona Chamber of Commerce for the benefit of local residents and visitors wanting to know more about the community. The organization also is involved in many areas of education, legislation, transportation, local government action, housing, code enforcement, community image, and special programs.

MT. SAN ANTONIO GARDENS

The concept was glorious: to establish a retirement home for "the continuance of significant living," a place that would go beyond just providing shelter and care for elderly people. It was also enormously ambitious. But to a group in the Claremont Congregational Church the idea was a challenge to their faith that "the things that matter the most" are attainable through prayer, dedication, and hard work.

The year was 1953, and they had no money and no land—only conviction, enthusiasm, and a lot of untapped talent. The first step toward the reality of their "prayer-vision" was taken when a gravely ill schoolteacher, Anna Peterson, made a $2,700 bequest to the group. That bequest became a catalyst in 1955 for them to convince the Southern California Conference of the Congrega-

tional Church (now the United Church of Christ) to throw its support behind the new venture.

Two key breaks came for the committee in 1957. The Federal Housing Authority established a special loan program that would allow the group to borrow 60 percent of the money it needed at low interest, and a 22.5-acre site straddling the northeast Pomona/Claremont line was discovered. But a problem surfaced: The owner of the land had to have $50,000 in cash within 10 days. A novel idea was proposed—to form a little syndicate of supporters and their friends who would tap their savings accounts to lend the money to the conference. A few days later the $50,000 was raised.

In September 1961 the first major buildings were completed on the 13-acre Pomona section (the nine acres in Claremont were developed two years later) and move-ins began. By the end of the year there were 189 residents, with more than 100 units

The future site of Mt. San Antonio Gardens in 1960, looking north toward the San Gabriel Mountains from Bonita Avenue.

The colorful oval flower garden adjacent to the dining room and administration offices.

waiting to be occupied.

Then it was decided to choose a name for the retirement center to accurately reflect its purpose and mission. After a long search Mt. San Antonio Gardens was selected in honor of St. Antonio de Padua, the patron saint of learning and culture, colleges, and churches.

Expansion and improvements, including a medical unit, continued throughout the 1960s and 1970s, much of them financially supported by the residents, now referred to as Gardeners and numbering 460.

The philosophy of Mt. San Antonio Gardens is perhaps best expressed in a booklet prepared for the first-anniversary celebration in 1962. "These Gardens came alive through four intangible, but very real forces. Our beginnings are not to be found in soil, steel, mortar, wood, and paint, but rather in fellowship, concern, faith, and vision."

The family of Gardeners today is the beneficiary of that philosophy into which life was breathed by the founders 35 years ago.

POMONA VALLEY COMMUNITY HOSPITAL

It was Christmas Eve, 1899, and the residents of the small agricultural community of Pomona were gathering to celebrate the holidays and prepare for a promising new century. Suddenly, news of a terrible train wreck on White Avenue shattered the festivities. There were more than 30 casualties, and Pomona citizens rushed to the victims' aid, opening their homes to care for the injured until they could be taken to Los Angeles hospitals by horse-drawn ambulance.

Spearheaded by Eliza B. Bradbury, the townspeople confronted the need for adequate hospital facilities by supporting construction of a 2.5-story frame house on Piedmont (now Kingsley) and Garey avenues. Completed in 1903, Pomona's first hospital included 12 patient rooms, an operating room, and living accommodations for the nurses. By the following year residents had joined together to officially create the Pomona Valley Hospital Association. Little did they know that 84 years later the tiny, 12-patient hospital would have become a 399-bed facility recognized for its specialty services, advanced technology, a distinguished medical staff nearing 500, and quality care.

The medical needs of the commu-

nity mounted as the area's population continued to swell. To help meet the need for more trained nurses, a Nurses Training School was established at the hospital in 1905 under the directorship of Clara Arbuthnot, R.N. The newly established hospital attracted new physicians into the Pomona Valley, bringing the total from 19 at the turn of the century to 44 in 1916. It is interesting to note that three female doctors were practicing in the area in those early years.

By 1910 overcrowding had become a serious problem. That year plans were initiated to construct a new facility on the five lots bounded to the north and south by Willow and Nemaha, and to the west and east by Garey and Orange Grove—the site of the present Pomona Valley Community Hospital complex. Just days after ground was broken for the new building, the existing 12-bed hospital was destroyed by fire. Fortunately, all patients were removed safely and transferred to temporary facilities nearby. In August 1913 a new hospital to accommo-

The charter class of the Pomona Valley Hospital Training School for Nurses (left to right): Addie Blewitte, Mauree DeBois, and Opal Chain. Clara Arbuthnot (seated) was founder of the school and served as its first superintendent.

date 30 to 40 patients was opened.

In 1924, under the leadership of benefactor and community leader Russell K. Pitzer, the hospital was reorganized from a stock company to a not-for-profit organization and rechristened Pomona Valley Community Hospital. With his magnanimous gift of $50,000 and an additional $100,000 generated by other influential civic leaders and community residents, a badly needed, four-story T-wing expansion was completed in 1928, boosting capacity to 65 beds.

The Great Depression years took their toll on Pomona Valley Community Hospital. The Nursing School was discontinued to cut overhead costs; all employees were given a 25-percent salary cut; and the hospital narrowly avoided bankruptcy.

These hard times inspired a group of 24 women, headed by Mrs. Paul Endicott, to band together and form the first Auxiliary. The Auxiliary celebrated its 50th anniversary in 1987, and the growth of the organization's services and contributions

Pomona's first 12-bed hospital and its medical and nursing staffs, pictured circa 1903. Today Pomona Valley Hospital is a 399-bed regional medical center with 2,000 health care professionals and a medical staff of 500.

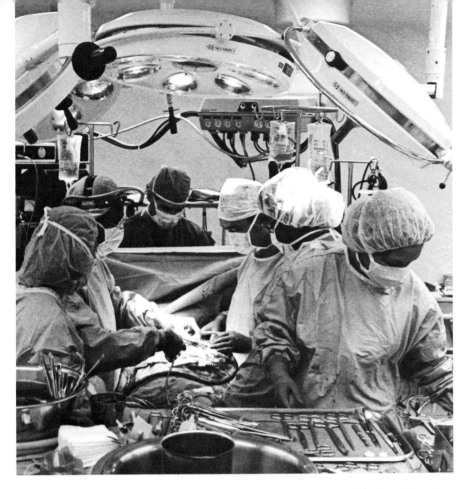

over the years reflect an astounding level of commitment and dedication. The 50th year boasted more than 500 members—both male and female—serving in 25 areas within the hospital and participating in several fund-raising activities and community events.

The years between 1937 and 1950 were comparatively peaceful. The late 1940s saw the addition of the radiology, or X-ray, department and auditorium. In 1951 Pitzer contributed a unique addition to Pomona Valley Community Hospital: the Pitzer Home. A separate building provided facilities on one side for 31 additional hospital beds, and on the other side, accommodations for 17 elderly residents.

The growth of Pomona, and of the entire valley, necessitated further expansion in 1954. A four-story north wing was built to house surgery, obstetrics, a laboratory, and, for the first time, physical therapy facilities. Funds raised by the Women's Auxiliary also financed a new pediatric department.

The 1960s and 1970s served to forge PVCH's long-term commit-

With the 1986 opening of the Stead Heart Center, complete with open-heart surgery and cardiac catheterization services, the hospital achieved a milestone in its commitment to provide the Pomona Valley area with a fully integrated, comprehensive cardiac care program.

ment to address state-of-the-art technology and to keep the hospital in the vanguard of new developments. In 1964 the six-story east-west wing was completed, and a fully appointed intensive-care unit opened. A coronary-care unit and radionuclide scanning section followed in 1968. Other advances were marked by the addition of a linear accelerator used for treatment of deep-seated tu-

mors through radiation, and the laminar air-flow surgery suite, which maintains a completely sterile airflow system during total hip and knee replacement operations. Also during this period the first of many regional services—a neonatal intensive-care unit—was opened in 1973 to treat sick and premature newborns who do not require surgical intervention. Today PVCH holds a high reputation for its specialized treatment of infants.

Additional building took place in the early 1970s, with a three-story wing completed in 1975, bringing the total licensed bed count to 389. On the technological side, a new computerized tomography (CAT) scanner, representing the most dramatic breakthrough in diagnostic capabilities since the discovery of X-ray, was installed in the radiology department.

Subsequent milestones at PVCH included the addition of an Alcohol/Drug Treatment Service, a neurological unit, day-surgery service, a cardiac rehabilitation program and expansion of diagnostic and therapeutic capabilities in noninvasive cardiology, a new birthing center, and a stoma clinic.

The mid-1980s saw yet another wave of tremendous growth for Pomona Valley Community Hospital,

The first operating room at Pomona Valley Community Hospital, circa 1910.

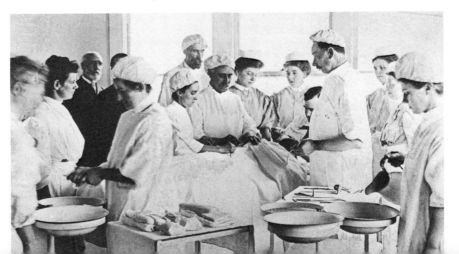

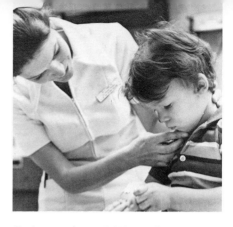

ushering in its evolution into a regional medical center. For the first time the hospital extended its geographical roots outside its existing campus to establish an affiliate urgent-care center, Central Avenue Urgent Care, and an adjacent physical-therapy annex in neighboring Montclair. Closer to the existing campus, the Alcohol/Drug Treatment Center was moved off-site to a 48-bed, 30,000-square-foot facility. Closer to the existing campus and indicative of the hospital's master plan to physically expand south is the Women's Diagnostic Imaging Center, offering mammography and osteoporosis screening.

The Regional Kidney Stone Center, Southern California's first free-standing outpatient facility for noninvasive, lithotripsy treatment of kidney stones, and the only such service within a 25-mile radius, was opened in 1986. Termed an authentic modern medical miracle, lithotripsy is a method of removing kidney stones utilizing high-energy shock waves to disintegrate the stone, providing an alternative to traditional surgical methods.

Perhaps the most significant milestone achieved by the hospital was marked in the fall of 1986, when the region's first cardiac-catheterization and open-heart surgery services were introduced. The Stead Heart Center could now offer a comprehensive center of heart care to the region's residents, who until that time had had to travel to Los Angeles or San Bernardino to receive the more critical surgical services. Led by highly respected, experienced medical teams, both programs have operated at peak capacity since their introduction. Partially in response to the tremendous demand, the hospital opened a new 10-bed critical-care facility in 1987.

In the technological arena, another first for PVCH was the opening of the regional Magnetic Resonance Imaging Center, featuring the most powerfully sensitive diagnostic equipment manufactured to date—the first of its kind in the country. MRI offers vital clinical data previously unavailable with other imaging modalities.

Other changes within the past decade include the addition of a popular Sports Medicine Center, physician referral services, a dedicated cancer program, and a wide array of community wellness activities.

Medical staff membership at PVCH now numbers nearly 500, and a new breadth and depth of medical subspecialties has been uniquely established, bringing new special ser-

Each year about 43,000 people turn to Pomona Valley Community Hospital for immediate, around-the-clock treatment of emergencies and other health-related problems.

vices to the local community and to the region as a whole.

As it looks to the future, Pomona Valley Community Hospital will continue to flex with the changing needs of its community as its history demonstrates, and to further establish its regional profile of services and technology that would not otherwise be available locally. But as current president Robert W. Burwell stated in the hospital's 1986 annual report: ". . . In the final analysis, however, PVCH's success is a direct tribute to its people and is not institutional in nature. The hospital provides only the organization, financing, and facilities. It is the individual doctors and professional people who have dedicated years of training and devotion to restoring health and caring, who have nurtured our success and recognition."

Historically recognized for its advanced, state-of-the-art technology, PVCH stays in the vanguard of new developments. The Magnetic Resonance Imaging Center, for example, features the most powerfully sensitive diagnostic equipment available.

A neonatal intensive care unit opened in 1973 to treat sick and premature newborns not requiring surgical intervention. Today PVCH is highly regarded for specialized treatment of infants and the security afforded the high-risk mother.

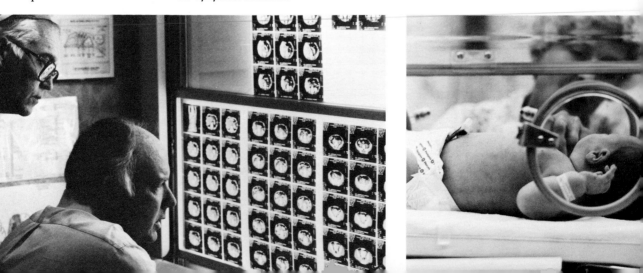

BANK OF AMERICA

For six decades of Pomona's first century Bank of America has been a partner in the city's progress.

The Bank of America presence in Pomona was established on February 19, 1927, when Bank of Italy (B of A's predecessor) and Liberty Bank of America consolidated their operations. It was an important historic event, for together with 174 other California communities Pomona was participating in the formation of the first statewide system of branch banks.

A.P. Giannini—the founder of Bank of Italy in 1904 and an early advocate of branch banking—faced strong opposition during the 1920s to his attempts to establish Bank of Italy as a statewide institution. After Bank of Italy was repeatedly denied permission to open or acquire new branches, Giannini—through the

Bank of America moved to this new, larger building in 1978.

The Pomona main office of Bank of America at Locust Street and Mission Boulevard.

Bancitaly Corporation—established several other banks in locations in which Bank of Italy was prohibited from operating.

Before it joined the Giannini family of branches, what was to become B of A's Pomona main office had operated as State Bank of Pomona, an institution founded in 1906. Its well-known and highly respected manager, E.R. Yundt, stayed on when the small local bank was bought out by Giannini's Bank of Italy and its name was officially changed to Bank of America-Pomona Branch.

By 1926 objections to Giannini's concept of statewide branch banking were crumbling rapidly. That year Giannini bought up the assets of Pomona's American National Bank and its affiliate, American Savings Bank, and moved to new quarters at the corner of Second Street and Garey Avenue. Then, on November 10, 1936, Trans-America Corporation, the former B of A holding company, purchased Pomona Commercial and Savings Bank.

Throughout its history Bank of

America has remained innovative in products and services. The consensus among most bankers in 1949 was that their lobbies should be open only until 3 p.m. Monday through Friday and not at all on weekends. Amid cries of protest from competitors, Bank of America in Pomona inaugurated experimental longer weekday hours and opened on Saturdays until noon. The arrangement won overwhelming approval from customers. As a result, some other banks began to follow suit.

By the mid-1950s Bank of America had outgrown its quarters at Second and Garey in Pomona, and soon a new Bank of America Building was opened on Garey Avenue at the corner of Fourth Street. In 1978 Bank of America Pomona moved into even larger facilities at Garey Avenue and Mission Boulevard, the present location of the Pomona main office.

The landscape of the Pomona Valley has changed considerably since Bank of America joined the partnership of enterprises that has been responsible for its development. A.P. Giannini had perceived Pomona as a key location in what was to become the Inland Empire. His vision was correct.

CLARION HOTEL/ONTARIO AIRPORT

Arriving by train and stagecoach, on horseback, and in wagons, weary travelers seeking a place to rest and eat had few options a century ago in the Pomona Valley and surrounding area. There was the Pomona Hotel, at Fifth and Garey avenues, erected in 1875 as Pomona's first building, and the Palomares Hotel, at Garey and Holt avenues, built in 1885 and destroyed by fire in 1911. And there were 14 saloons in the newly incorporated city in 1888.

But times would change dramatically and rapidly with the advent of the automobile and the airplane, creating a mobile society beyond the comprehension of those early pioneers. The demand for good rooms, food, and service at reasonable cost would create a huge new industry that eventually would bring to the Inland Empire such four-star establishments as the Clarion Hotel/Ontario

The Clarion Hotel/Ontario Airport, the first hotel in its chain built from the ground up by AIRCOA (above).

A last-minute check is made before guests arrive for a wedding reception in the elegant Clarion Ballroom (below).

Airport.

The area was perceived by AIR-COA (Associated Inns and Restaurants Company of America), a

Denver-based firm that owned 20 Clarions nationwide, as becoming significant in the hotel business because of its ongoing transformation from a predominantly agricultural region into a diversified commercial, industrial, and residential economy. Willis McFarlane, founder and chairman of AIRCOA, which now owns 43 hotels, opened the Clarion Hotel/Ontario Airport in the spring of 1986 as part of a major network of four-star hotels in the United States, including Alaska and Hawaii.

McFarlane hooked into Quality International's worldwide marketing network in 1987, under a joint-venture agreement that created a new system of 36 four-star hotels by merging Quality International's Royale system with AIRCOA's Clarion Hotels and Resorts. Quality International is the world's fastest-growing hotel system, with more than 1,000 hotels open or under development in the United States, Canada, Mexico, the Caribbean, the United Kingdom, Continental Europe, Australia, and New Zealand. These include hotels, inns, suites, and resorts marketed under the Comfort, Quality, or Clarion name.

Until 1983 AIRCOA had been solely a manager and developer of

Guests take advantage of the hotel's state-of-the-art Athletic Club facilities.

Guests enjoy the relaxed atmosphere in the "D" Street Tavern.

franchised Sheratons, Hiltons, Howard Johnsons, and other hotel chains. That year McFarlane decided to enter the hotel business for himself, and in 1984 he founded Wynfield Inns, which the company refers to as "budget luxury" hotels. McFarlane plans to become one of the major forces in the hotel industry and is constantly seeking locations as well as acquisitions.

Shanne Noble, director of sales and marketing for the Clarion Hotel/ Ontario Airport, sees the hotel vying "to compete head to head in drawing business away from the Los Angeles market." Ms. Noble does not like to hear Ontario referred to as a gateway to Los Angeles, saying, "'Gateway' implies that a place doesn't have anything of its own to recommend it." She and the Clarion management believe strongly in the growth potential of the Inland Empire and identify a growing number of large corporations that share their optimism for the area that includes Pomona.

The 300-room Clarion Hotel/ Ontario Airport, recently given the American Automobile Association's

A favorite dining spot is Guasti's Cafe, overlooking the lobby.

prestigious Four Diamond Award for quality, was built with the business traveler in mind, with a state-of-the-art meeting facility (called an Executive Conference Center); Preferred Chambers with concierge, turndown service, bathrobes, working desks complete with office supplies, a calculator, and video checkout; a full athletic club; fine dining; and its exclusive Executive Travel Club for frequent corporate travelers. It also has three hospitality suites and three presidential suites featuring libraries, fireplaces, and Jacuzzis. Free shuttle service is provided to and from the airport. Each of the sleeping rooms has a remote-control TV and AM/FM cassette player, two telephones, a desk, a hair dryer, and a mini-refrigerator. Nine rooms are designed especially for the handicapped.

The Athletic Club has three indoor racquetball courts and one outside lighted tennis court; there are also a heated lap pool, exercise equipment, a Jacuzzi, sauna, steam room, lockers, and showers. Separate shower facilities are provided for women.

The hotel's Learning Center provides a multitude of equipment and innovative features, such as ergometric chairs designed for up to 18 continuous hours of comfort in the 128-seat lecture hall and other meeting rooms. Ten soundproof meeting rooms in various sizes with seating for nine to 80 people surround the lecture hall, and an executive boardroom is available for small private meetings. The entire complex covers 16,000 square feet. High-tech audio-visual equipment, such as videotape

The executive boardroom in the Clarion's Learning Center is available for business meetings and conferences.

The Water Company bar in the Clarion's lobby follows the southwestern theme used throughout the hotel.

recorders, color monitors, color video cameras, 35-milimeter slide projectors, editing equipment, microphones, and lecterns with AV control, is available for all meetings and conferences. Continuous coffee/snack break areas are also provided, and a message center can handle any number of business needs, including typing and copying.

Guasti's Cafe and Deli highlights the hotel's southwestern theme in both food and decor. For casual dining there is the "D" Street Tavern, decorated with antiques, collectibles, an old English phone booth, and a jukebox. The full-size, brass-trimmed, stand-up Oyster Bar is surrounded by cocktail-table seating.

The Executive Travel Club Room has a full-service bar, big-screen TV, a pool table, and complimentary breakfast. Spouses of guests who qualify for membership in the Executive Travel Club stay free at the hotel.

Civic and public-service activities are considered by the Clarion Hotel/Ontario Airport to be a part of its responsibility to the community.

It hosts the annual national Clarion for Kids program to inform children under 12 and their parents about a variety of subjects, and invites local volunteer organizations such as the American Red Cross and police and fire departments to participate by offering advice and answering questions. The children are also entertained by dancers, gymnasts, singers, and acting groups from local schools. The event is free, but the hotel asks children and their parents

to donate new or used toys to be distributed to needy youngsters by Santa Claus, Inc., at Christmas.

In 1987, only 14 months after opening its doors, the hotel found itself already in need of additional room for catering and special events such as weddings and conventions. Shortly afterward it completed a 4,500-square-foot covered patio in the center court near the swimming pool. Built with permanent flooring and a permanent roof with skylights, it features unique side "walls" that can be taken down or retracted to convert an indoor setting to a casual outdoor one. Emphasis is placed on landscaping, with an atrium/greenhouse design.

Among the Clarion's security measures is the use of computer-coded magnetic metal cards instead of keys, whose electronic combinations are changed after every check-out.

The travelers of 1888 could not have imagined that a hotel such as the Clarion Hotel/Ontario Airport would one day stand on the then-dusty, desolate land east of Pomona. But their dreams were of new lives and progress, and they would not have expected anything less for those who were to follow them.

A view of the Learning Center's 128-seat lecture hall with specially designed ergometric chairs and sophisticated audiovisual equipment.

GLOBE PLASTICS, INC.

For Roy and Marion Kramer the dream of creating and owning their own business would depend, as it does for all entrepreneurs, on being in the right place at the right time with the right idea.

Roy, a tooling engineer at General Dynamics, had the technical know-how; Marion, a registered nurse, had excellent business sense and managerial abilities. They were in the right place: Pomona. The timing and the idea would come together when Roy discovered that window firms were experiencing

Roy Kramer (left), founder and president, working on specifications for a new product with quality engineer Len Groppell.

breakage problems with casement windows during installation. The window manufacturers regarded it as an inevitable cost of doing business, but Kramer saw it as a unique chance to put his inventiveness to work.

He designed, patented, and produced the Winlock, a disposable vent lock that solved the problem simply and inexpensively. He and his wife wrote to 28 window companies and soon had orders from 27 of them. It was a crucial point: They now had a product and a market, but what they did next would determine whether the business would ever be-

come more than a part-time operation.

The Kramers decided to concentrate on developing and providing items for the country's leading aerospace, electronic, and toy manufacturers, using the less expensive, more versatile, and stronger plastic materials. They established Globe Plastics in rented quarters in the 1400 block of Mission Boulevard in Pomona on October 15, 1958, and recorded sales of $1,000 that first year. Cautiously, Roy continued to work at General Dynamics while Marion ran the embryonic business.

But success came more rapidly than expected, and in October 1959 they moved into three large structures on Signal Drive. By April 1966, when the firm was incorporated, Roy left General Dynamics to devote full time to what had now become a $65,000-per-year business with projected annual sales of more than a quarter-million dollars within three years. Globe Plastics, Inc., was on its way and in 1970 would reach the half-million-dollar mark. Sales have been over the million-dollar mark since 1984, and the projected sales for 1988 is $2 million.

Today, with 15,200 square feet of space and 20 employees, the Kramers attribute their extraordinary growth to insistence upon high stan-

A view of part of Globe Plastics' manufacturing facilities on Signal Drive in Pomona.

The old building was torn down in 1967 to make way for the new Globe Plastics plant on Signal Drive. Roy Kramer (third from left) shares the nostalgic moment with his business associates.

dards of project reliability and accuracy. "Compromise for the sake of expediency has no place in Globe Plastics' engineering and design," Kramer says.

Globe manufactures injection and transfer molded parts by the millions, primarily for businesses in the industrial and electronics fields. The parts range in size from the head of a pin to more than a foot for such disparate uses as military weaponry, aerospace, and industrial products.

What the Kramers describe as "a knowledge of space-age technology and good old-fashioned hard work" is the source of Globe Plastics' success in a highly competitive business. That, and the ability to turn dreams into reality.

PIONEER ELECTRONICS TECHNOLOGY, INC.

When local political, business, and civic leaders gathered at an open house at the new Pioneer Electronics Technology plant at 1800 West Holt Boulevard in Pomona in early 1987, they were witnessing not only the expansion of a major worldwide Japanese corporation but also the reclamation of what had become a depressed and shabby part of the city. It was a bright and positive occasion for all present—a celebration of growth for the company and a new symbol of progress in the rejuvenation of Pomona as an industrial and business center.

Pioneer Electronics Technology, Inc., a subsidiary of Pioneer North America, Inc., the wholly owned holding company of the giant Pioneer Electronic Corporation headquarterd in Tokyo, Japan, was founded in America in May 1978 with the establishment of a modest-size plant on six acres in Duarte. Two months later the plant began operations with 26 employees turning out speaker cabinets and system components racks. Within a year Pioneer had expanded its plant to 121,000 square feet and its work force to 148. It was producing 10,000 speaker cabinets and 10,000 system components racks per month, and still was grow-

An Oriental-style carved monument attractively identifies Pioneer to passersby on West Holt Boulevard.

Yoshihiro Kawaguchi, president of Pioneer Electronics Technology, Inc., in Pomona.

ing so fast that immediately plans were begun to accommodate future expansion.

In 1987 those plans were realized when Pioneer opened its 180,000-square-foot building on 472,000 square feet of land in Pomona. Soon it was employing 355 people, and producing 66,000 speaker cabinets and 50,000 system components racks each month. The large, spotlessly clean plant with state-of-the-art automated equipment operates on an innovative 10-hour-day work shift, four days a week. Yoshihiro Kawaguchi, president of the Pomona firm, says that if business continues to grow at such a pace, the company will expand at its location on West Holt.

The parent organization, founded in 1938 in Japan by Nozomu

Matsumoto for the manufacture and sale of loudspeakers, was incorporated in 1947 under the name of Fukuin Denki Kabushiki Kaisha. Eight years later the company began the manufacture of audio amplifiers and turntables, and in 1961 assumed its current name, Pioneer Kabushiki Kaisha (Pioneer Electronic Corporation).

During the 1960s Pioneer expanded its line of products to include stereo sets and components, car stereos, and telephone answering devices. It was the first company in Japan to introduce "separate" (modular, console-type) stereo

Seiya Matsumoto, president of Pioneer Electronic Corporation in Tokyo, Japan.

equipment, and quickly took the lead in that nation's growing audio industry. In 1966 Pioneer looked to wider horizons and established marketing subsidiaries in the United States and Europe. Six years later it formed what was later named Electronic Engineering Research Laboratory for the development of new products.

Growth and progress continued throughout the 1970s. In 1974 the firm relocated to a new headquarters building in Meguro, Tokyo, a move accompanied by an audio boom created by its Project series of packaged stereo component systems. The following year Pioneer introduced Japan's first component-type car stereo products, creating a new demand. An unprecedented interactive cable-TV system was developed in cooperation with Warner Cable Corporation (now Warner Anex Cable Communications, Inc.) in 1977, followed by the formation of Universal Pioneer Corporation (UPC) in conjunction with the U.S. concerns to develop and manufacture laser-optical videodisc players.

In 1978, the year Pioneer began

the local production of speaker systems in the United States, the company became the first to introduce small, high-performance stereo components—microcomponents—which started a market explosion for that type of product in Japan. Other successes followed rapidly, with the adoption by General Motors Corporation of UPC's industrial-use laser-optical videodisc player for use in its dealer showrooms, and the development by Pioneer of the world's first interactive hotel cable-TV system.

The U.S. consumer market saw the debut of Pioneer's Laser Vision videodisc players in 1980, soon followed by Laser Vision discs and Compact Disc (CD) players. Pioneer started another sales boom in Japan in 1983 with its Laser Karaoke for videodisc sing-along entertainment in that country. In October of that year, with its developing optoelectronics technology, the way was paved for the creation of a new "video culture."

Continuing its growing list of firsts, Pioneer introduced in-car CD players and CD/Laser Vision-compatible players in 1984. Laser Vision disc titles topped the 2,000 mark by September 1985 in Japan, and demand for audio-video as well as dig-

ital products was expanding. The company introduced new audio-video packaged component systems, new CD players, and the Private S360 TV shelf-type packaged system, the latter two to meet the demand for compact, versatile, and affordable-priced products.

Pioneer, aptly named for its creative and innovative approach to the development and manufacture of new and competitive electronic products for consumers and industry, continues to expand its markets in Japan and throughout the world.

Seiya Matsumoto, president and representative director of the parent firm, who was present at the opening of Pioneer Electronics Technology, Inc., in Pomona, affirmed the company's commitment as a responsible and supportive corporate citizen of the areas in which it operates.

As Pomona looks toward its second century, it can do so with the same kind of confidence it had in 1888, knowing it can attract the kind of deep-rooted enterprises symbolized by Pioneer Electronics Technology, Inc.

Pioneer Electronics' 180,000-square-foot plant on West Holt Avenue brought new life to a depressed area of Pomona in 1987.

INDUSTRIAL BRUSH CORPORATION

Although Industrial Brush Corporation was founded on January 1, 1947, in Arcadia, California, its roots go back to 1896 to a company called Pioneer Brush in Los Angeles.

Pioneer Brush itself had little significance in the development of what was to become the major manufacturer of brushes that now is headquartered on East Philadelphia Street in Pomona. The real beginnings stemmed from a remarkably enterprising and inventive young man named Lloyd Jones, who, in 1927 at age 29, purchased Pioneer Brush.

Jones soon developed and patented the transverse brush fruit-washing process that today is found worldwide wherever fruit and vegetables are grown in commercial quantities. However, Jones sold Pioneer Brush and went to work for Food Machinery Company, spending the

next 18 years in the automated food-processing business until 1947, when he decided to once again strike out on his own.

He started Industrial Brush Corporation with himself as the sole employee. The first year nearly became his last, as the business showed a loss. But Jones was a man not easily discouraged, and he managed to end the second year of business with a microscopic profit of $29.80—hardly an overnight success story. The third year was not much better, even though he nearly doubled his profits to $55.

Jones knew that the firm's survival and growth would depend on having a wider range of brushes to offer, and in 1952 he developed his first strip brush-manufacturing machine. Elated by the possibilities that could now open up for IBC, he hired his first full-time salesman, Charlie Holmes, whose territory was the entire country. At that time IBC's primary products were for citrus, bus, truck, and train washing.

By 1954 IBC had the capability of

Founder Lloyd Jones (center) inspecting large industrial brushes at the Arcadia plant about 1950.

producing spiral-wound brushes by forming a strip brush into a coil or spiral shape. This important development allowed the firm to sell a cylindrical brush with a metal core that was far superior to the wooden cores used previously. Soon thereafter, IBC introduced a brush for the then-infant car wash business and quickly became the leading supplier of vehicle washing brushes.

Jones then turned his attention to the rapidly growing street-sweeping business and found that the mechanically driven broom on a street sweeper was made of natural fibers that had a useful life of only a few days. Why not, he thought, come up with a product to solve that costly problem?

IBC took its strip brush, with its rugged steel construction, and added the recently developed plastic fibers for the bristles. This new street sweeper broom became enormously

The basis of IBC's success: the strip brush. It is formed by crimping a metal channel around the bristles and anchor wire.

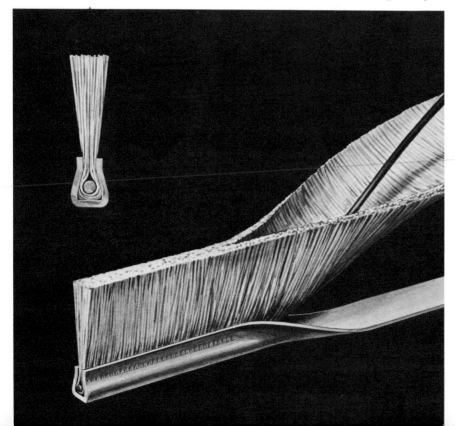

The present manufacturing plant on Philadelphia Street, Pomona.

successful and also opened another avenue for the company: its own plastic extrusion business to develop and manufacture improved plastic fibers for its brushes.

IBC's prowess in the street sweeper broom market did not go unnoticed. Wayne Manufacturing Company of Pomona, one of the largest makers of street sweepers in the world, approached IBC in 1963 to begin a joint venture to market street sweeper brooms. The partnership was so profitable that it led Wayne to purchase IBC in November 1965. Lloyd Jones then decided to retire.

Under the new ownership, IBC continued to grow and soon was producing brushes in the Wayne plants in both Canada and Holland. In 1967 IBC developed a new plastic bristle for vehicle washing brushes, and these quickly became its largest product line. At the same time it began making the plastic track used with Mattel's Hot Wheels toy cars.

That same year the company also left Arcadia for its present location in Pomona. Two years later, in a move to better serve the Florida citrus market, IBC opened a brush-manufacturing plant in Lakeland.

Following Lloyd Jones' retirement, IBC was directed by a series of presidents: Web Wiley, 1965-1967; Dick English, 1967-1969; Charlie

Holmes, 1969-1970; and Irv Belinkoff, 1970-1975. During Belinkoff's tenure both IBC and Wayne were bought by FMC Corporation and operated as separate subsidiaries.

In time it became clear to FMC that while IBC was operating successfully in the brush market, the parent company was more interested in concentrating on the street-sweeping machine business. Consequently, in 1985 FMC sold IBC to three employees: John Cottam, Bob Baldridge, and Bill Dawley. Today these three executives head up IBC.

Under the new ownership, IBC continues to grow at its plants in Pomona, Florida, and Canada, with sales up a dramatic 45 percent since 1985 and increasing at the rate of approximately 15 percent annually. The firm has successfully expanded its markets, from its beginnings in food processing, street sweeping, and vehicle washing, to include hundreds of different products ranging from mechanized cotton harvesting to automated glass washing, and from wood and metal finishing to brushes that convey, sort, clean, package, guide, or glue a myriad of different products. IBC has also found growth opportunities in high-technology industries such as circuit board manufacturing and high-speed printing. In a word, Industrial Brush Corporation offers the experience and manufacturing capabilities to provide the proper brush for virtually every application.

Lloyd Jones did not invent the brush—he recognized its potential and versatility. He knew that while it usually is the lowest part of the cost of a machine, it does the major work—a simple premise, but one that has resulted in a product line that affects the quality of our lives, indirectly or directly, in almost every area.

A section of the brush-manufacturing facilities.

COTTER & COMPANY

John Cotter has always had a different way of looking at things. In what appears to be a contradiction in terms, the founder of Cotter & Company, which is owned by approximately 8,000 True Value Hardware and V&S Variety Stores, is a "conservative entrepreneur" who approaches all new ventures cautiously, yet in a way that most people would consider unconventional and daring.

In 1947, attending a competitor's convention in Minneapolis for his employer, Tru-Test, he got into a marathon conversation with Bill Stout, general manager of American Hardware, about the potential of setting up a dealer-owned hardware wholesale house in Chicago. It was already being done successfully in other areas of the country, Stout argued, so why not in Chicago?

Cotter was sorely tempted. He had been thinking about the idea of establishing a dealer-owned cooperative since 1928, but "had the fear of God in me that I had to make a living." He was making $35,000 at Tru-Test, a very respectable sum in those days, and aspired to earn $60,000 to $70,000 a year eventually. He felt secure and didn't want to endanger his family's welfare. However, it didn't take him long to figure that $6 million or $7 million could be a reasonable expectation from a successful cooperative, and he knew similar ventures were doing well—a fact that satisfied his cautious side.

Ed Lanctot, who had worked with Cotter on and off for about 10 years and excelled in advertising and marketing, signed on immediately in the new venture.

Cotter, who had been given office space by his employer, Red Oakes of Tru-Test, mailed a long letter to 3,000 dealers outlining his plans and seeking their reaction to his idea. He received 300 responses, which encouraged him to send a second letter, inviting the dealers to a meeting in Sycamore, Illinois. He was told by the 12 dealers who showed up that he had a good idea, which they needed, but that his timing was wrong.

Undaunted, Cotter decided to go ahead and named his new firm Cotter & Company. The following day he and Lanctot began to look for 25 dealers who would make a $1,500 stock subscription and by the end of the year had them signed up. Another 25 were good prospects.

Cotter & Company became incorporated on January 15, 1948, with a working capital of $37,000 provided by the 25 dealers, and the venture was under way.

So successful did Cotter become with the idea of a 100-percent member-owned cooperative that he turned his attention west, buying out Great Western Hardware in 1960. What he was doing that was different was building a distribution cen-

John Cotter poses in front of a wall of plaques received by him and his company over the past 40 years.

ter and then establishing the stores around that nucleus, rather than the reverse, which was more common. It was working for him all across the nation, and Cotter's timing, as usual, was correct.

In 1979 Cotter & Company built the 320,000-square-foot Pomona distribution center for True Value Hardware and V&S Variety Stores at 2727 South Towne Avenue. Today it employs 100 people and serves 400 True Value and V&S stores in Southern California and Arizona. Another distribution center is located in Northern California and serves 350 stores.

John Cotter, who to a large degree was the savior of the independent hardware dealer in the United States, still is active in the business, his title now chairman. His son Dan has become chief executive officer, and his son-in-law Paul Fee executive vice-president and chief operating officer.

Forty years ago Cotter & Company had 25 retail members it was serving out of a 2,000-square-foot warehouse. Today it has nearly 8,000 member-owners in every state of the Union and 3,000 employees. Its annual revenues are close to $2 billion, and True Value has become the largest hardware distributor in the country.

Trucks are loaded at the Cotter & Company distribution center on South Towne Avenue in Pomona prior to delivery of products to 400 True Value Hardware and V&S Stores in Southern California and Arizona.

INTER VALLEY HEALTH PLAN

The idea was to create a new type of delivery system of affordable health care for the citizens of the Pomona Valley area. It would be independent and nonprofit, offering the advantages of a Health Maintenance Organization (HMO) linked to physicians in private practice and community hospitals, rather than centralized clinics where patients may see a different doctor at every visit.

By August 1977 a consultant had been hired to conduct a feasibility study, funded by 100 physicians whose contributions were matched by Pomona Valley Community Hospital. The results of the study were positive, and in December a joint committee of physicians and PVCH representatives decided to proceed, naming their new HMO the Pomona Valley Health Plan.

Moving quickly, the committee hired an executive director in April 1978 to develop the Health Plan, and the hospital's associated Valley Independent Physicians (IPA) became in-

Much of the success of Inter Valley Health Plan is credited to Lynn Rountree (left), retired education administrator, and Robert Burwell, president of Pomona Valley Community Hospital.

corporated as a nonprofit corporation.

In the early years the Health Plan was supported by the personal funds of the founding physicians and matching contributions from the hospital. The organization received its license from the State of California, and in July 1979 officially opened with a staff of two. By November 1980 it could count 4,200 members from local employers in the valley.

During the next two and one-half years the Health Plan became increasingly successful, experiencing such member and physician satisfaction that seven more community hospitals and independent physician associations were added. This expansion created a San Bernardino, River-

side, and East Los Angeles counties area, and it was decided to introduce a new name, Inter Valley Health Plan, to properly reflect the wider-ranging coverage.

Much of the credit for the creation and remarkable success of the Health Plan is attributed to four men in particular: Robert Burwell, Lynn Rountree, Richard Davis, M.D., and Lorin Spencer, M.D. Burwell is the president of the Pomona Valley Community Hospital; Rountree is a long-time Pomona Valley Community Hospital board member; Dr. Davis, in family practice in Pomona since 1960, was medical director for the Health Plan in the early years; and Dr. Spencer is a member of the Pomona Valley medical staff.

It has been 11 years since they first conceived the then-innovative prepaid health care plan. Today Inter Valley Health Plan continues in the forefront of meeting people's needs by constantly improving its services to its more than 31,000 members.

A member of Inter Valley Health Plan brings her children in for a checkup.

GARDEN STATE PAPER COMPANY, INC.

Garden State Paper Company's Pomona mill on Mount Vernon Avenue opened in 1967. It annually produces 130,000 tons of newsprint paper—all from recycled newspapers.

Garden State Paper Company, Inc., became a major manufacturer of recycled paper in Pomona in 1967. The Pomona mill was the second built by the firm, which is recognized today as a pioneer and leader in the area of resource recovery through recycling.

Shortly after World War II a newspaper publisher, Richard B. Scudder, an avid conservationist at a time when most people and industries were consuming Earth's natural resources as though they were limitless, looked at his own industry with deep concern. Each day thousands of tons of paper cascaded off the nation's newspaper presses on a journey of no return, to be discarded by readers without a thought.

Publisher of New Jersey's *Newark Evening News,* a major metropolitan newspaper, Scudder was one of the first to equate environmental and resource waste with economic waste. He asked himself why all the paper trimmings issuing from the presses, the badly printed newspapers that had to be thrown away, and the 5 percent or more of a newspaper's run that was returned unsold couldn't be remanufactured and used again. Better yet, he thought, why not also recover all newspapers and reuse them?

He knew what he was up against: Printer's ink would make remanufactured paper too dark for newspaper use, and there was no way to remove it. The technology existed to turn used newspapers into wallboard and cardboard—and had for generations—but not for transforming the paper into an identical product of acceptable quality.

Scudder, who was thinking about a process that later would be described as recycling, was undeterred by the fact that no one had ever been able to solve the problem. In 1950 he brought together a few fellow experimenters who shared his vision, borrowed a kitchen mixer from one of their homes, and began reducing old newspapers to pulp.

Separating the myriad of microscopic wood fibers interlocked by a hydrogen bond that are in a piece of paper was easily done with water in the kitchen blender. But getting the ink out was another matter. Years of frustrating research were to follow, with paper manufacturers and the trade press, skeptics all, jokingly calling the project "Scudder's Folly."

It quickly became evident that a full-scale laboratory was needed. In 1952 the inventors turned first to the Herty Laboratory in Savannah, Georgia, and then to Syracuse University in New York, which has one of the most highly regarded papermaking research laboratories in the world.

Scudder asked Robert H. Illingworth, chief engineer for the *Newark Evening News* and an electrical engineer, to take a crash home-study course in chemistry and to oversee the research. Working at the Syracuse laboratory with a small papermaking machine, a pulper, and other equipment, they made test runs of paper. These experimental rolls of paper were then taken to Newark and put on one of the giant presses at the *News* to be tested.

In 1956 the inventors rented the

Operators at right check controls of papermaking machines, which run 24 hours per day, 360 days per year.

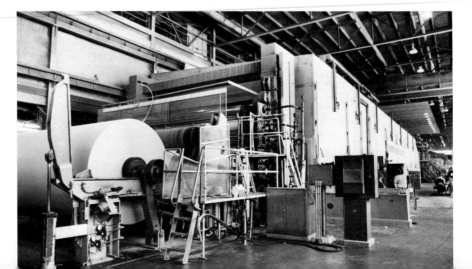

Hearst Corporation's paper mill in Maine and prepared enough pulp there to feed a papermaking machine for 10 hours. They invited 30 newspaper publishers to the demonstration and asked them to take some of the paper back to try out on their own presses.

The new product passed the tests, and Scudder decided on one final run of about a week at the Fitchburg Paper Company in Fitchburg, Massachusetts. He wanted to find out whether contaminants would build in the system, blackening felts, clogging wires, and making continuous operations difficult or impossible. Once again he confidently invited the publishers to watch and take test rolls of the newsprint home. And again the results were a success.

Scudder recognized then that he had a workable and economic process, and decided to begin newsprint manufacturing. Oddly, although they had witnessed the tests, tried the paper, and knew it worked, the publishers chose not to join Scudder in the manufacturing venture. They

Basil Snider, Jr. (left), president of Garden State Paper, and Royce Adair (center), vice-president and general manager of the western region, with Dave Hendrickson, mill manager, look over the production schedule at the Pomona mill.

did, however, contract to buy any satisfactory paper he produced.

That was enough for Scudder, and he decided to go it alone. He raised the necessary capital, and on July 15, 1960, ground was broken for the first mill of Garden State Paper Company, Inc., along the Passaic River in Garfield, New Jersey. Since the first roll of commercial newsprint

in 1961, Garden State Paper Company has remained in the forefront of industry developments.

Scudder, now a newspaper publisher, inventor, and manufacturer, took on yet another role, that of salesman. He went on the road, securing orders for 45,000 tons of newsprint and, as he recalls, "sold every ton of newsprint that came out of the Garfield mill, and those in California and Illinois, until 1968."

In 1967 the Garden State Paper Company opened its second mill, in Pomona at 2205 West Mount Vernon Avenue, which was followed by a third joint mill, in Alsip, Illinois, in 1968.

Media General, Inc., a diversified communications company headquartered in Richmond, Virginia, became the parent corporation of Garden State Paper in 1970, and in the years since has continuously expanded its paper-manufacturing and recycling operations nationwide.

Garden State Paper Company, Inc., today headed by president and chief executive officer Basil Snider, Jr., is a business that helps itself by helping the human environment, a fitting monument to a man who had the vision, perseverance, and courage to make "Scudder's Folly" one of America's great success stories.

All of the company's newsprint rolls are shipped by truck to customers primarily up and down the West Coast.

ITT POMONA ELECTRONICS

World War II had just ended, and the fledgling television industry was about to burst upon the nation's culture with the same impact as the invention of the automobile. Thousands—soon to be millions—of Americans were incredulously viewing the world on small electronic black-and-white screens in their living rooms.

Two brothers, Joe and Carl Musarra, recent arrivals in Pomona from New Brunswick, New Jersey, quickly saw the huge potential of this rapidly growing industry. What better way to climb aboard, they reasoned, than to get in on the after-market. Thus, Joe's Radio and TV Service was established in Pomona. Joe was the boss and repairman, and Carl, the salesman, who waited on customers and generally took care of the business end of things.

Business was slow: Most people's TV sets were too new to need repairs. Joe, who had become increasingly frustrated with the difficulty of checking TV cathode ray tubes, to-

Joe Musarra, who provided the engineering drive in the growth of ITT Pomona Electronics.

Carl Musarra, whose business acumen helped shape the future of the company.

gether with a friend, Dick Maggs, began to think of a practical and inexpensive solution. Creative and persistent men, they spent long hours experimenting while continuing with their day-to-day work. They knew that if they were to succeed in the development of a new tester for the tubes, they not only would

simplify the servicing of sets, but also quite possibly open the route to capitalize on what they had already identified as a relatively untapped and virtually limitless market of the future.

They developed a universal cathode ray tube test harness adapter, and in 1951 Pomona Electronics was officially born to produce it.

Joe, Carl, and Dick set up their new business in the back bedroom and garage of a home at 524 West Fifth Avenue in Pomona. They began to manufacture the test adapter while continuing the TV and radio repair business. The three entrepreneurs each put in $300 and, for the next three years, took no salaries. Maggs left the young firm, but the brothers continued, with Joe providing the engineering know-how and Carl the business acumen. Another brother, Frank, joined them shortly afterward, working in the molding department, and today still is employed by ITT Pomona Electronics.

The universal test adapter became a major success, and the Musarras entered the mainstream of the

A view of ITT Pomona Electronics' modern plant on East Ninth Street.

burgeoning television industry. Soon they moved to 1126 West Fifth Avenue, where they built a 2,500-square-foot building, later doubling the space.

In 1958 they purchased the land for the present 35,000-square-foot plant at 1500 East Ninth Street, and three years later moved to the new site. Later Joe and Carl Musarra donated their former building to a charitable organization in Pomona. Soon the firm added other models of the cathode ray test tube harness adapter, then test socket tube adapters, test socket savers, cable assemblies, and a wide variety of banana plugs and other products.

In December 1972 the thriving company became a part of ITT, changing its name to ITT Pomona Electronics.

Today ITT Pomona Electronics features more than 800 products (2,600, counting optional length and color variations) in its catalog. Although emphasis continues to be on the same type of item that brought initial success to the firm, capabilities now also include the design and manufacture of special electronics components to customer order.

ITT Pomona Electronics, which has always prided itself in keeping pace with advancing technology, serves a vast national and international market of industrial users that ranges from large government agencies to small TV service technicians. Its worldwide sales distribution includes customers in Canada, Mexico, Puerto Rico, Europe, Japan, Hong Kong, Taiwan, Singapore, Australia, New Zealand, and Israel. It is served by a nationwide network of sales representatives and distributors, and also by representatives throughout the world. It continues to create new products in keeping with its dedication to provide the most extensive line of electronic components available in its field, always with the

prime objective of producing the highest quality possible.

For more than 35 years ITT Pomona Electronics has been on the cutting edge of test technology, creating innovative devices for state-of-the-art electronic components. It has, for example, come up with solutions to the challenge of advanced ultraminiaturized electronic components such as Surface Mount Devices. Surface Mount Technology is considered to be the wave of the future and the Pomona firm is in the forefront

A few examples of the products provided by ITT Pomona Electronics to the electronics industry worldwide.

of its development, offering the broadest line of products designed to test Surface Mount Devices.

Joe and Carl Musarra, both now retired, can look with pride and satisfaction at ITT Pomona Electronics, whose enormous success must have exceeded even their wildest dreams back in the days of Joe's Radio and TV Service.

TELEDYNE CAST PRODUCTS

The creation of castings by pouring molten metal into a shaped cavity to form a replica is an ancient concept. But the casting industry has taken the process far beyond that basic idea and turned it into a complex, technical, and highly sophisticated technology.

Today, in a 231,000-square-foot building located on 18 acres at 4200 West Valley Boulevard in Pomona, Teledyne Cast Products, a division of Teledyne Inc. and its 460 employees, daily turn out castings in aluminum and magnesium for major airframe manufacturers, the defense industry, and consumer products producers.

Teledyne Cast Products, with an annual payroll of $12 million, today prides itself on its old artisan devotion to detail and quality while using modern production techniques. That approach has enabled the company to successfully cast such products as cascade thrust reversers and engine nacelle hinge fittings for Boeing aircraft, gas turbine engine gear boxes and compressor frames, missile fins and structural sections, and aircraft flaps. The Pomona foundry provides state-of-the-art casting design and development, tool and fix-

Teledyne Cast Products received the coveted Teledyne "Triple Crown Award" in 1986 for outstanding performance in marketing, production and financial management. Ross Anderson (center), president, is surrounded by employees who helped Teledyne Cast Products win the recognition.

ture fabrication, processing, a full range of testing to specification, machining, heat treating, protective coatings, full dimensional layout, and parts assembly.

Its major customers include the airframe and gas turbine engine manufacturers, missile producers, and other defense contractors. Among these are some of the best-known companies in the world: Boeing, General Dynamics, General Electric, Fiat, McDonnell Douglas Aircraft, Pratt & Whitney, Bell Helicopter, Rockwell International, Beech Aircraft, and Sundstrand.

The company poured the first gun mount casting for the U.S. Navy's Phalanx Close-In Weapon system in 1977. A one-piece aluminum casting weighing more than 1,200 pounds, it is one of the largest single thin-wall aluminum castings ever produced. To date, Teledyne Cast Products has made more than 650 of these gun mounts. In contrast,

it also makes castings weighing only a few ounces.

Before it was purchased by Teledyne Inc. in 1967, the foundry operated independently in Costa Mesa under the name of Precision Castings Company. John J. Hall purchased Precision Castings Company in 1955 from national Utility Company, beginning his ownership in the Southern California foundry industry.

In 1962 Hall acquired his second foundry, located on Violet Street in Los Angeles. This company employed a total of 80 workers and generated roughly a quarter-million dollars in sales to aerospace customers.

In October 1966 Teledyne Inc., then a young, emerging conglomerate, continued its acquisition program by purchasing both the Costa Mesa and Los Angeles plants from Hall and changing the name to Precision Castings of California. Hall continued to operate both plants under Teledyne's direction.

In 1967 Teledyne closed the Los Angeles plant when it went to a larger plant facility in Norwalk, California, buying the ARCEE foundry there. In 1970, when the Electronics Specialty foundry in Pomona was offered for sale by its parent organization, International Controls Corporation (ICC), Teledyne acquired this facility, closed down both the

Teledyne Cast Products plant at 4200 West Valley Boulevard, Pomona, is considered one of the outstanding sand casting foundries in the United States.

Ready for action is the proven Phalanx Close-In Weapon Support System on board a U.S. Navy frigate. Teledyne Cast Products is a key supplier of castings for the Phalanx gun mount shown here. The barbette base castings, train ring casting, and the large gun mount casting are visible in this photo.

Insert shows Paul Francis, Phalanx program manager, inspecting a gun mount casting at the Pomona plant prior to shipment. This casting weighs more than 1,200 pounds and is the largest high-technology casting in regular production in the free world.

struction machinery, and some one-half of all general aviation piston engines. A new Teledyne Continental liquid-cooled, high fuel efficiency engine was the power behind the *Voyager* aircraft on its 1986 record-breaking, nonstop, 216-hour, unrefueled 26,178-mile journey around the world.

This widely diversified corporation is also active in the consumer products arena. Teledyne companies manufacture such products as high-fidelity electronic components and speaker systems, oral hygiene appliances and shower heads, battery-operated hand lanterns, swimming pool and spa heaters, water heater and residential heating boilers, drafting room instruments and supplies, diazo whiteprint machines, and items for professional dental use.

Teledyne Cast Products in Pomona has good justification to call itself "a full-service foundry": It has total design, development, manufacturing, and testing capability under one roof. Teledyne Cast Products is a world leader that works closely with high-technology customers in the development and production of high-strength precision, light-metal castings.

Metal pouring crews in action at Teledyne Cast Products as they coordinate the pouring of a magnesium alloy casting for General Dynamics, Pomona Division.

Costa Mesa and Norwalk plants, and moved personnel and equipment to the current Pomona address. Just prior to this acquisition, William H. Dorricott had assumed the leadership role over the Costa Mesa and Norwalk plants, replacing Hall. He continued in this role until 1975, when Edgar W. Dansby was appointed president, and Dorricott assumed a more expansive role in the Teledyne organization as group executive of some eight companies, including Teledyne Cast Products. Ross K. Anderson became president in 1985, succeeding Dansby.

The parent company, headquartered in Los Angeles, is a high-technology, multiproduct corporation founded in 1960. It consists of more than 100 individual firms and has more than 44,000 employees. In addition to the Pomona casting foundry, Teledyne's various companies produce electronic components and systems, including advanced microelectronic hybrid devices, electromechanical and solid-state relays, analog and digital components and systems, high-speed general-purpose airborne computers, large-scale instrumentation systems, radar, mircowave, guidance and navigation equipment, and electronic warfare systems integration and management for a complete line of identification (IFF) equipment.

Other Teledyne companies also manufacture products for the aerospace industry, as well as subsonic and supersonic aircraft, airframes, heavy-duty turbocharged engines for military tanks and heavy con-

CASA COLINA CENTERS FOR REHABILITATION

On the same day that the Casa Colina Convalescent Home for Crippled Children in Pomona admitted its first patient—October 1, 1938—a letter arrived from President Franklin Delano Roosevelt expressing the hope that it would become the "Warm Springs of the West." His encouraging message was written to Frances Eleanor Smith, herself a victim of polio and the executive director of a rehabilitation center that was destined to exceed even FDR's expansive vision.

Frances Smith, who had been named American Mother of the Year in 1936, had been confined to a wheelchair for six years as a teenager. She had overcome her disability through her own rehabilitation techniques and wanted to dedicate her life to helping others.

A determined woman with a dream, she enlisted the help of Dr. Loyal Lincoln Wirt, Judge Edwin Rhodes, and other community leaders to found the center. With perfect timing, an old Spanish-style mansion in Chino called Casa Colina (House on the Little Hill) was offered to the group by Boys Republic, to which it had been bequeathed by Margaret Fowler "for some good purpose." Before the end of 1936 Casa Colina was incorporated. Gradually, with funds they were able to raise, beds, equipment, furniture, and other basic needs were purchased,

and repairs were begun on the old house.

"Mother Smith," as she became known, was chief fund raiser, surrogate mother to the children, sometime cook, and, above all, the inspiring force that kept the struggling institution going. It wasn't easy. Her treasury, usually meager, often dipped to as little as 15 cents. But she never panicked, confident that help would be found to support the 10-patient center, which in its first year provided $7,000 in services to about 30 patients with a paid staff

The corporate offices of Casa Colina Centers for Rehabilitation behind attractive landscaping on the Pomona campus.

Frances Eleanor "Mother" Smith smiles at four young patients being helped at the "House on the Little Hill" in the early days of her rehabilitation hospital. Photo circa 1940

of only three or four and several volunteer physicians.

Sometimes the support she received from local residents was in the form of home-canned products, fruit from their trees, and meat from their ranches, but enough was cash to help her pay the bills.

As the news of Casa Colina's work spread, more and more patients began to arrive. When medical advances reduced the number of children needing polio treatment, Casa Colina began addressing additional needs of children and adults disabled by birth defects, spinal cord injury, and other conditions.

By 1958 it had become clear that the old house was both inadequate and unsafe, and that a new center had to be found. Through a combination of state and federal funding and a major local fund-raising campaign, a new and ultramodern rehabilitation hospital was opened in Pomona on January 5, 1961.

Some believed that the new building was too large and the space

CASA COLINA

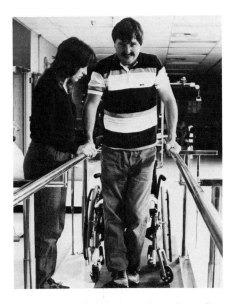

Hard work, but worth it. A therapist assists a patient in taking the first step toward leaving his wheelchair behind.

would never be fully utilized. But by 1971 it already was inadequate, and additions were being made. Within a decade even more space was needed, and new buildings were going up, nearby homes were being purchased, and the president had to move his office to a portable building.

During this period Casa Colina Hospital added comprehensive brain injury, spinal cord injury, and stroke rehabilitation programs. A unique Children's Services Center was opened as well as a Comprehensive Back Services Center that now serves as a national model for such programs. One of the nation's first day treatment programs opened in 1975, as Casa Colina recognized the need to develop less costly outpatient alternative programs for the future. New and innovative programs were developed in the areas of residential services, career development, physical fitness, and more.

Casa Colina has also become widely recognized for its work with sports programs for disabled children and adults, offering training in

tennis, bowling, water and snow skiing, camping, horseback riding, and even white-water rafting. In the 1970s Casa Colina introduced a wheelchair sports program and formed the Condors, a wheelchair basketball team that in 1979 won the national championship and continues to collect national and world championship trophies year after year, becoming a model for such activities.

In 1984, with the construction of a large, two-story administrative headquarters building and an adjacent outpatient treatment center on the Pomona campus, Casa Colina seemed complete. Today, however, there is a new need for further expansion.

When Dale E. Eazell became president and chief executive officer of Casa Colina in 1973, about $1.5 million worth of rehabilitation services was being provided annually. Most of Casa Colina's major growth has taken place since then, with the value of services escalating by approximately $5 million each year.

World renowned, this voluntary, nonprofit, fully accredited, commu-

nity-supported organization currently provides more than $40 million in rehabilitation and related services to nearly 8,000 disabled children and adults in more than 20 locations nationwide.

A Casa Colina subsidiary, Advanced Rehabilitation Management, provides consulting, joint venture, and management contract services on a national and international level. Through this subsidiary Casa Colina programs are being replicated in multiple locations, including sites in Alaska and Florida.

Casa Colina also operates the Casa Colina Foundation, which supports clinical and research activities, assists economically disadvantaged patients, and funds special programs for the disabled.

Casa Colina today is even more than was envisioned by Mother Smith and hoped for by FDR back in 1938. The Casa Colina of tomorrow will be even more than can be envisioned today.

The Casa Colina Condors, five-time National Wheelchair Basketball Champions, celebrate another victory.

POMONA VALLEY CHIROPRACTIC CENTER

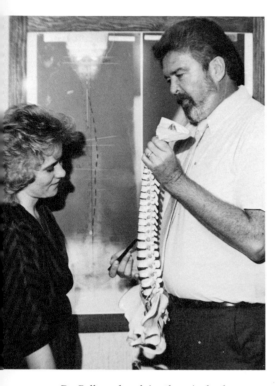

Dr. Bellwood explains the spinal column to a patient following examination.

There are few career choices more influenced by personal experience or role models than the decision to become a health care professional. An underlying desire to want to help people overcome the mental and physical agonies of pain, injury, and disease is frequently triggered by receiving or observing successful treatment of a health problem. So it was in the lives of Dr. L.W. Bellwood and Dr. George B. McClellan, partners in the Pomona Valley Chiropractic Center.

Bellwood, born in Lowell, Massachusetts, received an early, but unrecognized, hint when he was seven. Suffering severe neck pain, he was diagnosed as needing surgery, a solution his parents were not ready to accept. They took him to a chiropractor, who enabled him to avoid surgery.

Later, after the family had moved to Southern California, young Bellwood entered Mount San Antonio

College, not knowing what he wanted to do. His parents suggested he visit their chiropractor in Covina for advice. Soon after Bellwood applied to Palmer College of Chiropractic in Davenport, Iowa, graduating in 1965. Today he is married to a chiropractor.

McClellan, who was born in Detroit, Michigan, belonged to a family of physicians and surgeons. But he, too, was unsure of what he really wanted, until one day a chiropractic student treated him successfully for chronic headaches he had suffered all through high school.

For the moment, though, he stayed on the traditional path, first as a premed student at Creighton University in Omaha, Nebraska, for two years, and then at California State University, Los Angeles, for another two. Ready now to enter medical school, he chose instead to attend Los Angeles College of Chiropractic, graduating with the D.C. degree. In 1980 he set up his practice in Pomona.

Two years later he and Dr. Bellwood became partners, establishing the first of what today is a practice of three offices: in Pomona, Rancho

Cucamonga, and Covina. The two chiropractors are associated with a psychologist, an internist, an orthopedic surgeon, and a psychiatrist. They specialize in industrial and personal-injury cases and have nine employees.

Both Dr. Bellwood and Dr. McClellan are past presidents of the Citrus Chiropractic Society, and both were named Doctor of the Year in 1986-1987. They belong to the International Chiropractic Association, the American Chiropractic Association, the California Chiropractic Association, and Business Industrial Chiropractic Services, a nationwide organization of 5,000 chiropractors who work with companies specifically on back care. They are also members of the Pomona Chamber of Commerce, where Dr. McClellan is active on the Special Events Committee. For the past few years the partners have sponsored an annual poster contest on good posture at Harrison Elementary School, and they are involved in Pomona's Adopt-A-School program.

Dr. McClellan prepares a patient for X-ray.

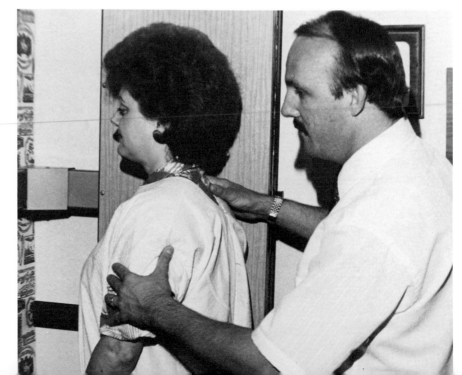

FIRST INTERSTATE BANK OF CALIFORNIA

In 1886 First National Bank of Pomona opened for business in a little one-story building that fit inconspicuously into the settlement's dusty scenery of unpaved roads, wooden sidewalks, and oil street lamps.

Its capital of $50,000 and deposits of $62,000 were equally modest, but the aspirations of its founders, under the leadership of Carlton Seaver, were not. They were as tall as those of Andrew Chaffey who started American Savings Bank in 1903. American Savings was the direct progenitor of United California Bank, which, in 1981, became First Interstate Bank of California, the 14th-largest bank in the United States. Unknown to either man, the futures of the two institutions would one day converge. First National Bank eventually would become the main Pomona branch of UCB.

Within a year of its organization First National Bank purchased its present site on the northeast corner of Second and Main streets for $7,000, and in 1889 built a three-story pressed brick building that was a landmark in the growing town.

The bank's resources by then had increased to more than $500,000, and business was booming, with settlers flocking to the Pomona Valley in growing numbers. By 1924 First National Bank had succeeded so well that it needed larger, more modern quarters and completed construction of the impressive five-story and basement structure it occupies today.

As the years went by the bank prospered, and in 1936 it had resources of $5 million and deposits of $4.4 million. Pomona's population had grown from 1,500 in 1886 to 22,000, and the future remained bright.

In time First National Bank's accomplishments attracted the attention of United California Bank, which had attained major stature as one of the top financial institutions in the state and in the country, and First National was acquired.

UCB's founder, Andrew Chaffey,

First Interstate Bank's main Pomona branch against a backdrop of the snow-capped San Gabriel Mountains.

began his banking enterprises in the early 1900s with three successful banks: First National Bank of Imperial, First National Bank of Ontario, and First National Bank of Upland. His father, George Chaffey, a land developer and irrigation genius, was playing a major role in opening up California and the West to settlers, and Andrew quickly seized the opportunity to provide financing for these pioneers. All three towns, now prosperous and growing, had been made possible by his father's irrigation projects 20 years earlier, and the Chaffey name was a highly regarded one.

Over the ensuing years Andrew continued to use his magic touch, creating successful banking institutions that ultimately resulted in First Interstate Bank of California, with its more than 900 branch offices throughout the western United States.

Today First Interstate's Pomona branch is a vigorous, living symbol of two pioneering enterprises that have had major impact on the history of a community.

Ornate tellers' windows adorned the lobby of First National Bank of Pomona in the mid-1920s.

COOPERVISION CILCO

There was a time, not too many years ago, when a person who had cataract surgery could see reasonably well again only by wearing thick glasses or contact lenses. Then, by pure chance, a whole new world became possible in 1948, when a medical student at St. Thomas Hospital in London, watching his first cataract operation, remarked, "It's a pity you can't replace the cataract with a clear lens."

Hearing the comment, surgeon Harold Ridley felt a memory click into place: During World War II he had worked on airmen who had suffered eye injuries when hit by fragments of Perspex from bullet-shattered airplane canopies. He remembered noting at the time that these foreign bodies caused little significant reaction unless a sharp edge touched a mobile or sensitive portion of the eye.

It was just a thought, but it led him to pursue the idea with Imperial Chemical Industries, manufacturer of polymethylmethacrylate, and Rayner of New Bond Street, London, which made ophthalmic lenses. Soon a prototype intraocular lens was developed and implanted in a female patient's eye, restoring the miracle of sight.

Dr. Ridley's innovative develop-

ment transcended the popular wisdom and current technology of the time, just as did Benjamin Franklin's invention of bifocals in 1785, freeing people from the need to rely on more than one pair of glasses.

Following several experimental procedures a residual refractive error was identified and corrected, resulting in what was to become the standard lens. Over the next few years, although modifications and improvements continued to be made in the lenses, complications continued to arise. Eventually the concept was perfected through research and clinical work, resulting in today's sophisticated intraocular lenses.

In 1975 California Intraocular Lens Corporation was formed in Baldwin Park, California, to manufacture intraocular lenses. Begun with only 10 employees, it did so well that in 1977 it opened another facility in Huntington, West Virginia, and changed the company name to CILCO, Inc.

The California division moved to its current facilities at 2865 Pomona Boulevard, Pomona, and in February 1986 CILCO was acquired by Cooper-

A portion of the modern headquarters of CooperVision CILCO in Pomona.

Vision, Inc., and renamed Cooper Vision CILCO, with corporate headquarters located in Bellevue, Washington. CooperVision CILCO is a division of The Cooper Companies, Inc. (TCCI), headquartered in Palo Alto, California, and traded on the New York Stock Exchange.

TCCI develops, manufactures, and markets automated medical diagnostic systems and reagents for the analysis of blood and other body fluids, a broad range of ophthalmic surgical products, plastic and reconstructive surgical products, and optometrically related products.

CooperVision CILCO concentrates on the manufacture of intraocular lenses. One of 16 companies in the United States that makes these lenses, CVC markets its products worldwide to physicians and medical facilities. In the United States, approximately 97 percent of the 1.3 million patients who have cataract operations each year receive lens implants.

The CooperVision CILCO division ranks number one in worldwide sales of intraocular lenses. Its future growth is seen as based on the increasingly large population of el-

CooperVision CILCO workers preparing and inspecting intraocular lens loops.

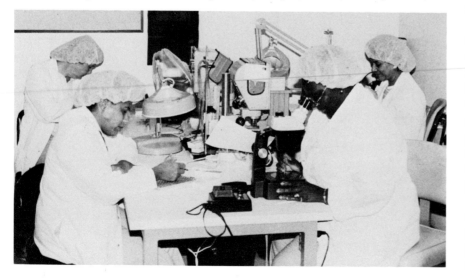

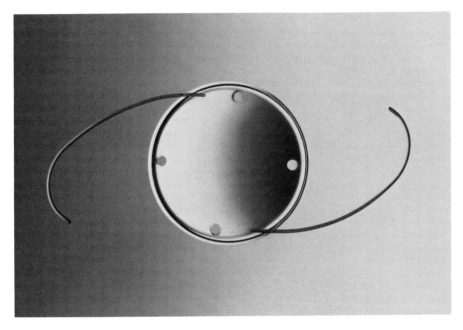

An intraocular lens with loops designed to secure it within the eye.

tion, and very little magnification. Once implanted in the eye, they are permanent and require no care.

Intraocular surgery is an option for most patients where the cataract is replaced with a clear plastic IOL implant. There are a number of different types of IOLs, with the particular kind a patient receives depending largely on the surgical procedure used. The surgery, which is exceptionally safe, is performed in a hospital, a surgery center, or a clinic and usually takes less than an hour. Many people are able to go home the same day. Although complete healing of the eye may take a couple of months, many patients notice significant improvement in vision almost immediately after surgery.

Since intraocular lenses were first introduced in 1949 they have been continuously improved and refined. CooperVision CILCO is in the forefront of that research and development to improve technology and, like Benjamin Franklin and Dr. Ridley, sees "no limits" to what can be accomplished in the future.

derly people and a desire by patients to avoid reduced vision caused by cataracts, a condition usually associated with aging.

CooperVision CILCO's Pomona facility today has a total of 100 of the 925 employees nationwide, which include 175 in West Virginia, 32 in North Carolina, and the remainder in Washington State. The company's primary products are single-piece, multipiece, and foldable intraocular lenses.

A cataract, from the Greek word meaning "to break down," is a clouding of the eye's lens that casts a blurred image onto the retina. Located behind the pupil, the lens is shaped like a magnifying glass and transmits and focuses light rays onto the retina at the back of the eye. From there the retina transmits impulses to the brain, which registers the visual images. A cataract disrupts that process by preventing light rays from doing their job.

While a cataract ordinarily is a natural consequence of the aging process, it is not life-threatening. However, if severe and untreated, it can result in total blindness. Cataract surgery is not only necessary but

also is the sole effective therapy.

Intraocular lenses (IOLs) are offered as an alternative to cataract spectacles or contact lenses and have great potential for improved vision after cataract surgery because they substitute most closely the eye's own lenses. IOLs offer full peripheral vision, good depth percep-

Technicians performing the crucial task of heat-welding loops to intraocular lenses.

TITECH INTERNATIONAL, INCORPORATED

Founder Edgar A. Williams beside a model of TiTech's foundry, which was completed in July 1969.

worked for the Loud Machine Works in Pomona, a supplier of major parts forged out ot titanium for use in the construction of the Lockheed SR-71. Titanium, the fourth-most-abundant metal on earth, is extraordinarily light in weight, strong, and corrosion resistant, but Williams also knew the problems: The metal was extremely difficult to work with, and the idea that parts would be as strong and could be more accurately shaped if cast instead of forged was considered at that time by many people to be a technological pipedream.

Williams persuaded W.H. Burgess, president of the Electronic Specialty Company, to share his conviction about the future role of titanium as a "miracle metal," especially in the aerospace industry, and a $300,000 study was initiated with M.I.T. Soon afterward, in 1969, the firm entered into a joint venture with the Carpenter Steel Company of Reading, Pennsylvania, forming a new venture called Titanium Technology Corporation (TiTech). The idea was that Carpenter would turn the California company's titanium ingots into mill products, billet, tubing, wire, etc. It was expected that they

When Edgar A. Williams stood on a hill overlooking 30 acres of undeveloped land on West Valley Boulevard in Pomona in the late 1960s, he knew he had found the ideal site for a new plant for his employer and, in the back of his mind, for a daring venture into an uncharted area with an exotic metal called titanium.

A professional engineer and a senior officer of the Electronic Specialty Company in Los Angeles, Williams had over the years recommended the building of seven manufacturing plants, all of them

successful. This new Pomona plant would produce aluminum and magnesium castings for the aerospace industry, but he was eyeing an unexplored market that he believed had a potential beyond anything the company had ever envisioned: the quality-grade casting of titanium for aerospace applications.

He had first become aware of titanium metal in 1956-1960 when he

TiTech's Pomona plant (1971) when it was a subsidiary of the Carpenter Steel Company.

would provide large amounts of titanium for the then-planned U.S. Supersonic Transport (SST), but the project was canceled in 1971, and Carpenter's interest in titanium quickly evaporated. Along the way a hostile corporate takeover also had occurred, resolved when Carpenter became sole owner.

Williams was disappointed but far from defeated. He and a group of fellow believers, A.L. Donlevy, J.R. Newman, and W.A. Rohrbach, bought out the Titanium Technology Corporation in 1972 from Carpenter and formed TiTech International, Incorporated. James R. Kostoff also joined the new firm as a board member, legal counselor, and founding stockholder.

"The future of TiTech continues to look promising," said Williams at the time, "and the restructuring will enable the company to pursue its growth program." TiTech's goal was to become a prime supplier of titanium castings for the aerospace, missile, jet engine, marine, and petrochemical industries. The new firm already had 56 employees and an annual payroll of more than one million dollars. Between 1972 and 1977 it came close to failure several times. But TiTech persisted in the face of its many setbacks, confident that its reputation for making a superior product would prevail in the expanding Space Age market.

Throughout those difficult early years the nucleus of engineers, craftsmen, technicians, and other professionals remained loyal to the company, sharing the commitment and dedication of its management to cast titanium, which *Smithsonian Magazine* recently called "The metal without which the Space Age would never have got off the ground," and "the most glamorous metal in the world today."

The applications for titanium are almost unlimited, ranging from sunglasses to submarine hulls to artificial joints, but in the 1970s, when TiTech was struggling to succeed, the firm undertook the task of learning to develop a process to cast the wing for the Sparrow Missile for the Raytheon Company Missile Systems Division. Eventually TiTech became the only titanium-casting company in the world to produce the part successfully, and since then has made thousands of cast-titanium wings for Raytheon and General Dynamics. It

Family of life-critical attachments and cast-titanium fittings, which connect the external fuel tanks to the space shuttle.

was the turning point for the young firm, and TiTech's future became assured. Soon new products were developed, early orders were repeated, and applications multiplied.

In 1979 TiTech was selected by the Martin Marietta Company to produce the highly stressed, major attachment fittings that hold the external fuel tank to the space shuttle. These life-critical parts have been used on every space shuttle since. TiTech's corporate offices and plant at 4000 West Valley Boulevard now occupy 13 acres of the original 30, which have been fully developed for industrial use. It has 180 employees, a payroll of $5 million, and annual sales in excess of $12 million. The founder's son, Richard D. Williams, Ph.D. in physics, who joined the firm in 1982 in the engineering department, became president and chief operations officer in 1986. In turn, his son and daughter have joined TiTech, making three generations of the family directly involved in its operation. Edgar A. Williams serves as chairman and chief executive officer.

TiTech's list of customers reads like a who's who of the world's leading manufacturers, and the company continues to grow and prosper as its reputation for excellence in producing complex titanium castings attracts customers with a constantly expanding range of applications.

Seated in his comfortable office, surrounded by memorabilia of his productive and interesting life, the founding chairman is only a stone's throw away from the hill he stood upon in the late 1960s—the busy plant outside his door now the substance of his dream.

Edgar Williams (center) inspects one of Ti-Tech's titanium ingot melting furnaces in 1969 with C.R. Harmon (left), executive vice-president of Electronic Specialty Company, and A.L. Donlevy, chief engineer / TiTech.

LAW OFFICES OF PARKER AND DALLY

John F. Parker, president.

For most people, the dream of setting up their own business remains just that—an unattainable idea full of risk and uncertainty, but attractive to speculate about.

Attorneys John F. Parker and Robert L. Dally had no such hesitations. Both were working for large firms in their primary specialty fields of the defense of workers' compensation cases for self-insured employers and insurance carriers. As they went their separate ways in Los Angeles, appearing before the Workers' Compensation Appeals Board, they would constantly meet each other.

Eventually Parker decided to go out on his own and set up a practice in San Bernardino, later moving his office to Pomona. At this point Dally was practicing in San Bernardino. Once again they found their paths crossing frequently and began to talk about the possibility of forming a partnership. Both agreed it would be a good idea to pool their resources and skills, and on September 1, 1964, they formed the law firm of Parker and Dally, retaining their offices in San Bernardino and Pomona. From

the outset a major client of the new firm was Kaiser Steel Corporation in Fontana.

The Pomona office was in the Buckeye Building at 435 West Fifth Street in microscopic quarters, and the San Bernardino office was at 255 North "D" Street. As the firm grew in Pomona, an additional attorney was added, but when he began describing his four-foot-square office as a closet, it became clear that it was time to move. The firm's next stop was the Barrister Building, but again the practice soon outgrew it and moved to the Home Savings Build-

Robert L. Dally, corporate secretary.

ing in 1971, where it stayed until 1985.

In March 1967 Ross C. Irwin joined the firm in Pomona, later to become one of the senior principals and one of the three officers when the firm incorporated on April 1, 1977, with Parker as president, Dally as corporate secretary, and Irwin as chief financial officer.

From the beginning the firm has been committed to providing quality legal representation for its clients

and has controlled its growth at a slow but steady pace to preserve that standard. Since 1964 it has added approximately one attorney each year, until today it has 20 attorneys—eight in San Bernardino and 12 in Pomona.

Continuing its growth pattern, the firm will be moving in the summer of 1988 into larger quarters. Over the years its clients have included the City of Pomona, Pomona Valley Community Hospital, Pomona Unified School District, General Dynamics Corporation, Garden State Paper Company, Aerojet Electro Systems Company, and private employers and insurance companies. Legal areas covered include, in addition to workers' compensation, wills and probate of estates, and civil litigation and subrogation.

It is 24 years since Parker and Dally decided to turn their acquaintanceship into a partnership. In that time they have participated in Pomona's first century of progress with the same kind of enterprising attitude that has marked the city from its beginnings.

Ross C. Irwin, chief financial officer.

PARKVIEW COUNSELING & PSYCHOLOGICAL CENTER

"Helping people help themselves" may seem cliche, but it truly describes the work and philosophy of Drs. Ben and Marge Allen. As co-founders of Parkview Counseling & Psychological Center, and previously, Pomona Valley Psychological Center, they strive to meet the needs of children, adolescents, and adults by helping them find their own satisfying solutions to life's most difficult problems. In this way, they not only promote growth and self-fulfillment, but also strengthen self-confidence and dignity.

The center's programs deal with most of life's problems: personal growth, marital conflicts, family problems, parenting, depression, anxiety, substance abuse, eating disorders, mid-life crisis, and others. A full range of psychological testing and evaluation is also available, including medi-legal evaluations in the areas of worker's compensation, personal injury, rape and molestation, child abuse, and custodial situations. All of the center's work encourages new ways of thinking that allow for individual differences in the process of becoming more confident, assertive, and competent.

Ben and Marge Allen come from a background of service to others. Marge received her bachelor of arts and master of arts degrees in psychology from California State University, Long Beach. Later she received a Ph.D. in theology. She is highly regarded as a caring person who is capable of genuine empathy with her clients and excels in helping others find solutions to problems relating to women's issues, interpersonal relationships, and family conflicts.

Ben is a native of Upland and is well known in the valley for his involvement with others, including 18 years of teaching in the Psychology Department at Mt. San Antonio College (he retired in 1987). After receiving his Ph.D. from the University of Southern California, he completed his clinical internship at the Tri-City Mental Health Center in Pomona. He quickly realized the need for a comprehensive counseling center in the valley and founded the Pomona Valley Psychological Center in 1977. It was well received by the community, and nine years later he and Marge created a new entity, Parkview Counseling & Psychological Center. Located at "The Cabin" at 1248 North White Avenue in Pomona, the center is a surprising oasis of peace right at the White Avenue offramp from the I-10. The uniqueness of The Cabin is that it offers a calm and relaxed atmosphere—far different from the typical medical look.

Drs. Ben and Marge Allen, co-founders of Parkview Counseling & Psychological Center on White Avenue.

Working with the Allens is their daughter, Vicki Bloom, who will soon complete a Ph.D. program in psychology, and a staff of psychologists and counselors. All are experienced in helping others find their own individual solutions to life's problems. Their philosophy of the practice of psychology stems from a belief in the independent nature and needs of each individual.

"The uniqueness of the center is in the recognition of the complexity of human nature," Ben explains. "No single theory can fully explain how lives can be transformed. There just are no simple, universal rules for easing the pain in one's life. The process of therapy involves exploring both the self and the range of alternative solutions. This is true of individuals, families, and groups.

"Yet, while the techniques and individual goals of therapy can differ greatly from one person to the next, the broad goal remains the same: achieving awareness and a sense of wholeness, enabling responsible choices to be made. Toward this goal, we encourage a multidisciplinary approach to treatment, in both outpatient and inpatient settings."

"The Cabin," an oasis of calm within sight of the I-10 freeway.

SIMPSON PAPER COMPANY

Pomona's oldest paper mill, now owned and operated by Simpson Paper Company, originated in 1926 under the name of the California Fruit Wrapping Mill.

The major citrus associations and many independent citrus producers had a need for tissue to wrap fruit. The tissue was treated with a mold-retarding oil, and each piece of fruit was wrapped before packing in the shipping crates.

Most of the citrus growers in the area had a private emblem for their wraps, and the printing was done at the mill. At one time five printing presses were needed to maintain production. There were several large packinghouses in the Pomona area, and they were the major employers in the Pomona Valley.

In the early 1930s the name of the mill was changed to Fernstrom Paper Mill, after the family from Sweden that provided the initial financing for the construction of the mill. In the early 1950s new technology in the chemical treatment of the liners used in the fruit packing crates was developed that made it unneces-

The California Fruit Wrapping Mill was surrounded by citrus groves in 1936. Originally owned by Fernstrom Paper Mills, it was purchased by Potlatch Forest, Inc., before being sold to the Simpson Paper Company in 1979.

John Fannon (right), president of the Simpson Paper Company, with Pomona Mayor G. Stanton Selby, cuts the fifth-anniversary cake at SPC's Pomona mill in 1984.

sary to wrap each piece of fruit. In a short period of time the packinghouses started shutting down, and the need for the treated tissue paper no longer existed.

Fernstrom sold the mill in 1952 to Potlatch Corporation. Potlatch, a forest products company, had a surplus of wood pulp from its Lewiston, Idaho, mill, and the Pomona mill provided a market for the surplus pulp. Potlatch changed the product line to include household papers such as napkins, toweling, placemats, garment hanger covers, and waxing base paper. In 1958 it added a fourth paper machine for the manufacture of business papers.

In 1978 Potlatch expanded its paper production capacity at its Lewiston mill through the addition of a new paper machine. The Pomona mill was no longer needed for its wood pulp, and it was sold to the present owner, Simpson Paper Company, in 1979.

Simpson Paper Company was founded in 1889, the year after Pomona's incorporation as a city. A young man named Sol Simpson traveled from Canada to the state of

Washington to work on the construction of a logging railroad. A man of extraordinary vision, he quickly realized that land was a fundamental resource and trees a renewable crop. Within a year he started the first business bearing his name, and in 1895 the Simpson Logging Company was incorporated. The family has retained ownership of the Simpson organization for these many years.

Today the firm owns more than a half-million acres of timberland, of which about 300,000 acres are in California and the remainder in the Pacific Northwest. It also holds rights to harvest from one million acres in the Whitecourt forest in Alberta, Canada.

Soon after the company was organized, Simpson management recognized that the wise use and replenishment of the timberland was important to the future of the firm. Such practices as planting superior seedlings, fertilization, and proper spacing for tree growth enabled Simpson to more than double nature's own rate of growth.

In a major strategic move, Simpson started buying California land in 1945 and quickly recognized that fiber manufacture and use was essential to the long-term growth of the company. In 1951 it entered the pulp and paper business through the purchase of the Everett Pulp and Paper Company in the state of Washington. Everett was an old mill built in 1891 by the Rockefeller interests. This action was followed by the purchase of the Lee Paper Company in Vicksburg, Michigan, in 1959. Also in 1959 a modern specialty mill was built in Ripon, California. The mill in Everett, Washington, was shut down in 1971, and some of the equipment was moved to the company's Anderson, California, mill. With other acquisitions, Simpson now owns four pulp mills and nine paper mills throughout the United States.

Simpson Paper Company president John Fannon conducts a tour of the Pomona mill for local civic leaders in 1984.

The company employs approximately 4,200 workers in the pulp and paper part of its business and nearly 7,700 in all. In addition to the logging, lumber and pulp, and paper operations, Simpson is also a major producer of plastic water pipe and related plastic products.

Simpson is a major supplier of high-quality printing and writing papers in the western market. It is also a leader in the industry for text and cover papers. At the Pomona mill, 120,000 net tons of paper is produced per year with a work force of 480 employees and an annual payroll of $16 million. In the tradition of Simpson, the mill is referred to as the San Gabriel Mill because of the San Gabriel Mountains to the north of Pomona. The firm's pulp and paper mill located in Anderson, California, is called the Shasta Mill because of the closeness to Mt. Shasta, and its mill in Pasadena, Texas, is called the San

Jacinto Mill after the famous battleground in that area.

Simpson has invested $35 million in modernization since purchasing the Pomona plant in 1979. It has also installed a cogeneration plant that produces 32 megawatts of electric power per hour. Simpson Paper Company, with corporate offices in San Francisco, is a subsidiary of Simpson Investment Company of Seattle, Washington.

As the company has grown its management has retained a strong desire to support the communities where the firm does business and it is pleased to be a part of Pomona in the celebration of its centennial year. The Simpson Paper Company is currently making plans for its own centennial celebration in 1989.

CALIFORNIA STATE POLYTECHNIC UNIVERSITY, POMONA

W.K. Kellogg's California home shortly after its completion in 1926. Now surrounded by trees and part of the Cal Poly Pomona campus, it is passed by thousands of motorists each day on Kellogg Hill.

The evolution of Cal Poly Pomona, celebrating its 50th anniversary in 1988-1989, began in 1938. One hundred fifty acres of land in San Dimas, the former site of the Voorhis School for Boys, was donated to the State of California by the Charles B. Voorhis family. Shortly thereafter it became the campus for Cal Poly Pomona, founded as a men's agricultural college and operated as a Southern California branch of Cal Poly San Luis Obispo.

Slightly more than a decade before, in 1926, breakfast cereal magnate W.K. Kellogg began construction of a California family home located on 813 acres of land on the western edge of Pomona. The family mansion, manor house, and several ranch buildings were all of Spanish-style architecture and designed by architect Myron Hunt of Los Angeles.

It was there that Kellogg decided to carry out a lifelong dream to develop the purebred Arabian horse. He purchased the first horses from Poland, Egypt, Arabia, and England, and built large stables around a training ring and courtyard. The Kellogg Arabian horses soon became the third-largest collection of Arabian horses in America.

The Kellogg Ranch quickly became one of the beauty spots and attractions of Southern California. After constructing a grandstand for several hundred spectators, Kellogg opened the ranch to the public in 1926 for Sunday Arabian horse shows. Many Hollywood film stars, including Rudolph Valentino and Douglas Fairbanks, rode Kellogg Arabian horses in such movies as *Son of the Sheik, Lives of a Bengal Lancer,* and *The Garden of Allah.*

From 1932 to 1949 the ranch was sequentially the property of the University of California, the U.S. Army, and the U.S. Department of Agriculture.

In 1949 the Kellogg Ranch was deeded to the State of California for use in the expansion of the education program of Cal Poly. The deed agreement specifically stipulated retention of the Arabian horse breeding and training program, and continuing the Sunday horse shows.

In 1956, 550 male students and 30 faculty members teaching six courses of study moved three miles from the original Voorhis site to the Kellogg campus. Women were enrolled for the first time in 1961 when 322 coeds entered the academic program. In 1966, 28 years after its founding, Cal Poly Pomona separated from the San Luis Obispo campus to become California's 16th state college.

Officially granted full university status in 1972, Cal Poly Pomona today occupies a 1,400-acre campus that is one of the largest of the 19 campuses of The California State University (CSU) system. Approximately 2,000 persons are employed as members of the faculty and staff.

More than 19,000 students, 40 percent of them women, are enrolled in one of 44 departments in six academic colleges: Agriculture, Arts, Business Administration, Engineering, Environmental Design, and Science, and in the Center for Hospi-

Audiences of 2,000 to 3,000 were common at the famous Kellogg Sunday Arabian horse shows beginning in 1926 and still continuing today. Note four airplanes tied down on the private landing strip in the upper left.

tality Management and Teacher Preparation Center. Cal Poly Pomona currently offers 56 undergraduate and 15 graduate degrees, and 7 credential programs.

The university has been served by three presidents: Julian A. McPhee, president of Cal Poly San Luis Obispo as well as Cal Poly Pomona (1938-1966); Robert C. Kramer (1966-1977); and Hugh O. La Bounty, who joined Cal Poly Pomona in 1953 and was acting president for one year before being appointed in March 1978 to the position he still holds.

Cal Poly Pomona is accredited as a degree-granting institution by the Western Association of Schools and Colleges. Its curricula have been awarded professional accreditation by the Accreditation Board of Engineering and Technology, American Chemical Society, American Planning Society, American Society of Landscape Architects, California State Commission for Teacher Preparation and Licensing, Committee on Postsecondary Accreditation, Council on Social Work Education, and National Architectural Accreditation Board. In addition, 17 special programs and 30 special university centers or institutes have been created to better serve the student body.

The College of Engineering has

the largest undergraduate engineering enrollment of any university west of the Rocky Mountains. In the last available report Cal Poly Pomona ranked second in California and 16th nationally among 284 college and university engineering programs in numbers of minority graduates. In numbers of students, the College of Business Administration is the largest of the six colleges, with an enrollment of approximately 4,800, some 25 percent of the total student body.

Both undergraduate and graduate degree programs in the three academic disciplines of the College of Environmental Design—architecture, landscape architecture, and urban and regional planning—are recognized by professional accrediting agencies.

More than 700 students are enrolled in the Center for Hospitality

A portion of the university's 1,400-acre campus today, one of the largest of the 19 campuses of The California State University system.

The Cal Poly Pomona campus shortly after operations moved to the Kellogg property in 1956 from the Voorhis campus in San Dimas.

Management, which offers the oldest and largest four-year degree program in hotel and restaurant management in California. The James A. Collins Center for Hospitality Management, a multipurpose facility dedicated to professional hospitality management education for both traditional students and industry practitioners, is being built to house the program.

The Kellogg family home and other buildings have been painstakingly preserved and today are in daily use. The original stables, built around a courtyard and Spanish fountain, have been refurbished for use as offices for student groups. Several new structures have been added, with red tile roofs and Spanish architecture that faithfully restate the heritage of the Kellogg Ranch.

The tradition of Arabian horse shows started by Kellogg in 1926 also continues; 1988 marks the 63rd year that the popular programs have been presented for the public. The shows are held on the first Sunday afternoon of each month, October through June. The handling and training of the horses is done exclusively by Cal Poly students and staff, and these purebred Arabians from the oldest Arabian horse breeding program in the United States continue to delight the public as they perform tricks, stunts, and demonstrations during the popular program.

TODD MEMORIAL CHAPEL

When Walter B. Todd and his wife, Emily, lived in Norwalk, Ohio, in 1895, a good home could be built for $900 and annual taxes on it were $12—a good deal, even by the standards of those days. But attractive as it was, the Todds were not ready to put their roots in Huron County and decided to head west.

They ended up in Pomona, which was a thriving and fast-growing village whose friendliness and potential opportunities impressed them enough to settle there. Soon, in April 1907, Walter founded Todd Memorial Chapel in a small two-story building at 570 North Garey Avenue, establishing not only what was to become a Pomona institution but also one of the valley's leading families. Today, 81 years and four generations of Todds later, Todd Memorial Chapel continues at the same location, but is housed now in one of the city's most beautifully landscaped and attractively designed buildings.

The wisdom of the Todds' decision to leave Ohio and settle in Pomona became increasingly clear early on. It wasn't long before their ornately carved horse-drawn hearses were a familiar part of the

Todd Memorial Chapel as it is today, on the same Garey Avenue site where it was founded 81 years ago.

community as the young firm assumed a position of leadership in the mortuary field throughout California. Over the years Todd Memorial Chapel prospered and grew, expanding its facilities and adding personnel.

Walter Todd died in 1933, leaving active management of the firm to his son, John, who continued his father's dedication to broaden and increase the scope of the services offered to the community. Following John's sudden death in 1947, his widow, Grace, and their sons, Richard K. and John W. (Jack), along with their partner, the late Lawrence C. Smith, carried on the business. Grace Todd died 31 years later.

The management of the firm today, in addition to Richard and Jack Todd, consists of fourth-generation John R. and a partner, Keith E. Pewe. Together they have increased the choices offered by Todd Memorial Chapel to encompass all types of services, ranging from traditional funerals to direct cremation. They also provide various types of prearrangement plans, including pre-need trusts and insurance.

Since its founding in 1907 Todd Memorial Chapel has taken pride in

its commitment to maintain price structures that enable even those with limited means to turn to the company. It is a legacy left by Walter Todd, who always viewed the business as a hometown, family-oriented institution and an intrinsic part of the community, stressing neighborly, helpful, and compassionate services to meet the needs of all faiths.

Todd Memorial Chapel also extends this feeling of obligation to be a good citizen to include membership in the Pomona Chamber of Commerce and, through its management, participation in the Rotary Club, Kiwanis, Lions, and Jaycees. Richard Todd, who is a licensed pilot, serves on the board of Pomona Valley Community Hospital and actively supports the YMCA. Jack Todd is on the boards of the Los Angeles County Fair Association and the Pomona Civic Center Corporation. John Todd serves on the board of the Volunteer Center of Greater Pomona Valley, Inc., and Keith Pewe is on the board of Inland Hospice Association.

Drivers in top hats and a hearse with a matched pair of white horses wait outside the first home of Todd Memorial Chapel in 1907.

INDUSTRIAL WIRE PRODUCTS CORPORATION
INDUSTRIAL ALLOYS, INC.

In Pomona only since 1981, Industrial Alloys, Inc., on West Valley Boulevard, can trace its origins back to the 1930s, when two young men were helping to shape the early independent wire-drawing industry in California.

Although Earl R. Potter and Kenneth H. Davis had enjoyed a personal and business relationship for many years, it was not until the 1940s that they combined their talents and business acumen into a partnership. Potter had founded Industrial Wire Products Corporation in 1944 in San Francisco with R.B. Flynn, but the partnership had not worked out. Displaying the same kind of perseverance and courage that marked his approach to all his business ventures, Potter refused to toss in the towel and turned to his friend Davis. An astute businessman, Davis agreed to purchase Flynn's interest in the young company.

While Potter took an active role in running the firm, which primarily functioned as a jobber selling wire cloth and weaving wire mesh, Davis concentrated on his own company, K.H. Davis, which manufactured drawn wire. Industrial Wire Products prospered, and in 1948 the partners opened a plant in Los Angeles to take advantage of the growth there. It was a good move, one that would set the stage for fu-

ture successes. A year later they decided that the company could serve the San Francisco area from Los Angeles and closed the original facility. During the next 10 years the firm would move three times in order to accommodate the expanding line of products being manufactured and the rapid growth of sales, finally settling on East 23rd Street in Los Angeles.

In 1956 Davis passed away, his death resulting in the reorganization of Industrial Wire. During the 1960s the newly reorganized company continued to expand its products and processes, and Potter's son, Charles, joined the firm.

In 1965 Ed Westendarp asked Industrial Wire to draw stainless-steel welding wire, and a decision was made that the product was different enough to warrant the setting up of a new, separate company, Industrial Alloys, Inc., in South El Monte. Westendarp became the president but within a year relinquished the post to Charles Potter. During the next 15 years Industrial Alloys became a major supplier of stainless-steel wire, growing so fast it had to move four times, ultimately locating in Pomona. Two years earlier Earl Potter resigned as president of Industrial

This monument identifies the corporate headquarters of Industrial Alloys, Inc., on West Valley Boulevard, Pomona.

Wire Products Corporation, to be succeeded by Marshall R. Bull as president and chief executive officer. Potter then joined his son at Industrial Alloys.

Shortly after the move to Pomona a severe economic recession hit the steel industry, but while Industrial Wire managed to escape the worst of it, Industrial Alloys was not so fortunate. Charles Potter believed the company's best chance of survival was to sell it to Fundamental Management, Inc., a subsidiary of Industrial Wire, which is a holding company to facilitate acquisitions. Subsequently, Industrial Alloys rebounded and today is a major domestic manufacturer of stainless-steel wire, selling to and serving the entire country from Pomona.

All administrative, accounting, and sales offices for the four companies, which also include Our Computer, Inc., a data-processing firm formed in 1980, were combined and centralized at the Pomona location in 1983. Together the companies employ more than 200 people and occupy in excess of 200,000 square feet of manufacturing space.

Material exits from bright annealing furnaces into coils for wire belts.

LOS ANGELES COUNTY FAIR ASSOCIATION

The Los Angeles County Fair is envisioned by these six men in 1922. A.E. Andrews, a building contractor (right), discusses plans with (left to right): Joseph M. Paige, Charles B. Curran, L.E. Sheets, Fred E. Whyte, and George Cob.

The 49,461 people who visited the first Los Angeles County Fair, held on a 43-acre beet and barley field in Pomona in 1922, probably had no idea that they were participating in a historic event: the creation of what was to become the largest county fair in North America.

A year earlier Clinton B. "Jack" Afflerbaugh, a druggist, and several other local businessmen had held a highly successful merchants' industrial exposition along the Southern Pacific Railroad siding in downtown Pomona. Why not establish a county fair and capitalize on that success, and on the area's agricultural influence and location in the heart of Southern California's citrus belt? It would be an ideal and effective way to promote agricultural, horticultural, and animal husbandry interests of the region. Wasting no time, they incorporated the Los Angeles County Fair Association in Pomona in 1922.

Led by Afflerbaugh, the organizers and first directors included L.E. Sheets, music store proprietor; Charles B. Curran, lumberyard owner; Fred Reynolds, car dealer; Fred E. Whyte, who ran a laundry and linen supply service; and W.A. Kennedy, banker.

They then purchased a field from the Vejar estate, that of a local pioneering family tracing its ownership of a Mexican government land grant back to Don Ricardo Vejar in 1837. Tents, temporary buildings, and a half-mile racetrack were put in place, and the Los Angeles County Fair began its five-day run, from October 17 to October 22, 1922. Delighted crowds strolled among the displays of oranges and other produce, admired the show horses and cattle, and watched harness racing, chariot races, and an airplane wing-walking demonstration. It was all very exciting and very successful, well worth the $63,000 it cost the promoters.

Shortly afterward, in 1923, a $75,000 bond issue was approved by the city for the purchase of an additional 62 acres—deeded to the county 10 years later and then leased back to the fair—for the first major development of the association. Construction of permanent buildings and a grandstand then began.

When the association realized in 1924 that it needed full-time leadership, Afflerbaugh was appointed the first paid manager, a post he held until 1960, when he was succeeded by Philip B. Sheperd. Sheperd was the son of B. Chaffey Sheperd, one of the early members of the board of directors.

By 1928 the fair was attracting the attention of newspapers worldwide, including the press of Sweden, France, England, Mexico, and South America. That same year 145,062 people attended the fair.

The first Los Angeles County Fair, held under canvas on a beet and barley field in October 1922.

The Pomona racetrack became the first in Southern California to offer horse racing with pari-mutuel wagering in 1933, the year that betting on the sport became legal in the state, and attendance soared to 334,759 for the fair's 10 days.

Disaster struck in 1937, when the livestock barns were destroyed by fire. But recovery was speedy, and the fair soon became firmly reestablished. The grounds now had a day care center and six exhibition buildings, including what was then the largest exhibit building in the world. Measuring 800 feet by 135 feet, it had a stage at one end and seating for 16,000 people. That massive structure stood until the early 1940s, when it too was destroyed by fire. It was rebuilt following World War II.

During the war years fair activity came to a halt, and from 1942 to 1947 the grounds became home for troops of the United States Fourth Army. When the fair reopened in 1948, all of the lost momentum was regained, and attendance topped the one million mark for the first time with 1,254,503 visitors. It was to prove to be a long-term trend: Attendance has exceeded one million every year but 1963, ranking the fair first in attendance among all county fairs.

A magnificent Court of the Redwoods was introduced in 1961, and a mile-long monorail circling the exhibit area was installed the following year. In 1965 the popular Golden Empire Mine made its debut. Also dur-

ing this period of major development the grandstand was expanded to accommodate a clubhouse and permanent seating for 10,000 spectators, and indoor exhibit space was increased to 370,000 square feet.

In 1978 Philip B. Sheperd decided to retire. He was followed in that position by Ralph M. Hinds, who in 1978 was appointed general manager of the LACFA.

Under the leadership of Hinds and his board of directors, chaired by James R. Kostoff, a Pomona attorney, the LACFA moved into a third era of major development, with special attention focused on the non-fairtime use of its 487 acres and facilities. Then, in 1983, a decision was made to call the overall operation Fairplex, the Los Angeles County Fair and Ex-

A rich gathering of glass objects and bottled preserves in an exhibit lighted by chandeliers at the 1932 Los Angeles County Fair.

hibition Complex, to more accurately reflect the increasing array of events and activities at the fairgrounds.

This new chapter in Fairplex history has seen a $4-million renovation of 105,000 square feet of building area for year-round exhibition use, a move that proved so successful that it was decided to expand other facilities to meet the needs of non-fairtime exhibitors and other potential users. More than one million people attend year-round trade and consumer shows, agricultural fairs, rodeos, horse shows and sales, dog shows, championship drag races, swap meets, and conferences. Also, there has been the expansion of the original half-mile racetrack to five-eighths of a mile and the upgrading of the grandstand and clubhouse, with new lighting added for night harness racing, which was introduced in 1986, and of livestock and equestrian areas.

Ambitious and imaginative plans are under way today to keep pace with Fairplex growth and the changing demands being made upon it, continuing the positive vision and innovative ideas that have marked it since the beginning.

Aerial view of Los Angeles County Fair in full swing, with the recently renovated racetrack in the center.

THE SADDLER CHIROPRACTIC CLINIC

Dr. Leslie Saddler, Jr., founder of The Saddler Chiropractic Clinic at 1238 North Park Avenue in Pomona.

Getting banged about as a high school football player in Baltimore, Maryland, J. Leslie Saddler, Jr., often ended up getting treated for his aches and pains by a chiropractor. While he appreciated the help at the time, many years and a World War would intervene before he realized the true significance of those early encounters with that particular health care practitioner.

Saddler graduated from Baltimore City College before joining the United States Marine Corps, in which he served for six years. During World War II he was stationed aboard the USS *Wichita* and later in the Southwest Pacific in amphibious tanks. While in the service, Saddler learned a love for the sea that was never to desert him and which today is his principal form of recreation.

Once the war ended Saddler's subliminal desire to do something in the health care field came to the surface, traced back, he now thinks, to those early high school years and his experience with the chiropractor. He entered Palmer Chiropractic College in Davenport, Iowa. Three years later he graduated and decided to pursue additional studies at four-year Logan Chiropractic College in St. Louis,

Missouri, from which he graduated. Believing that he should have even more training before hanging out his shingle, he then took a postgraduate course in physical therapy at Los Angeles College of Chiropractic.

On May 1, 1954, Dr. Saddler established his practice on Park Avenue in Pomona, calling it The Saddler Chiropractic Clinic. Thirty-four years later he continues his busy practice at the same location. Dr. Saddler has a staff of three Chiropractic Assistants: his wife, Alyce, Patricia Larkins, and Mara Thim, all of whom have worked with him for the past 18 years, a longevity of service that particularly pleases him.

Dr. Saddler is a member of the International Chiropractic Association, the California Chiropractic Association, the Pomona Chamber of Commerce, and the First Marine Division Association.

A man who enjoys the outdoors, Dr. Saddler has decorated his clinic with pictures and carvings of fish, boats, and other reminders of his passion for the ocean. He is a member of the United States Power Squadron, the California Sports Fishing Association, and, as a part of his shore-based sports activities, of the American Bowling Congress.

Active members of The Pomona First Baptist Church, the Saddlers have been married for 46 years and have two daughters, Susan and Kathy, and three grandchildren.

It is possible, Dr. Saddler likes to think, that some of the young patients he treats may eventually be inspired in the same way he was to become chiropractors.

From left: Patricia Larkins, Alyce Saddler, and Mara Thim, each of whom has worked at The Saddler Chiropractic Clinic for 18 years.

BRASWELL ENTERPRISES, INC.

Perceiving a need to provide housing and care for retired Christian workers and other elderly persons living on fixed incomes, the Reverend A.L. Braswell, Sr., a retired Church of the Nazarene minister, assisted by his son, C. Allen "Chuck" Braswell, a public schoolteacher, decided to do something about it by forming a nonprofit corporation in Pomona in the early 1960s. Although their dream was not realized, it did lead to a partnership with L.H. Lambert, a builder/owner of convalescent hospitals.

By early 1964 Towne Avenue Convalescent Hospital had opened its doors in South Pomona. Nora Lambert, wife of L.H. Lambert, served as the original administrator, followed later by James W. Braswell, who in turn was succeeded by Glen A. Crume in 1966. Under Crume's direction and with the support of his wife, Jeanne, daughter of A.L. Braswell, Sr., convalescent and rehabilitative services have been provided to hundreds of patients since that time. Also in 1966 the family group, under the leadership of C. Allen Braswell, opened a facility in Yucaipa and formed Olive Medical Development, Inc., for the purpose of building a long-term psychiatric hospital in Pomona.

Subsequently they built Olive Vista just west of Towne Avenue Convalescent Hospital, opening it in 1968 to serve 80 geriatric psychiatric patients and 40 patients requiring medical treatment of alcoholism. During this period C. Allen Braswell was instrumental in the development of the Pomona Valley Council on Aging, which evolved into an agency serving seniors now funded by Los Angeles County and the City of Pomona. He also served on the board of directors of the Pomona Valley Mental Health Association, which founded and governed the Tri-City Mental Health Authority. In 1970 the firm led in the organization of the Pomona Open Door, a youth crisis resource center that is still providing services to troubled young people.

A 43-bed skilled nursing facility was acquired in northwest Pomona in 1973, which became Laurel Park. Along with Olive Vista it was to form the nucleus for special treatment programs for chronically mentally disordered young adults. Treatment of this clientele became the major thrust of the company. Facilities were later acquired in San Bernardino and Riverside counties to expand the scope of psychiatric services.

In 1976, as some of the family members began to move in different

The Reverend and Mrs. A.L. Braswell.

directions, Olive Medical Development, Inc., was reorganized, and the name was changed to Braswell Enterprises, Inc. The Reverend Braswell, A.L. Braswell, Jr., C. Allen Braswell, and Glen and Jeanne Crume have continued to provide convalescent and psychiatric services in the Pomona Valley. In 1976 B.R.I.D.G.E.S., a nonprofit corporation, was formed by Braswell Enterprises, Inc., for the purpose of providing child care and rehabilitation services. A.L. Braswell, Jr., Ph.D., became the executive director and continues in that role today.

The Braswell family has been active in civic, service, and church activities. C. Allen Braswell served on the Pomona School Board from 1975 to 1979 and is a past president of Kiwanis. Glen Crume has filled many roles in the Pomona Chamber of Commerce and is a past president of Rotary. Cheryl Braswell-Jumonville has also been active in the chamber.

Braswell Enterprises, Inc., purchased a historic building at the corner of Monterey and Gibbs streets in 1982. For more than 40 years the building had housed a medical clinic and offices, and at one time had been a church. It has been restored to its art-deco heritage and is now the corporate headquarters.

Towne Avenue Convalescent Hospital in Pomona is the flagship facility of Braswell Enterprises and was opened in 1964.

PO-TEL FEDERAL CREDIT UNION

Po-Tel Federal Credit Union moved into these new quarters on East Second Street in 1986.

When the Pomona Valley Associated Telephone Federal Credit Union was chartered on April 2, 1937, it had eight members who each purchased one $5 share. The idea was a simple one, based on a concept born in Germany in the mid-1800s: A group of people who share a common bond, such as their place of work, would pool their savings and make low-cost loans to each other, a practical form of self-help and a way to promote thrift.

The foundation of the credit union movement in North America was established at approximately the turn of the century by a French-Canadian journalist, Alphonse Desjardins, operating out of his home in Levis, Quebec. It immediately became a huge success, and soon he was organizing other credit unions throughout Canada. Desjardins then turned his sights toward the United States, but believed that credit unions would only be successful there if the initiative and leadership were to come from Americans.

Coincidentally, and unknown to him, a wealthy Boston department store owner, Edward A Filene, who had a lifelong desire to better the lot of the working people, was about to "discover" credit unions on his own, not from Canada or Germany, but during a trip to India in 1907. Filene's guide in Bengal was associated with an organization called the Agricultural Cooperative Banks, which was composed of villagers who used their savings to make small loans to each other at reasonable interest rates. This self-help principle appealed to Filene, and he began to dream about importing the idea to America.

Upon his return to the United States, he began a campaign to establish credit unions nationwide, using his own money to finance the project. Unlike Desjardins' experience in Canada, Filene found it heavy going in the United States. By 1920 fewer than 200 credit unions were operating under workable laws in only four states. At that point Filene met a lawyer from Lynn, Massachusetts, who was to become the organizational architect he so badly needed.

Roy F. Bergengren took up the task with relish, and within 15 months had created the Massachusetts Credit Union League, the first such organization in the nation. He was so successful that by 1925, 15 states had enacted legislation en-

Three of the original charter members: Clara M. Johnson (left), Mary Lydon (representing her late husband, William H. Lydon), and Harold Frater.

abling 419 credit unions to serve 108,000 members. By 1933 there were 32 state credit union laws on the books and 2,400 credit unions serving 420,000 members. When President Franklin Delano Roosevelt signed into law the Federal Credit Union Act in 1934, the way was cleared for the organization of credit unions under federal charters anywhere in the country, and the long-awaited Credit Union National Association (CUNA) became a reality.

Today, 54 years later, the credit union idea continues to spread throughout the free world. They now operate in more than 50 countries and in many places have dramatically improved living conditions.

Later, recognizing a need to protect the survivors of members who died with loans still outstanding, the national organization formed its own insurance company, CUNA Mutual Insurance Society, to ensure that "The Debt Shall Die with the Debtor."

It was against this backdrop (culled from a history of CUNA Mutual Insurance Society selected for printing by the Newcomen Society in North America) that the Pomona Valley Associated Telephone Employees Credit Union came into being.

On April 28, 1937, the eight charter signers—J.A. Essex, Wilbur R. Parrish, Clara M. Johnson, G.E. Christianson, Harold Frater, William H. Lydon, Louis D. Yard, and Alick R. Daines—held their first meeting at the Women's Community Center office at Third Street and Garey Avenue in Pomona. Their first item of business was the election of a board of directors, composed of Essex, Parrish, Johnson, Yard, Frater, Christianson, and Grant A. Smith. The fledgling credit union had 27 members, $150.50 in the bank, and

$143.75 in shares. Membership was limited to "employees of the Associated Telephone Company, Ltd., in Pomona, Ontario, Upland, Covina, and San Bernardino; members of their immediate families; and any organization of such families." Before the year ended there were 115 members and total assets had reached $1,993, a modest but encouraging beginning that presaged a successful future.

In 1953 the charter was amended to change the name to Po-Tel Federal Credit Union. The following year saw a credit union organized in San Bernardino, the Covina members moved under the Whittier Group, and Po-Tel's membership restricted to Pomona, Ontario, and Upland. That arrangement continued until 1971, when the San Bernardino Gentel Co. Employees Federal Credit Union merged with Po-Tel, with a branch office in San Bernardino. For many years Po-Tel only offered savings accounts and loans. Recently, it has become more of a full-service financial institution.

By 1984 the credit union had 7,000 members and assets of nearly $17 million, and it was time to seek larger and more modern quarters. Following a feasibility study, a search for a suitable building was begun and, toward the end of the year, it was discovered that a local bank was planning to sell its facility in downtown Pomona. One year later, after remodeling was completed, Po-Tel moved into its attractive new quarters at 401 East Second Street on the Pomona Mall.

Today, with 7,800 members and $28 million in assets, Po-Tel Federal Credit Union has come a long way since its founding in Pomona more than a half-century ago, when credit unions still were struggling for acceptance and recognition. It has contributed importantly to the history of a proud city made possible by pioneers with the ability to create reality out of visions.

A view of Po-Tel's modern and tastefully decorated new offices.

RICHTER
"THE PACKAGING PEOPLE"

One man, staring glumly into the ashes of a disastrous fire that had destroyed his manufacturing plant, saw his dreams gone up in smoke. Another looked at the blackened debris and saw an opportunity. It was more than a difference in viewpoint, for the fire had taken the second man's job. But what had caught his eye was a key piece of machinery that somehow had survived the flames, damaged but intact. Later it would have a significant role in his life.

The second man's name was Al Richter, the son of immigrants who had come to the United States from Germany in 1921 and settled in Sierra Madre. Following service in the Coast Guard during the Korean Conflict, Richter went to work for a major paper manufacturer who assigned him Pomona as his first sales territory. It was to give him a familiarity with an area and its people that in time would prove to be important to his future.

Eventually Richter joined a firm in San Dimas, which was the first manufacturer of crepe cellulose wadding material. Located in an old former orange-packing shed, the entrepreneurial venture appeared to have a lot of promise, and he was excited by the potential he perceived. Then, in January 1966, a fire burned the building to the ground and suddenly everything was over.

The owner decided to retire, and Richter found himself at a crossroads: He could either look for a new job elsewhere or try to pick up the remnants of the business by taking care of its customers. He opted for the latter, and arranged through a competitor to continue to serve the customers. Soon, however, he recognized the weakness of the competitor and decided he could do better by starting his own business.

Shortly before the fire Richter had become acquainted with Mike Abbinante and was impressed by his ability. He promptly invited Abbinante to join him in his new venture. In February 1966 the two men formed Richter Manufacturing Corp., and soon after built their first machine to make paper cushioning material and installed it in a warehouse in Los Angeles.

Richter recalls that the young organization had a total of five employees in those days, all of whom had worked for the old firestruck firm, and they drove from San Dimas to Los Angeles each day in one car. "Mike and I used to worry that if the car were ever to break down, we'd be out of business," Richter laughs.

Things went well for them during the next two years, and when they learned that someone they had previously worked with had purchased the tissue-making machine that had survived the 1966 fire, they were interested. Located in an old building in Pomona owned by the Votaw brothers (Pomona Box Company), the machine seemed to be beyond the ability of its owners to repair, and they had run out of money. Richter and Abbinante thought they could get it operating and purchased it. They proved to be right, and it was not long before they had it producing tissue in the Votaws' building, which they had also bought.

In 1968 Richter moved a part of its Los Angeles plant to its newly ac-

President Al Richter (seated) and vice-president Mike Abbinante—two entrepreneurs who turned a dream into a successful reality.

Special polyethylene foam packaging materials made by Richter are used to wrap and protect vulnerable products that range from fruit to TV sets.

quired building, marking the beginning of the company's operation in Pomona and its ultimate departure from Los Angeles. Later on Richter purchased buildings and land next to the railroad tracks from Loud Machine, a manufacturer of landing gears for aircraft that had gone out of business. As the firm continued to grow, Richter demolished all but one of the old structures and erected new facilities in their place, eventually expanding onto the old Pomona High School athletic field south of Holt Avenue, which Richter had purchased from Occidental Petroleum.

Today Richter, which also has a plant in Kent, Washington, and a warehouse in Hayward, California, has a 225,000-square-foot plant at 159 North San Antonio Avenue in Pomona and employs 105 people. It has increased its line far beyond just paper packaging to include plastic products that serve a wide variety of needs.

Richter's many innovative packaging materials include Cushion-Pak, a cellulose wadding used to safely ship furniture, hand-blown glass, machinery, gauges and instruments, aircraft parts, cosmetics, hard-

ware, trophies, and china and glassware, and to absorb excess juices in meat and poultry trays; Astro-Foam, a polyethylene foam for the surface protection of furniture and appliances, circuit boards, polished marble, and mirrors, the air-freighting of flowers, the cushioning

of cameras and other delicate instruments, and the wrapping and insulation of fragile candles; Astro-Packaging, air bubble cushioning in sheet or bag form to protect delicate instruments and other items during shipping; and Astro-Foam, a low-density polyethylene made up of millions of air cells that is used to protect such vulnerable products as art objects, cosmetics, radios, and, in a special antistatic form, electronic components.

In addition to manufacturing and distributing literally hundreds of packaging items, Richter Manufacturing Corp. offers its customers the ability to meet special requirements and to work with them in determining the most effective product to meet specific needs.

The firm, today still headed by its founders, Al Richter as president and Mike Abbinante as vice-president, is an enterprise that almost literally has risen from the ashes of that old orange-packing shed 20 years ago to become a major part of the city's history and economy.

Richter Manufacturing Corp.'s Cushion-Pak, a cellulose wadding, is shown among some of the many products it protects.

CARE ENTERPRISES, INC.

A philosophy of independence begins with good rehabilitation programs.

Entrepreneurs seldom come in identical pairs, but twin brothers Lee R. and Dee R. Bangerter did, sharing the same dreams and aspirations that resulted in Care Enterprises, one of the nation's largest nursing home companies.

In 1965 the brothers turned 21 and became eligible to receive $22,000 from the War Orphan Fund as a result of their father's death in World War II. At the same time Opal Winn, the twins' mother, had inherited a nursing home from her husband. Opal ran the nursing center with assistance from Lee during his school holidays. Using their familiarity with operations of the nursing home, the brothers decided to go into the business for themselves.

Using the War Orphan money, the Bangerters and their half-brother, Ted Nelson, bought their first facility, Garfield Convalescent Hospital of Huntington Beach. The successful operation of Garfield

spurred them on to look for other acquisitions.

In the early 1970s nursing home values dropped dramatically, due to a 10-percent MediCal reimbursement reduction in the state of California. More than 100 facilities went into bankruptcy.

Most people would have given up, but not the Bangerters. They saw the difficulties as an opportunity to grow. By 1973 the Bangerters owned 500 beds, and continued to acquire other facilities. In 1978 the newly incorporated Care Enterprises was operating 11 nursing homes with a total of 1,300 beds in California and Utah.

Care purchased its first multifacility company in 1979, 800-bed Med Inc. in Northern California. In 1983 it took another giant step with the purchase of Casa Blanca Convalescent Homes, consisting of 34 facilities.

Riding the crest of their remarkable success, the Bangerters bought North American Health Care, bringing their holdings to 10,000 beds in California and Utah. During the first half of 1985 Care added Americare Corp., operator of 26 facilities with 2,770 beds in Ohio, West Virginia, New Mexico, Arizona, and Florida. The company, now headquartered in Tustin, stretched across the country, owning and operating 110 nursing homes in seven states, 10 home health agencies, and 12 pharmacies.

Care's earlier purchases of Casa Blanca and North American brought the firm to the Pomona area in 1983, where today it operates three skilled-nursing facilities: CareWest-Pomona Vista, CareWest-Palomares, and CareWest-Claremont—for a total of 406 beds. All of the nursing centers specialize in 24-hour care, activity programs, and physical, occupational, and speech therapies.

In only 23 years the Bangerters have built an enormously successful company based on a humanistic philosophy—to return as many of their nursing home residents as possible back to their families and communities, and to encourage those who are permanent residents to lead as active and independent lives as they can.

Lee Bangerter, chief executive officer of Care Enterprises.

INLAND ENVELOPE COMPANY

When Gregor Kloenne arrived in America in 1955 from Germany, he was like many young immigrants: restless with ambition and eager for a new life, but uncertain about how to begin.

After several months in Newark, Ohio, he headed for New York City and later Detroit, with high hopes that soon crumbled. Then he met two young men who, like himself, were searching for their own unrealized dreams. It was a simple proposition: They had some money and he had a car, so why not pool their resources and drive to Los Angeles.

Once on the West Coast, Kloenne decided to use his training as a tailor in Germany and eventually opened a small tailoring and dry cleaning shop in Los Angeles. Married by then, he knew that what he was doing was not going to give him the success he still felt possible. It was then that things began to come together. He and his brother-in-law, who had worked for a firm in Germany that built envelope-making machines, decided to start their own envelope company. But not in highly competitive Los Angeles; they found an old grain warehouse in Pomona in 1967 and started the Inland Envelope Company with a few second-hand machines.

Working in shifts around the clock, Kloenne and his brother-in-law managed to produce some 60,000 envelopes per day, all one size. But a national paper shortage oc-

curred in 1973, and the future of the small company looked bleak. Kloenne decided to stick it out; he bought Inland Paper from his partner in early 1974. First he obtained a bank loan to keep the plant operating, then called personally on each of his customers and offered them a reduction of one dollar per 1,000 envelopes. It brought in orders and enabled the firm to survive.

Soon paper became plentiful again, and Inland Envelope began to prosper. Kloenne added new equip-

The original Inland Envelope Company plant still in use as part of expanded manufacturing facilities.

Greg Kloenne (right), founder of Inland Envelope, and son Bernard look at plans for a new plant under construction in January 1988.

ment and bought a lot next to his plant on North Gordon Street and put up another building.

In 1985 his son, Bernard, a CPA who had worked for an international stockbrokerage firm in Japan and New York, joined Inland Envelope and today is president, with his father, who has retired to Hawaii, as chairman of the board and consultant.

In the spring of 1988 Inland Envelope opened a new state-of-the-art plant across the street which, together with the original facility, brings the firm's total operating area to 65,000 square feet. It employs 45 people who produce close to 75 million envelopes per month for annual sales of approximately $7 million.

The journey from Germany to Pomona so many years ago has been long and hard, and the reward has been well-earned by a man who held on to his perception of America as a country of unparalleled opportunity.

POMONA FIRST FEDERAL SAVINGS AND LOAN ASSOCIATION

Pomona First Federal Savings and Loan Association is the oldest and largest savings and loan headquartered in eastern Los Angeles County. The beginning of Pomona First Federal dates back to 1892, when Pomona boasted a population of 3,900. A group of forward-looking citizens met on Christmas Eve and incorporated the Mutual Building and Loan Association of Pomona, one of the first of its kind in California. Included among the officers and directors of the new association were many of the pioneer citizens of the 1890s: J.D.H. Browne, president; Oliver Youngs, vice-president; Charles C. Zilles, treasurer; C.I. Lorbeer, secretary; W.A. Bell, attorney; and John L. Means, Stoddard Jess, J.T. Brady, G.W. Hill, J.D.H. Browne, and Walter A Lewis, directors.

The organization was completed and the books of the association kept in the residence of C.I. Lorbeer at 629 West Holt Avenue. The first formal quarters of the association consisted of desk space in the offices of Walter A. Lewis in the American National Bank building, which was located on the southwest corner of Second and Thomas streets on what is now the Pomona Mall. Mutual paid a monthly rent of four dollars for the space.

The founders immediately established the policies of thrift and the promotion of home ownership that have enabled PFF to grow steadily

from that date. Then, as now, carefully planned home loans formed the basis for most of the lending at PFF. The first loan was made for $500 on a home that still stands at 859 East Second Street. In those days loans were due in full at maturity, and monthly payment home loans were an innovation not available before the early 1890s.

Formed to facilitate thrift and home ownership, Pomona First Federal was the first savings and loan to be established in the Pomona Valley, just 61 years after the first such association in America was founded in 1831 in Frankford, Pennsylvania. At the end of its first year in business Mutual Building and Loan Association's assets totaled $8,900.

In 1906 Mutual Building purchased property at 260 South Thomas Street, where it occupied a single small room until 1924, when the building was remodeled and larger quarters were provided. In 1917 the company had changed from a mutual to a capital stock association, and in March 1931 its name became Pomona Mutual Building and Loan Association.

By 1933 the United States government had recognized the importance of savings and loan associations and

Pomona First Federal's first formal home occupied desk space in the American National Bank Building, on the southwest corner of Second and Thomas. The monthly rent was four dollars.

created, by an Act of Congress, the system of federal savings and loan associations. Conversion to Pomona First Federal Savings and Loan Association was completed on July 27, 1938, under that federal charter.

The head office was opened in February 1956 at Garey Avenue and Center Street with facilities for administrative officers. Formal administrative offices were opened at 350 South Garey Avenue in November 1985, after renovation of the former Wells Fargo Bank building. This two-story office building is in the 44-block area of the historic Pomona Landmark Quarter.

Today, in addition to PFF's administrative offices, the head office, Indian Hill office, and Loan Support Center in Pomona, 18 other branch offices are scattered throughout the Southland. These include two in Upland; those in Chino, San Dimas, Glendora, La Verne, Rancho Cucamonga, Alta Loma, Montclair, Claremont, Rowland Heights, Yucca Valley, Twenty-nine Palms, Palm Desert, Palm Springs, and Cathedral

The interior of Pomona First Federal's quarters, complete with heater in a converted fireplace, in the early 1900s.

City; and two offices in Orange County, in Yorba Linda, and Tustin. A Consumer Loan Office, which processes home improvement, mobile home, auto, boat, R.V., and equity loans, is located in Upland.

The administrative offices of Pomona First Federal at 350 South Garey Avenue were opened in November 1985 following renovation of the former Wells Fargo Bank building.

PFF also maintains PFF Insurance Service, a wholly owned subsidiary at 393 West Foothill Boulevard, in the Claremont Office. The firm is licensed with the State of California Insurance Commission and is a multicompany independent insurance agency. It carries property and casualty insurance (both personal and commercial lines), plus life, health, and disability insurance.

At the end of June 1987 the association had total assets in excess of $1.165 billion, with a net worth of $61.7 million, and approximately 137,244 savings and checking accounts and 18,225 loans. Even more notable than the growth indicated by the figures is the continued increase of community confidence in Pomona First Federal as a sound financial institution.

Through the years the association also has gained a reputation for its contributions to the community. This tradition of civic service received great impetus during the tenure of well-known community

Ellson F. Smith (left) became chairman of the board of directors of Pomona First Federal in January 1988, and W.F. Montgomery (center) served as board chairman from 1978 to 1988. Robert D. Nichols (right) has been president/chief executive officer since August 1986 and also is a member of the board.

leader Paul D. Walker, who served as PFF president and board chairman from 1954 to 1976. The tradition for both corporate financial assistance and volunteer support by PFF officers and employees to community causes has continued through the

leadership of presidents William F. Montgomery, Fred W. Mack, Jr., Thomas W. Jones, and current president Robert D. Nichols.

The hope expressed by longtime PFF president Fred B. Palmer in 1942 is echoed today by the board of directors, officers, and staff of PFF: "Like the early-day pioneers who envisioned a greater Pomona and planned to help in its building, so we, the PFF officers and directors of this age, look ahead to a far greater growth and development of our beloved Pomona. We venture the hope that Pomona—and indeed the entire Southwest—grows during the next half-century as it has since 1892 . . . We of PFF want to grow with it and contribute our share to a future that will bring happiness and prosperity to our children and their children's children."

Pomona First Federal's head office at Garey Avenue and Center Street was first occupied in 1956.

LANTERMAN DEVELOPMENTAL CENTER

The main entrance to Lanterman Developmental Center on Diamond Bar Boulevard.

Half hidden in a grove of pepper trees and surrounded by acres of green lawns, more than 70 white-walled buildings roofed with red Spanish tile looked to unsuspecting motorists on Brea Canyon Road like an exclusive country club. In fact, what they were seeing was Pacific State Hospital, as it was known in 1960, a facility for 3,000 developmentally disabled people.

Surrounded by bare Southern California hills, brown most of the year, without a house visible anywhere, the hospital's only public entrance was on Pomona Boulevard. Only after entering the 494-acre grounds, passing between the homes of employees, and driving under the Union Pacific railroad tracks, would a visitor become aware of the isolation of the facility. Many Pomona residents still called it Spadra Home, even though that had never been its name, and the little stagecoach settlement of Spadra had long since vanished.

Lacking adequate staff and money, the hospital was remarkably self-sufficient, even to the point of having its own source of water and making its own bread and bakery products. Also, because there was no public transportation available, many employees lived in dormitories on the grounds. There was a good source of labor in the mildly retarded patients, who were able to perform unskilled work under supervision.

There was no lack of patients. A history of overcrowding and long waiting lists went back to the hospital's beginnings in the 1920s. But the 1960s were to see the start of dramatic progress in the understanding of, and care for, the mentally retarded. Scientific breakthroughs and an increased political awareness encouraged by President John F. Kennedy, whose own family included a retarded member, resulted in a flood of new legislation at both the state and federal levels.

In California, State Legislator Frank D. Lanterman introduced bills that, along with other legislation, resulted in a drop in the population of the state's hospitals for the mentally retarded. By 1973 the number of patients had fallen to 5,030 from a staggering 42,894 in 1952. One bill in particular, the Lanterman Mental Retardation Services Act of 1969, created 19 regional centers that were responsible for diagnosis and counseling, with the hospital as one of many resources, usually the last resort for those clients who had multiple and severe problems. Other improvements, such as home care and day-patient programs, were initiated, further reducing the need for full hospitalization for many patients.

In 1964 Pacific State Hospital's grounds were annexed to the City of Pomona, transferring responsibility for police and fire protection from

This modern building houses the George Tarjan Research Center on Lanterman's spacious grounds.

the facility.

As the 1960s advanced, new strides continued to be made and the word "rehabilitation" began to attain increasing importance, combining recreation, physical therapy, occupational therapy, education, and volunteer and fund-raising activities. Toward the end of the decade the results of all the efforts for improvement in the care of the mentally retarded began to become evident throughout the hospital. The sense of isolation that had previously been a feature of life in the facility became a thing of the past, with more contacts being made with the community and bus service right onto the grounds inaugurated for the first time. A research building was constructed, but no additional facilities were contemplated; the focus was turned toward improving the environment of the patients. Air-conditioning was installed, the large wards were partitioned to provide increased privacy, and colorful carpets and fresh paint were added.

The hospital's George Tarjan Research Center for Mental Retardation, opened in 1964, was the first such facility to be constructed on the grounds of a hospital for the mentally retarded. By the end of the decade more than 100 research projects were in progress, supported by funding at the local, state, and federal lev-

els. It had become the largest program of its kind in the state, if not the nation.

Throughout the 1970s Pacific continued to enhance its national reputation as one of the country's leading institutions for the care and study of the mentally retarded. It was also to survive an attempt by the Department of Mental Hygiene to phase out all state hospitals over a 10-year period, with regional centers and community centers assuming services for the patients. In 1973 Governor Ronald Reagan shelved the plans to close down the hospitals, and in 1974 the legislature passed a bill to prevent any such attempts in the future without prior approval by that body.

On January 1, 1979, Pacific State Hospital was renamed Lanterman Developmental Center to honor the state assemblyman who had contributed so much to the welfare of the mentally ill and the developmentally disabled, and also to more accurately reflect the center's function.

In 1983 Lanterman regained its status as a fully accredited institution, a designation it had lost in 1973 because it was unable to meet qualifying standards that were designed

The attractive Spanish-style administration building.

Lanterman's rustic camp and equestrian center.

for smaller facilities for mildly or moderately retarded patients. The following year Rowena J. Taylor, a registered nurse, became the first woman to be appointed executive director of the facility, a position she retains today.

Driving onto the grounds in 1988, crossing the bridge over the freeway, a visitor sees a scene vastly different from that in 1960. The pepper trees still remain, however, many have been replaced by evergreen ash trees; homes have been built all over the hills of the Diamond Bar Ranch; and there is a new sense of openness and bustling activity. With a resident population of 1,100, and predictions that it will remain at that level, Lanterman Developmental Center today remains one of the best resources for the mentally retarded in the United States.

K.K.W. TRUCKING, INC. & FURNITURE TRANSPORTATION SYSTEMS

Art Shelton, like a lot of other people, had a personal dream that one day he would start his own company. But unlike most others, he actually did something about it—and with stunning results.

In 1954, after working for the Van Vorst Mattress Company for 13 years and Furniture Fast Freight for 10 years, he decided to go into the furniture transportation business for himself. He called his new company Blue Truck Line and did so well that he soon joined forces with Lad's Furniture Freight to enable him to ex-

Dennis Firestone, chief executive officer.

pand into Northern California. The partnership gave Shelton the opportunity to introduce a number of innovative systems and ideas that he had been thinking about for a long time, such as Drom-type tractors and square-nose trailers.

But though it was a fulfilling and rewarding time of Shelton's life, it was not destined to last. By 1961 he and his partners had made a mutual decision to go their separate ways, with Shelton selling his equity in Lad's-Shelton Trucking.

He said he was retiring, an announcement greeted with skepti-

cism by those who knew him best. And they were right. The following year Shelton founded another company, K.K.W. Trucking, Inc., named from the first initials of two friends and a nephew who became his board of directors: Carl Krager, Thomas Kane, and Donald Walls.

The tiny firm began to serve the Northern California area with two tractors and two trailers to transport blanket-wrapped furniture. Soon business grew to the point that two more trailers were added, and a search was begun for a larger warehouse.

It was then that fate took a hand in a way that was to have a far-reaching effect on the future of K.K.W. Shelton moved his company into a 12,000-square-foot warehouse on Maie Avenue in Los Angeles, already partially occupied by another firm, Nikkola Express, which also specialized in transporting blanket-wrapped new furniture. He had known Nikkola's owners, Fred Krocker and G.T. "Sarge" Sarjeant, for many years and believed not only that it would be a good place to settle down but also that the two firms could cover the entire state between them.

At that point two other men entered the scene, E. Carl Sarjeant, son of "Sarge," and Dennis Firestone, although the two had not yet met. They would have such a major impact on K.K.W. and Nikkola Express that eventually they would own the business.

As a teenager Carl had learned about the trucking business from his father, but he had chosen a career in architecture instead. Then, in 1964, Nikkola Express needed some help, so Carl took a "little" time off to assist Sarge. With an all-family office staff and an almost all-family dock crew, they received furniture and made deliveries during the day and loaded trailers at night. All the hard work

The late Art Shelton, founder of K.K.W. Trucking, Inc.

paid off, and by 1967 Nikkola was thriving.

Meanwhile, Dennis Firestone was building his own enterprise. After attending San Jose State for a year, he dropped out to start his own business. In 1963 he bought a used stake-bed truck and began making deliveries to various retail outlets in

E. Carl Sarjeant, president.

the San Fernando Valley under the name of Safeway Delivery. Operating out of North Hollywood, Firestone developed a respectable list of customers, but his biggest break came when he landed Ortho Mattress as an account. As Ortho grew, so did Safeway.

In March 1967 Firestone was ready to expand. He formed a new company, Stonelin Industries, with Miller Collins, and upon the signing of a contract with McMahan's, Santa Monica Division, they were off and running.

It was in that same year that Firestone chanced to meet Shelton. Firestone purchased K.K.W., and the circle was closing. Soon he and Carl were discussing merger, and before the year was out an agreement was made that would make K.K.W. the second-largest blanket-wrapped new-furniture transporter on the West Coast.

Eventually a new idea was born: If shipments could be consolidated and then transferred by the truck-

Fulfillment of a dream. Dennis Firestone (left) and Carl Sarjeant flank Pomona Mayor G. Stanton Selby in a symbolic ground-breaking ceremony in 1985 for the company's new 100,000-square-foot terminal and corporate headquarters on Pomona Boulevard.

load, it could mean business for K.K.W. Consequently, a consolidation was begun under the name Furniture Transportation Systems (F.T.S.), headed by Sarge, and it wasn't long before it too began to

grow. By 1980 K.K.W. was the largest blanket-wrapped furniture carrier on the West Coast and was operating from two terminals, in Gardena and Milpitas, while F.T.S. was in a new 50,000-square-foot warehouse in the City of Industry.

They were riding high. Then the aftershock of a recession hit, and thousands of furniture stores and many furniture factories went under. It was time to reorganize and make changes. So in 1982 all "less-than-truckload" business was dropped and "truckload" customers were sought. It was the right move, and soon K.K.W. and F.T.S. were back on the fast track again.

Business continued to thrive, and in 1985 ground was broken in Pomona on a 9.3-acre site for a 100,000-square-foot terminal and corporate headquarters at 3100 Pomona Boulevard. In October of that year the state-of-the-art facility began operations, and a new era began for K.K.W./F.T.S.

Founder Art Shelton is gone now, and G.T. Sarjeant is retired, but the two young men, E. Carl Sarjeant and Dennis Firestone, whose paths crossed so luckily in 1967, continue to nurture their dream.

Aerial view of K.K.W. Trucking's terminal and corporate headquarters.

ELIAS CONSTRUCTION, INCORPORATED

Elias Construction prepares a local street for rebuilding.

An early memory of Cedric C. Elias, founder and president of Elias Construction, Incorporated, is of Welsh farmers working the local area beet fields with horse-drawn ploughs. "There was a lot of open land in those days," he says, and for the future, a lot of room for the vast growth that was to begin in Southern California and Pomona at the end of World War II.

Following graduation from high school in Pomona, Elias recognized the opportunities awaiting someone who could provide professional, economical construction services to this exploding market. In 1945 he started a small construction company that became his foundation for establishing himself as a reputable contractor who did quality work. By 1958 he was beginning to attract larger contracts, one of which was with Pomona to grade and landscape areas in the northern part of the city for $7,000, a substantial sum in those days.

Business was flourishing, and Elias continued as an independent contractor doing work for cities and private customers under the name Cedric C. Elias Paving Company.

In the meantime two of his sons, John A. and Edward M., were successfully building their own construc-

tion businesses, and Elias got the idea to invite them to join him and consolidate all of the companies into a family-owned organization. The new corporation, Elias Construction, Incorporated, was formed in 1981, and two other sons, Anthony, secretary, and Gregory, director, also came into the firm at that time. Since then the company has done work for Cal Poly Pomona, Claremont, Rancho Cucamonga, Union Pacific Railroad, and many other major cities, universities, businesses, and government agencies, primarily in the central Los Angeles and San Bernardino counties.

Edward Elias, now vice-president of Elias Construction, entered the construction business as a pick and shovel laborer for his father's Cedric C. Elias Paving Company, gradually learning new skills and receiving increasing responsibilities. In 1976 he decided to capitalize on his experience by starting a company called Edward M. Elias Construction.

His younger brother, John Elias, who today is treasurer of Elias Construction, followed a similar path. His career in construction began with part-time summer work as a laborer. Following graduation from high school he joined the U.S. Army, serving for two years in Korea as a demolitions expert. Between 1969 and 1976 he worked for various construction companies, including Cedric C. Elias Paving Company, giving him extensive experience that encouraged him to found his own business, Elias and Son Construction, in 1977.

The merging of all three companies into Elias Construction, Incorporated, is a heartwarming Pomona story, uniting members of a family for the common good in much the same way as did many of the early pioneers who settled the area a century ago.

A freak snowstorm in 1960 did not stop Cedric C. Elias from fulfilling a contract.

JAMES S. BAKER, POMONA CENTENNIAL COMMITTEE CHAIRMAN (January 6, 1888-1988)

Like the early pioneers of a century ago, Jim Baker came to Pomona from someplace else. And also like many of them who became leaders, he was destined to contribute to the city's growth and progress in significant ways.

Baker, a native of Los Angeles, graduated from the University of Southern California with a bachelor's degree in political science in 1939. Two years later he received his J.D. degree, passed the state bar, and spent a year practicing law in the office of the Los Angeles County Counsel before entering the U.S. Army.

Upon separation from the service in 1946, Baker moved to Pomona and was employed for eight years in a family-owned citrus business. In 1954, convinced that Pomona was a warm, wholesome community, Baker, with the support of his wife Ganell, son Stephen, and daughter Martha, returned to the practice of law, and in 1956 was admitted to practice before the United States Supreme Court.

In 1955 Baker believed he should become involved in Pomona's growth and direction, and he campaigned and won a seat on the city council, served the four-year term, and was reelected in 1959. Two years later he resigned his council seat and entered the race for mayor, which he won in the primaries. These eight years became known as the Golden Years of Pomona, when many important civic accomplishments were commenced and achieved.

Supported by a large number of enthusiastic citizens, Mayor Baker and city administrator Fred Sharp successfully convinced the County of Los Angeles to locate its Superior Court Building in the city's Civic Center, and Pomona became the hub of the Eastern District judicial system.

It was a major coup. But there were to be others. In 1962 the Pomona Mall was completed, the first

Jim Baker still actively practices law in his office in Pomona.

Mayor James S. Baker in 1963.

open-air pedestrian shopping center in the western United States.

Led by Baker, Sharp, and the council, the citizens voted bonds to construct sorely needed underpasses at White, Garey, and Towne avenues. Baker's term in office left yet other important legacies to Pomona, including one of the first university-related industrial parks in Southern California, and dedications of the city library and police and fire headquarters in 1964.

Baker married Celeste Sanders Baer in 1969, joining her family of five children, Barbara Epstein of Alta Loma, Bob and Jim Baer of Palo Alto, and John and David Baer of Menlo Park.

Perhaps owing to his seniority in the community, Baker was chosen as chairman of the Pomona Centennial Committee, ably assisted by Rosanne Bader, John Fowlkes, Terry Stemple, and Stanley Adams.

As chairman of the Centennial Committee, he has seen his role as helping "to encourage the citizens of Pomona to enjoy the opportunity to look proudly back . . . and proudly forward."

MONEY RADIO, KMNY 1600 AM

Popular Southern California broadcaster Buz Schwartz was taking telephone calls after a 1986 program, when a Pomona listener requested advice on how to change the format of a business. "What kind of business?" asked Schwartz. "A radio station," replied Dean Wickstrom, owner of Pomona's Magic Oldies Radio, 16 K-WOW AM.

The rest is radio history; Schwartz happened to be in the market for a station. His show, "Investors Club of the Air," had drawn such a faithful following that Schwartz and partner Vera Gold knew a larger destiny beckoned: the creation of radio's first format "all about money, all the time."

Originally K-WOW was not for sale, but discussions ensued for various airtime arrangements. Eventually, however, Wickstrom saw that "Money Radio" was a viable concept whose time had come, and he agreed to sell. After individual partnerships closed in January 1987, the new KMNY 1600 AM thanked its 1,300 investors with a special theatrical ex-

An overflow audience listens to Buz Schwartz, general managing partner and cofounder of Pomona-based Money Radio, during the station's Investment Fair in November 1987.

travaganza.

Things moved rapidly thereafter. Award-winning announcers, managers, and engineers went to work. Following the February 27 ownership transfer, Money Radio, based in Los Angeles' Pacific Stock Exchange building, introduced the world's only all business/finance/investments format. From its Pomona transmission tower, KMNY's 5,000-watt signal saturated a 10,000-square-mile area throughout eastern Los Angeles County, all of Orange County, and the Inland Empire.

By April the station was broadcasting 24 hours a day, every day. Marketing breakthroughs attracted additional listeners, advertisers, and the broadcasting industry to the new station, establishing it as the industry leader in its special niche.

By autumn Money Radio's coast-to-coast syndication plans were racing a year ahead of schedule, with stations as far-flung as Long Island negotiating a Money Radio relationship. Syndication made sense considering KMNY's national—even global—content scope. Program guests included Apple Computer's John Sculley, best-selling authors, economists Eliott Janeway and Arthur Laffer, plus Congressman David Dreier and U.S. senators com-

menting on taxation and fiscal legislation.

Today Money Radio also presents direct telephone reports from overseas stock exchanges; live in-studio interviews with leading traders, analysts, market timers, entrepreneurs, and business experts; and constant updates on investment and financial news. The station's Investment Fair in November 1987 drew 18,000 people. "Everyone is interested in money," Gold explains.

In mid-1988 KMNY 1600 AM made Pomona its broadcast headquarters by locating most newscasters and engineers to the transmission studio there. "Pomona is the ideal location for Money Radio," Gold believes. "Here, we're in the heart of our listening audience, which is now expanding west to the high-demographic coastal communities and east to the desert's glittering retirement cities.

"Pomona is growing," concludes Gold, "and we look forward to continue growing with Pomona in the years ahead."

Vera Gold, executive vice-president and cofounder of Money Radio, KMNY 1600 AM, America's first all-financial/business news and talk radio station.

PATRONS

The following individuals, companies, and organizations have made a valuable commitment to the quality of this publication. Windsor Publications and the Pomona Chamber of Commerce gratefully acknowledge their participation in *Pomona: A Centennial History.*

James S. Baker, Pomona Centennial Committee Chairman (January 6, 1888-1988)*
Bank of America*
Bill's Tree Service
Braswell Enterprises, Inc.*
California State Polytechnic University, Pomona*
Care Enterprises, Inc.*
Casa Colina Centers for Rehabilitation*
Clarion Hotel/Ontario Airport*
College of Osteopathic Medicine of the Pacific
CooperVision CILCO*
Cotter & Company*
Elias Construction, Incorporated*
Emerson Village
First Interstate Bank of California*
John A. Forbing - State Farm Insurance
Garden State Paper Company, Inc.*
Globe Plastics, Inc.*
Industrial Alloys, Inc.
    Industrial Wire Products Corporation*
Industrial Brush Corporation*
Inland Envelope Company*
Inter Valley Health Plan*
ITT Pomona Electronics*
K.K.W. Trucking, Inc., & Furniture Transportation Systems*
Lanterman Developmental Center*
Law Offices of Parker and Dally*
Claudette C. Leever, CFP
Los Angeles County Fair Association*
May-Midkiff Construction Corp.
Money Radio, KMNY 1600 AM*
Mt. San Antonio Gardens*
Parkview Counseling and Psychological Center*
Pioneer Electronics Technology, Inc.*

PIP Printing of Pomona Valley
Pomona First Federal Savings and Loan Association*
Pomona Valley Chiropractic Center*
Pomona Valley Community Hospital*
Po-Tel Federal Credit Union*
Richter "The Packaging People" *
The Saddler Chiropractic Clinic*
Simpson Paper Company*
Teledyne Cast Products*
TiTech International, Incorporated*
John Todd
Todd Memorial Chapel*
Trophy King Awards, Inc.
Western Fireplace Distributors, Inc.
Williams Sign Co.

*Partners in Progress of *Pomona: A Centennial History.* The histories of these companies and organizations appear in Chapter Eight, beginning on page 125.

BIBLIOGRAPHY

CHAPTER ONE

Beck, Warren A. and Ynez D. Haase. *Historical Atlas of California.* Norman, Oklahoma: University of Oklahoma Press, 1974.

Belmont, John and Timothy Seymour. "Smallpox, Poverty and Death at Ganesha Park." *Mt. San Antonio Historian,* vol. 15, no. 2 (Spring 1979): 47-66.

Hart, James D. *A Companion to California,* rev. ed. Berkeley: University of California Press, 1987.

Johnston, Bernice Eastman. *California's Gabrieleno Indians.* Los Angeles: Southwest Museum, 1962.

Kroeber, Alfred Louis. *Handbook of Indians of California.* Washington: Bureau of Ethnology, Bulletin 78, 1925.

Long Beach Museum of Art. *Prehistoric and Indigenous Indian Art.* Long Beach, California: Long Beach Museum of Art, 1959.

Reid, Hugo. *The Indians of Los Angeles County.* Los Angeles: Privately printed, 1926.

Rolle, Andrew. *California, A History,* 4th ed. Arlington Heights, Illinois: Harlan Davidson, 1987.

Steiner, Rodney. *Los Angeles: The Centrifugal City.* Dubuque, Iowa: Kendall/Hunt Publishing, 1981.

CHAPTER TWO

Baker, Charles C. "Mexican Land Grants on California." *Historical Society of Southern California Annual Publication,* vol. 9, no. 3: 236-243.

Bancroft, Hubert Howe. *California Pastoral, 1796-1848.* San Francisco: A.L. Bancroft, 1888.

———. *History of California,* 7 vols. San Francisco: A.L. Bancroft, 1884-1890.

———. *Register of Pioneer Inhabitants of California 1542-1848.* Los Angeles: Dawsen's Book Shop, 1964.

Brackett, Frank P. *Brief Early History of the San Jose Rancho and Its Subsequent Cities.* Los Angeles Historic Record Company, 1920.

Cahoon, Burton. "The Palomares Cemetery." *Pomona Valley Historian,* vol. 6, no. 3 (July 1970): 120.

Cleland, Robert Glass. *The Cattle on a Thousand Hills: Southern California; 1850-80.* San Marino, California: The Huntington Library, 1951.

Cole, Martin. "When Camels Came to Pomona Valley." *Pomona Valley Historian,* vol. 5, no. 3 (July 1969): 121-135.

Cowan, Robert G. *Ranchos of California, A List of Concessions 1775-1822 and Mexican Grants 1822-1846.* Los Angeles: Historical Society of Southern California, 1977.

Engelhardt, Zephyrin. *San Gabriel Mission.* Chicago: Mission Herald Press, 1927.

Fryer, Roy M. "Pomona Valley before the Americans Came." *Historical Society of Southern California,* vol. 21, no. 4 (December 1939): 91-101.

Garner, Bess (Adams). *Windows in an Old Adobe.* Pomona: *Progress Bulletin* in collaboration with Saunders Press, 1939.

Hoover, Roy. "The Adobe de Palomares." *Historical Society of Southern California Quarterly,* vol. 43 (December 1961): 415-420.

Northrop, Marie E. *Spanish-Mexican Families of Early California: 1769-1850,* vol. 2. Burbank, California: Southern California Genealogical Society, 1983.

Pitt, Leonard. *The Decline of the Californias: A Social History of the Spanish-Speaking Californians, 1846-1890.* Berkeley: University of California Press, 1970.

Robinson, W. Wilcox. *Land in California: The Story of Mission Lands, Ranchos, Squatters, Mining Claims, R.R. Grants Landings, Homesteads.* Berkeley and Los Angeles: University of California Press, 1948.

———. "Meanwhile, Back at the Ranchos." *Westways,* vol. 58, no. 10 (October 1966): 19-22.

The Story of Pomona. Pomona: Todd Memorial Chapel, n.d.

CHAPTER THREE

Beasley, T.D. "Selling Pomona in 1887." *Pomona Valley Historian,* vol. 4, no. 2 (April 1968): 81-92.

Brackett, Frank P. "Beginnings of Pomona." *Pomona Valley Historian,* vol. 11, no. 3 (Summer 1975): 94.

Bunnelle, Floyd R. "Pre-Pomona: A Mirror of the 70's." *Pomona Valley Historian,* vol. 11, no. 4 (Fall 1975): 156-161.

Dodge, Mark. "Railroad Violence in Early Pomona." *Mt. San Antonio Historian,* vol. 16, no. 4 (Fall 1980): 162-169.

Dumke, Glenn S. *The Boom of the Eighties in Southern California.* San Marino, California: Huntington Library, 1970.

"An Early Description of Pomona." *Pomona Valley Historian,* vol. 3, no. 1 (January 1967): 20-30.

Echeverri, Mark. "A History of Pomona: The Early Years, 1875-1920." *Mt. San Antonio Historian,* vol. 17, no. 4. (Fall 1981): 139-181; vol. 18, no. 1 (Winter 1982): 1-45; vol. 18, nos. 2, 3, 4 (Summer 1984): 47-169.

Fryer, Roy M. "When the Americans Came to Pomona Valley." *Historical Society of Southern California Quarterly,* vol. 23, nos. 3 & 4 (September-December 1941): 156-176; 165-166; 157-177.

Gridley, Emily Brady. "Pioneering in Southern California." *Pomona Valley Historian,* vol. 1, no. 2 (April 1965): 68-72.

Guinn, James Miller. *The Great Real Estate Boom of 1887.* Los Angeles: Historical Society of Southern California, 1890.

———. *Historical and Biographical Record of Southern California.* Chicago: Chapman Publishing, 1902.

History of Pomona Valley, California with Biographical Sketches. Los Angeles: Historic Record Company, 1920.

Holt, Christine. "The Los Angeles Immigration and Land Cooperative Association." *Pomona Valley Historian,* vol. 9, no. 1 (Winter 1973): 1-30.

Holt, Raymond. "L.M. Holt: The Man Behind the Avenue." *Pomona Valley Historian,* vol. 9, no. 1 (Winter 1973): 31-46.

Jensen, James M. "Thomas Andrew Garey." *Pomona Valley Historian,* vol. 5, no. 3 (July 1969): 115-120.

Klotz, Esther H. "Pomona's Palomares Hotel." *Pomona Valley Historian,* vol. 6, no. 1 (January 1970): 32-39.

McDonald, S. Dennis. "Cloud Over

San Jose." *Pomona Valley Historian,* vol. 4, no. 2 (April 1968): 47-70.

Moses, Vincent. "Oranges for Health' California for Wealth: The Billion Dollar Navel and the California Dream." *The Californians,* vol. 3, no. 4 (July/August 1985): 27-37.

Newmark, Harris. *Sixty Years in Southern California, 1853-1913.* New York: Knickerbocker Press, 1916.

Nilleen, Linda. "Pomona Fire Department: The Early Years, 1883-1934." *Pomona Valley Historian,* vol. 12, no. 1 (Winter, 1976): 1-33.

Nordhoff, Charles. *California: For Health, Pleasure and Residence.* N.p.: Centennial Printing, Ten Speed Press, 1973.

Pomona History Book Subcommittee of the Pomona Centennial-Bicentennial Committee. *Pomona Centennial History.* Pomona Centennial-Bicentennial Committee, 1976.

"Pomona Valley Railroad." *Historical Society of Southern California Quarterly,* vol. 47 (September 1965): 149 ff.

Rhodes, Edwin. *The Break of Day in Chino.* Chino, California: P-B Press, 1951.

Robinson, W. Wilcox. *Land in California.* Berkeley: University of California Press, 1948.

Saturday Beacon. *Pomona City Directory 1890, A Complete Resident and Classified Business Directory.* 1890.

Shorb, J. DeBarth. "Address at Unveiling of Goddess Pomona." *Pomona Valley Historian,* vol. 2, no. 4 (October 1966): 139-150.

Smith, Frederick J. "Pomona in the 1880's." *Pomona Valley Historian,* vol. 3, no. 4 (October 1967): 165-179.

Tinsley, Henry Griswold. "Charles I. Lorbeer' Pioneer Promoter." *Pomona Valley Historian,* vol. 2, no. 3 (July 1966): 104-108.

Warner, J.J., Judge Benjamin Hayes, and J.P. Widney. *An Historical Sketch of Los Angeles County.* Los Angeles: O.W. Smith, 1876.

Wilson, John Albert. *Reproduction of Thompson and West's History of Los Angeles County, California.* Berkeley, California: Howell-North, 1959.

CHAPTER FOUR

Bess, Michael. "Early Agriculture in Pomona Valley." *Pomona Valley Historian,* vol. 6, no. 2 (April 1970): 47-63.

Bunnelle, Floyd. "Gold is the Cornerstone." *Mt. San Antonio Historian,* vol. 17, no. 2 (Spring 1981): 47-66.

Dreher, Peter J. "Early History of Cooperative Marketing of Citrus Fruit." *Pomona Valley Historian,* vol. 3 no. 4 (October 1967): 139-157.

Jones, Willis S. "Our Important Natural Resource—Water." *Pomona Valley Historian,* vol. 5, no. 4 (October 1969): 175-184.

McWilliams, Carey. *California: The Great Exception.* Santa Barbara: Peregrine Smith, 1976.

_____ . *Southern California: An Island on the Land.* Santa Barbara: Peregrine Smith, 1979.

Palmer, Frank L. "Eleven Years in an Orange Grove (1891-1901)." *Pomona Valley Historian,* vol. 1, no. 2 (April 1965): 55-61.

Patton, H.W. "Pomona, Past and Present." *Pomona Valley Historian,* vol. 2, no. 2 (April 1966): 87-90.

Pflueger, Donald H. *Covina: Sunflowers. Citrus. Subdivisions.* Covina, California: Castle Press, 1964.

Stone, George G. "Financing the Orange Industry in California." *Pomona Valley Historian,* vol. 2, no. 4 (October 1966): 159-174.

_____ . "Financing the Orange Industry." *Pomona Valley Historian,* vol. 2, no. 1 (January 1967): 31-46.

Thrall, Will H. "Our Unusual Rains." *Pomona Valley Historian,* vol. 13, no. 4 (Fall 1977): 168-170.

Van Gelderen, Joe Beth. "Sunkist's Southland." *Mt. San Antonio Historian,* vol. 17, no. 1 (Winter 1981): 1-21.

Young, Floyd. "Frost Warnings in the Early Days." *Pomona Valley Historian,* vol. 5, no. 4 (October 1969): 171-174.

CHAPTER FIVE

Amrine, William J. and Susan. "Brackett Field: Dirt Strip to Modern Airport." *Pomona Valley Historian,* vol. 6, no. 2 (April 1970): 72-86.

Armour, Richard. "Books, Libraries and My Home Town." *Pomona Valley Historian,* vol. 1, no. 2 (April 1965): 45-54.

Baur, John E. "A County for Early Pomona." *Mt. San Antonio Historian,* vol. 15, no. 2 (Spring 1979): 67-91.

_____ . "Early Pomona's Youngest Editor: Edward E. Stowell." *Pomona Valley Historian,* vol. 7, no. 1 (January 1971): 1-11.

Burt, Arthur W. "Adventures in Light and Power." *Pomona Valley Historian,* vol. 2, no. 3 (July 1966): 93-103.

Cahoon, Burton W. "History of Historical Society of Pomona Valley." *Pomona Valley Historian,* vol. 2, no. 2 (April 1966): 47-64.

Crump, Spencer. *Henry Huntington and the Pacific Electric, a Pictorial Album.* Corona del Mar, California: Trans-Anglo Books, 1978.

Daniel, Evelyn A. "Russell K. Pitzer—A Man of Vision." *Pomona Valley Historian,* vol. 10, no. 1 (Winter 1974): 1-26.

Driscoll, Roy, ed. *Pomona Valley Community Book.* Pomona: n.p., 1950.

Escher, Steven T. "The Y.M.C.A.: Pomona's Investment in Its Youth." *Pomona Valley Historian,* vol. 7, no. 2 (April 1971): 73-92.

Federal Writers Project. *California: A Guide to the Golden State.* New York: Hastings House, 1939.

Fryer, Ron. "Early Schools in Pomona Valley." *Pomona Valley Historian,* vol. 3, no. 2 (April 1967): 56-69.

Gebhard, David and Robert Winter. *Architecture in Los Angeles: A Compleat Guide.* Salt Lake City: Peregrine Smith Books, 1985.

Gelbach, Alice M. "The Catholic Church in Pomona." *Pomona Valley Historian,* vol. 3, no. 3, (July 1967): 112-123.

Holt, Raymond M. "Pomona—Presidential Battlefield of 1888." *Pomona Valley Historian,* vol. 2, no. 1 (January 1966): 1-8.

Kennedy, Erin. "Early Doctors in the Pomona Valley." *Pomona Valley Historian,* vol. 7, no. 4 (October 1971): 139-168.

Kester, Kathleen. "Serving the Valley—The Pomona Chamber of Com-

merce." *Pomona Valley Historian,*
vol. 10, no. 3 (Summer-1974): 120-
138; vol. 10, no. 4 (Fall 1974): 174-
184.

Kohler, Hugh. "Pacific State Hospital,
1921-1965." *Pomona Valley Historian,* vol. 8, no. 1 (January 1972): 1-
29.

Los Angeles: 1900-1961. Los Angeles:
History Division of the Los Angeles County Museum, 1961.

Mallory, Lynn. "Life on the Kellogg
Ranch." *Pomona Valley Historian,*
vol. 8, no. 3 (July 1972): 93-114.

McKelvey, Kathleen. "The Restoration
of the Palomares Adobe." *Pomona
Valley Historian,* vol. 12, no. 2
(Spring, 1976): 47-78.

Mead, Louise Richards. "The Ragtime
Era in Pomona, part II." *Pomona
Valley Historian,* vol. 12, no. 4 (Fall
1976): 169-184.

Nally, Timothy F. "Long Distance,
Please." *Pomona Valley Historian,*
vol. 6, no. 3 (July 1970): 110-117.

Nunis, Doyce B. *Los Angeles: A Bibliography of a Metropolis.* Los Angeles:
n.p., 1973.

Parkinson, Mary Jane. "The Kellogg
Ranch a Half Century Ago." *Pomona Valley Historian,* vol. 12, no. 4
(Fall 1976): 163-168.

Polos, Nicholas C. "A Jewel in Pomona's Crown—Her City Schools."
Pomona Valley Historian, vol. 7, no.
3 (July 1971): 93-102.

Smith, Gertrude. "Health Care for the
Valley: The Pomona Valley Community Hospital." *Pomona Valley
Historian,* vol. 11, no. 2 (Spring
1975): 70-92.

Warren, Marcia Fredendall. "The Fox
Theatre—Pomona's *Grande Dame.*"
Mt. San Antonio Historian, vol. 15,
no. 1 (Winter 1979): 1-30.

Webb, Carl. "Little Theatre in the Pomona Valley." *Pomona Valley Historian,* vol. 9, no. 2 (Spring 1973):
69-92.

Winton, Marcia. "An Act of Kindness—
Pomona's Reaction to the San
Francisco Earthquake." *Mt. San Antonio Historian,* vol. 16, no. 4 (Fall
1980): 156-161.

CHAPTER SIX

Banham, Reyner. *Los Angeles: The Architecture of Four Ecologies.* New
York: Penguin Press, 1971.

Bigger, Richard and James D. Kitchen.
*Metropolitan Los Angeles, A Study
in Integration: How the Cities Grew.*
Los Angeles: Haynes Foundation,
1952.

Brienes, Marvin. "Smog Comes to Los
Angeles." *Southern California Quarterly,* no. 58 (Winter 1976): 515-
532.

Brodsky, David. *L.A. Freeway: An Appreciative Essay.* Berkeley: University of California Press, 1981.

Chapman, John L. *Incredible Los Angeles.* New York: Harper & Row,
1967.

Community Guide to Greater San Gabriel.
Los Angeles: Security First National Bank, 1967.

Developmental Research Association.
Economic Analysis of Pomona, California. Los Angeles: 1968.

Durrenberger, Robert W., ed. *California:
Its People, Its Problems, Its Prospects.* Palo Alto, California: National Press Books, 1971.

From Agriculture to Aerospace. Los Angeles Area Chamber of Commerce,
1987.

Los Angeles Chamber of Commerce.
*The City and County of Los Angeles
in Southern California.* Los Angeles:
Kingsley-Barners & Neuner Company, 1897.

McIntyre, Joan. "The Wayne Sweeper
Story." *Pomona Valley Historian,*
vol. 9, no. 3 (Summer, 1973): 110-
121.

Penalosa, Fernando. "Class Consciousness and Social Mobility in a Mexican-American Community." Ph.D.
diss., University of Southern California, 1963.

Rabinovitz, Francine. *Minorities in the
Suburbs: The L.A. Experience.* Lexington, Massachusetts: D.C. Heath,
1977.

Sell, Ted. "Storm of Ethnic Change."
Los Angeles Times (January 1971):
part 3, pp. 1-3.

Trasin, Walt. "Saving the Barbara
Greenwood Kindergarten Bungalow." *Mt. San Antonio Historian,*
vol. 14, no. 2 (Spring 1978): 47-60.

CHAPTER SEVEN

City of Pomona. *Economic Profile.* Pomona Economic Development Corporation, 1987.

———. *Bulletin.* Department of Regional Planning, 1987.

County of Los Angeles. *Inside the First
District.* Winter 1988.

Facilities Masterplan for Fairplex. Montclair, California: Cashion, Horie,
Cocke, Gonzalez, Architects, 1986.

Finnegan, W. Robert. "The Facts About
Doing Business in Pomona." *Vis a
Vis* (March 1988): 1-4.

"Hot Economy for Pomona, Agency
Claims." *Progress Bulletin.* February
3, 1987.

Katz, Jesse. "Booming Pomona Bursts
with Pride—And Critics." *Los Angeles Times* (April 5, 1987): part 9,
p. 1 ff.

*Los Angeles County Fair Association 1986
Annual Report.* Pomona.

Los Angeles Department of Regional
Planning. *Los Angeles County Data
Book.* Los Angeles County, 1987.

Mt. San Antonio Community College.
*Directions Toward the Year 2000:
Strategic Plan.* Walnut, California:
1952.

Pomona Business Monthly. N.p., March
1988.

Pomona Economic Development Corporation. *Ped Corp: A Publication
for Shareholders.* (Winter 1987-88).

Pomona Unified School District. *Handbook 1987-88.* Community Information Office, 1987.

Security Pacific Bank. *The Sixty-Mile
Circle.* Los Angeles: Security Pacific Corporation, 1987.

INDEX